Dilly

The Man Who Broke Enigmas

Dilly

The Man Who Broke Enigmas

MAVIS BATEY

biteback

First published in Great Britain in 2009
This paperback edition published in 2010 by
Biteback Publishing Ltd
Westminster Tower
3 Albert Embankment
London
SE1 7SP

ISBN 978-1-906447-15-1

A CIP catalogue record for this book is available from the British Library.

Set in Garamond by SoapBox
Printed and bound in Great Britain by CPI Cox & Wyman, Reading, RG1 8EX

For Keith

(Keith Batey died on 28 August 2010)

Contents

Foreword

Dillwyn (Dilly) Knox was a renowned classical scholar and a codebreaker of genius. Although a number of codebreakers served in both the First and Second World Wars, Dilly was probably the only codebreaker in any country to make a successful transition from breaking manual ciphers and book codes in the First World War to solving complex cipher machines such as Enigma, and their traffic, in the Second World War.

George Steiner has described the British codebreaking effort at Bletchley Park as 'the single greatest achievement of Britain during 1939–45, perhaps during [the 20th] century as a whole'. Signals intelligence (Sigint) was Britain's most important source of intelligence during the war, and eventually led to the Government Code and Cypher School (GC&CS) and its outstations such as Berkeley Street (diplomatic work) and Knockholt (interception of Tunny – enciphered teleprinter traffic), employing 10,500 people by January 1945. However, the skilled work of breaking the codes and ciphers of the Axis powers and of selected neutral countries was carried out by a relatively small number of highly talented cryptanalysts. A few, such as Alan Turing, are now household names, but sadly most of them are largely unknown to the general public, despite their magnificent achievements in breaking Enigma and other ciphers.

Very little was known about Dilly's codebreaking work until the publication of Penelope Fitzgerald's enchanting *The Knox Brothers* in 1977. Penelope Fitzgerald knew very little herself about codebreaking, but consulted various experts, including Mavis Batey and Peter Twinn, the first professional mathematician to join GC&CS. Her book disclosed that Dilly had penetrated various versions of Enigma, including one used by the Abwehr (the Wehrmacht High Command's intelligence service), and that he had failed by the narrowest of margins to solve the wiring of the Wehrmacht Enigma's rotors. However, due to the then swingeing

Official Secrets Acts and the government's refusal to release a single file about the work of Room 40 (the Admiralty's codebreaking section in the First World War), she was prevented from giving a full picture of Dilly's considerable achievements. Although the Ministry of Defence went so far as to tell her that the Room 40 files would never be released, claiming that to do so would endanger national security, the government later relented, and they were transferred to the Public Record Office. Mavis Batey has therefore been able to use them and Second World War papers on Dilly's work in writing this book.

Regrettably, the Government Communications Headquarters (GCHQ) has only released a few pages of a technical history of which Mavis Batey was a co-author. Since amateur cryptanalysts can now solve Wehrmacht Enigma messages that frustrated the codebreakers at Bletchley Park and no one would dream of using a cipher machine that is now over eighty years old, it is virtually impossible to conceive of any valid reason for withholding most of that history. Most unfortunately, this is not an isolated example of GCHQ's heavy-handed treatment of GC&CS's wartime histories. This not only deprives the codebreakers involved of the recognition and credit that they so richly deserve; more importantly, it endangers national security since, as any security officer knows, that is an inevitable consequence of over-classifying documents, which brings the whole classification system into disrepute. Over-classification also leads to a culture of secrecy and bad decision-making and undermines public trust in government. It facilitates the politicisation of intelligence by allowing its selective use to 'sell' specific policies and results in individuals handling classified documents carelessly, believing that they are 'not really classified'. Paradoxically, the American 'Commission on Protecting and Reducing Government Secrecy' concluded that 'Secrets can be protected more effectively if secrecy is reduced overall'. The US Homeland Security Advisory Council recently reported that the American 'classification system is broken and is a barrier (and often an excuse) for not sharing pertinent information with homeland security partners'. It would be arrogant to assume that the British classification system is in significantly better shape, with all that that implies about the efficient sharing of British intelligence.

Dilly specialised in solving Enigma, which does not merely refer to breaking messages enciphered on an Enigma machine. Before a single message could be broken, the complex wiring of the rotors of the relevant Enigma, and the manner in which they operated (mainly the turnover motion of the rotors, which was irregular), had first to be solved. And since Enigma was really a family of machines, and not a single model, as often supposed, this process had to be repeated with each Enigma model being attacked. The original A, B and C commercial machines evolved into the D model. A later version of D, the K commercial machine, with rewired rotors, was also bought by the armed forces of various countries such as Italy and Spain.

Dilly solved the Italian naval K machine in 1937. However, his finest achievement was his solution in October 1941 of a version used by the Abwehr, which led to the establishment of a special section at GC&CS under Dilly's leadership, 'Intelligence Services Knox' (ISK). The main Abwehr Enigma was essentially a model G, with rewired rotors. Most regrettably, the British official history of intelligence merely credits 'Knox's section' with the breaking, in December 1941, of 'the Enigma key' used by the Abwehr for 'most of the traffic between its headquarters and its controlling stations in occupied and neutral countries'. This grossly underestimates Dilly's achievement, and that of his gifted staff, since he first had to reconstruct the G machine being used, including the wiring of its multi-notched rotors, which was a much more difficult task than solving daily keys. ISK1, the first decrypt of a message enciphered on the main Abwehr Enigma machine, was issued on 25 December 1941. In fact, Knox's section (which was headed by Peter Twinn after Knox died in January 1943) solved the wirings of no fewer than ten different Enigmas (seven Abwehr and SD Enigmas, two Italian naval Enigmas, and the Spanish military attaché Enigma). By the war's end, GC&CS had circulated about 140,800 decrypts of Abwehr Enigma messages, a figure that excludes routine signals such as weather reports, which were not disseminated.

Mavis Batey describes how Dilly and other members of GC&CS also attempted to solve Wehrmacht Enigma, and how close Dilly was to success before the war started. The German army had added a plugboard to its rewired and modified version of commercial Enigma in 1930, greatly increasing its complexity. Since GC&CS, unlike the Poles, was receiving virtually no German Enigma signals, which were mostly transmitted on low power on medium frequencies, Dilly largely had to use intuitive methods when attacking Wehrmacht Enigma. The Poles, being close to Germany, intercepted a considerable amount of traffic, enabling Marian Rejewski to employ mathematical methods, including permutation theory, in his successful attack on it in 1932. But it required an inspired guess by Rejewski about the first section of Enigma's wiring before he could make the final breakthrough. Dilly was understandably furious when he learned from the Poles that the relevant wiring was not random as he had feared.

Dilly was a fascinating personality. He was the very epitome of an absent-minded professor – he even forgot to invite two of his three brothers to his wedding. He was somewhat unworldly, yet he could cut to the heart of a problem, and devise methods to protect the use of intelligence from Enigma, by ensuring that there was adequate 'cover' to convince the enemy that any disaster suffered by their forces, as at the Battle of Matapan, could not have been based on Sigint. If Dilly had known about it, he would have protested about the Admiralty's horrendously risky plan, based on Enigma decrypts, to send a British submarine to attack two U-boats at a rendezvous in the remote Cape Verde Islands in September 1941. When the attack failed, and both U-boats escaped, Admiral Karl Dönitz, the admiral commanding U-boats, immediately requested an investigation into Enigma's security. Dilly always knew that it was vital to protect the 'source' of any action based on Sigint.

Dilly showed remarkable judgement and was highly prescient in his views about the imperative need to share intelligence. He saw, at an early stage in the war, that cryptanalysis was becoming so complex that its results needed to be circulated to all the GC&CS cryptanalytic sections, in order to avoid any harmful effects of the 'need to know' policy, under which information is tightly compartmentalised, and only supplied to people who require it. Unfortunately, it was not until November 1942, when Professor Eric Vincent was appointed as the co-ordinator of cryptographic research, that this step was taken. 'Need to know' carries a hidden flaw:

it assumes that it is possible to know in advance who will require access to specific intelligence, yet that is completely impractical. Dilly too often had to protest about the 'burials of essential documents', insisting that he could not tell whether he needed anything until he had seen it. Over sixty years later, the National Commission on Terrorist Attacks upon the United States (the American 9/11 Commission) reiterated Dilly's concerns, complaining that 'each agency's incentive structure opposes sharing, with … few rewards for sharing information. … Agencies uphold a "need-to-know" culture of information protection rather than promoting a "need-to-share" culture of integration.'

Dilly ensured that the immense task of producing a complete set of 'perforated sheets', invented by the Poles to solve Enigma messages, was completed quickly, although to do so he had to disobey orders from Alastair Denniston, the operational head of GC&CS. When GC&CS completed a second set of sheets around 7 January 1940, he had to threaten to resign to ensure that they were sent to the Poles, who were by then working with the French army in Gretz-Armainvillers, near Paris; for some reason Denniston had apparently been most reluctant to let the Poles have them. In the event, Alan Turing took them and learned crucial information about rotors IV and V from the Poles, enabling Hut 6 (army and air force Enigma) to solve its first Enigma key immediately after he returned. Within a few weeks Dilly had found a method, 'cillies', which greatly eased the task of using the perforated sheets – without it, the sheets would almost have been unworkable in most cases. As late as mid-1944, Hut 6 was still finding 'cillies' to be an invaluable tool for penetrating German army Enigma ciphers.

GC&CS also broke the Abwehr's hand ciphers in a section called ISOS (Illicit Services Oliver Strachey), after the cryptanalyst at GC&CS initially in charge of that section. ISK intelligence was a perfect complement to ISOS, not least because an agent's report using a hand cipher could be traced as subsequently sent from an Abwehr sub-station to its local station in Germany or an occupied country, or to its war station in a neutral country such as Spain. At times ISK decrypts therefore provided excellent 'cribs' (probable plain text) to help in breaking new ISOS hand ciphers – but not vice versa. ISOS was generally used during the war to describe all decrypts of signals sent by any German intelligence service however enciphered, to disguise the fact that Abwehr Enigma was being solved. References to ISOS in wartime files therefore need to be approached with considerable care, since they often include ISK decrypts, and therefore mask the vital contribution made by Dilly and others in breaking Abwehr Enigma.

GC&CS was a meritocracy, where rank and age were irrelevant. Only talent and an ability to do the work well counted – Harry Hinsley (later the professor of the history of international relations at Cambridge, and the principal author of the magisterial official history, *British Intelligence in the Second World War*), who was only twenty-one and still an undergraduate when he joined Hut 4 (Naval Section), consorted with admirals and by 1943 held a higher grade than some former senior university staff in Hut 4. Until February 1942, when there was a major reorganisation, GC&CS was a very informal institution. Even after that reorganisation it was not rigidly hierarchical. However, the same could not be said of its master, the Secret Intelligence Service (SIS), which controlled the distribution of its results. This led to unfortunate results in relation to the product of ISK and ISOS until good sense prevailed.

Intelligence from ISK and ISOS was the principal British weapon against the Abwehr and other German intelligence agencies. The real art in employing it, as with any intelligence, was in doing so without betraying its source. To be of value, it had to be distributed to people who required it for operational, planning and other purposes. However, its distribution was controlled by the SIS's Section V (counter-espionage outside the United Kingdom) under Colonel Felix Cowgill, who was obsessed with security and all too conscious of his position in the SIS hierarchy. The Admiralty and other users of ISOS and ISK in the armed forces found that Cowgill wanted to stop virtually any use being made of them. They constantly had to struggle against his restrictions and were even forced to disobey orders by swapping information with each other, to avoid an enormous loss of intelligence.

Cowgill was much too possessive of the intelligence from ISK and ISOS and later admitted that he denied MI5 (the Security Service) access to some of it because he 'did not like the look of the people' involved

– a completely inadequate approach to personnel vetting, and one that signally failed with one of his senior staff, the Soviet double agent Kim Philby. Eventually most of Cowgill's restrictions were relaxed, but they should never have been imposed in the first place. Intelligence from ISK and ISOS proved to be invaluable in a number of ways, such as enabling the British to build up a detailed picture of the Abwehr's and SD's 'order of battle' and providing a check on how far information supplied by British-controlled double agents (the Double-Cross (XX) operation) was believed by the Abwehr. Perhaps its most important contribution was in connection with the Allied deception operations before the invasion of Sicily in July 1943 and the Normandy D-Day landings in June 1944 (Operations Mincemeat and Fortitude South, respectively). Most notably, a message sent on 9 June by the double agent known as Garbo (Juan Pujol Garcia) resulted in the Germans halting the movement of two armoured divisions so that they would be available to fend off feared – but wholly imaginary – landings in the Pas de Calais and Belgium.

Mavis Batey is ideally suited to write this delightful biography, as she worked closely with Dilly as one of his star 'girls' from shortly after joining GC&CS (as Mavis Lever) in January 1940 until his untimely death in February 1943. Dilly, who was devoted to his staff, thought the world of her expertise and Margaret Rock's (her colleague in ISK), writing: 'Give me a Lever and a Rock and I can move the universe.' She was one of only about three skilled female cryptanalysts at GC&CS throughout the war, together with Margaret Rock, and Joan Clarke (later Joan Murray) in Hut 8. She has an extensive and detailed knowledge of Dilly's work and of ISK, and an exceptionally accurate memory about events from over sixty-five years ago. She is also an accomplished author, with many books to her credit. Her fascinating account of Dilly's genius and quirky 'Carrollian' way of thinking demonstrates a unique insight into Dilly's mind and personality, and brings him vividly to life. It will rightly ensure that he will 'ne'er be forgotten'.

Ralph Erskine

Acknowledgements

My chief debt of gratitude is to my husband Keith, and to Michael Smith and Ralph Erskine, who encouraged me to write this book, giving due credit to Dilly as an outstanding cryptographer, and for their assistance throughout. I should also like to thank John Gallehawk, Frank Carter and Brian Oakley for their help. Rosamund Twinn kindly supplied the photograph of Peter Twinn, Eugenia Maresch that of Rejewski, Pam Brewster that of John Jeffreys and Kathleen Warren that of Admiral Godfrey. Pam Smith, the Naphill local historian, was most helpful in supplying information and photographs of Dilly's woodlands. The Bletchley Park Trust has been generous with archives and photographs and I am very grateful to Kelsey Griffin for all her help. Frank Carter and Ralph Erskine's appendices are valuable additions to the book which show the extent and originality of Dilly's contribution to wartime cryptography. It has been a great pleasure for me to work with Michael Smith as editor and to be the author of the first book to be published by Dialogue.

Mavis Batey
July 2009

Preface

Normally an obituary in *The Times* provides a framework for a biography, but that is not true of the eulogy of Mr Alfred Dillwyn Knox, CMG, fellow of King's College and 'a classical scholar and editor', who died on 27 February 1943. Truly, as stated, he was a son of Bishop Knox of Manchester and brother of Mr E. V. Knox, editor of *Punch*, and of the Catholic theologian Monsignor Ronald Knox, and during the First World War he was a lieutenant in the Royal Naval Volunteer Reserve in the Admiralty. It also credits him for the erudition required to piece together the fragments of the Herodas *Mimiambi* and describes him as 'a pioneer in a particularly difficult field'; but no mention could be made of his pioneering work in another even more enigmatic field, for which he had just received his CMG 'for services to his country' on his deathbed.

Those services were only revealed thirty years later when F. W. Winterbotham published the story of Bletchley Park in *The ULTRA Secret*. Dilly, as he was known to family, friends and close colleagues, was then first mentioned by name as 'the mastermind' behind the Enigma affair. Winterbotham added: 'He was quite young, tall, with a rather gangling figure, unruly black hair, his eyes behind glasses, some miles away in thought. Like R. J. Mitchell, the designer of the Spitfire fighter aircraft, which tipped the scales in our favour during the Battle of Britain, who worked himself to death at the moment of triumph, Knox too, knowing he was a sick man, pushed himself to the utmost to overcome the problems of Enigma variations, which also helped to tip the war in our favour. He too died with his job completed.'

His biography is long overdue. Like all those who worked for him at Bletchley Park and shared his Enigma successes, I have affectionate memories of a brilliant, humane, intuitive, if eccentric, genius with an unfailing sense of humour, loyalty and fair play.

John Tiltman, the chief cryptographer, who collaborated with Dilly on many occasions in the 1930s, saw cryptography 'as much closer to art than science, and that is what makes the personal factor so important'. This is particularly true of Dilly Knox and we are therefore fortunate to have first-hand accounts from his family, colleagues and friends of his early life, personality, motivation and talents, which were the making of a cryptographer.

Chronology of events

1920	Marries his Room 40 secretary Olive Roddam.
1921	Moves to Courns Wood, near High Wycombe, Buckinghamshire.
1922	GC&CS placed under Foreign Office. Dilly works on diplomatic messages.
1922	Publishes the Headlam/Knox Herodas.
1923	Offered professorship of Greek at Leeds University as result of dissertation on Cercidas and his work on Herodas.
1923	Arthur Scherbius markets a new electro-mechanical cipher machine which he calls Enigma.
1925	GC&CS moves to share offices with Secret Intelligence Service (SIS) at Broadway Buildings. Dilly said to acquire an Enigma in Vienna for his own use.
1926	Dilly works with John Tiltman to break messages passed by clandestine network of Comintern agents. Codebreaking operation is codenamed Mask.
1928	GC&CS acquires a commercial Enigma machine.
1929	Dilly publishes new translation of Herodas for Loeb Classical Library edition.
1929	Hugh Foss breaks commercial Enigma machine as part of GC&CS test of its security for possible use by British government. Deems it too insecure.
1930	Germany adds plugboard to commercial machine, significantly enhancing its security. Dilly and Tiltman continue to concentrate on Comintern and Soviet codes and there is little interception of German messages.
1931	Gustave Bertrand obtains German spy 'pinches' of material from a French agent inside the German war ministry codenamed Asché. Bertrand offers more documents but demands payment. Offer not taken up but photographs taken during assessment of material reveal the addition of the plugboard.

1931	Offer of Bertrand's Asché 'pinches', including daily army machine settings, eagerly accepted by Poles.
1932	Polish codebreaker Marian Rejewski breaks the Enigma machine theoretically using permutation theory.
1933	Poles begin reading German Enigma messages. Hitler comes to power and begins building up the German armed forces.
1935	Mussolini's Italy invades Abyssinia. Joint Anglo-French wireless intercept station set up in southern France.
1936	Germany sells commercial Enigma machine to Italy and Spain. German plugboard Enigma messages intercepted when German navy carries out manoeuvres in the Mediterranean.
1937	Dilly uses his own 'rodding' techniques to break the wiring on the wheels of the 'K' model commercial machine used by Italy in the Spanish Civil War. Wilfred Bodsworth, another GC&CS codebreaker, uses Dilly's 'rodding' techniques to break the Enigma machine used by the Spanish naval attaché. Dilly turns his attention to breaking German army and air force messages through their indicators.
1938 March	Germany annexes Austria. Admiral Hugh Sinclair, the SIS Chief , buys Bletchley Park as a 'war station' for both SIS and GC&CS.
August	Codebreakers make practice visit to Bletchley under cover of 'Captain Ridley's Shooting Party'.
November	Bertrand is invited to meet codebreakers and hands over spy 'pinches', known here as 'Scarlet Pimpernels.' These include an operator's manual which gives ninety letters of clear text and its enciphered equivalent together with the key setting. Dilly now only needs to know the

diagonal, the order in which the machine's typewriter keys are connected to the entry plate to break the German army and air force Enigma. The diagonal on the commercial machines followed the keyboard and so was called the QWERTZU by Dilly.

1939 January	Meeting between the British, Polish and French codebreakers in Paris produces nothing new for the British.
1939 July	Meeting in Pyry Forest just outside Warsaw tells Dilly what he needs to know. The diagonal was not QWERTZU as in the commercial machines but ABCDE, such a simple order that the British codebreakers had dismissed it without even testing it. Dilly sends the information back to GC&CS and the wheel wiring is broken within two hours. By now he has been diagnosed with lymphatic cancer.
1939 August	GC&CS moves to Bletchley Park 'war station'. Dilly put in charge of research section in the Cottage, assisted by Tony Kendrick, John Jeffreys, Alan Turing, Peter Twinn, Gordon Welchman and three female clerks. Sets up workshop in the stable-yard, where engineers work with Turing on experimental electro-mechanical codebreaking, which leads to the creation of the *bombe*.
1940 January	First current German Enigma message broken in Cottage. Dilly invents 'cillis' to speed up codebreaking process and solves weather codes which give away daily plugboard settings. Success of Turing's *bombe* turns Bletchley Park into a production line, leaving Dilly feeling sidelined. In March, he is given a new Enigma research section in the now enlarged Cottage and sets to work breaking the machines no one else can manage.

1940	German railway Enigma broken by Hut 8 using Dilly's methods. Turing's *Treatise on Enigma* explains Dilly's methodology to newcomers.
1940 September	Italian navy Enigma messages broken.
1941 March	Cottage breaks details of Italian navy plans for Battle of Matapan, leading to British success.
1941 October	Dilly breaks Abwehr multi-turnover 'Lobster' Enigma, allowing SIS to monitor German secret service messages. This is vital to the Double Cross system of captured German agents used by MI5 and SIS to feed false information to the German high command about allied intentions during the invasions of north Africa and Italy and most particularly for the D-Day Normandy landings.
1942	Dilly's team, now known as Intelligence Services Knox (ISK), breaks the Abwehr GGG machine used for communications with Spain. Dilly is now so ill that he is only able to work from home. Twinn takes over temporarily as head of section, but Dilly is still very much at work behind the scenes.
1943 27 February	Dilly dies at home, aged fifty-eight, having been given the CMG on his deathbed by an emissary from the Palace. He sends the decoration to his ISK section, saying that it was really earned by them.

ONE

The making of a codebreaker

The Knox family was a remarkable one by any standards. Alfred Dillwyn Knox, born on 23 July 1884, was the second of the four brilliant sons of Edmund Arbuthnott Knox, later Bishop of Manchester. Dilly and his elder brother Eddie were born in Oxford, where their father was sub-warden of Merton College, one of the oldest colleges. Merton was founded in 1264 as an independent academic community for training the secular priesthood. Ordained and elected as a fellow in 1870, the Rev. E. A. Knox's reading was not entirely confined to theological works as he was fond of Jane Austen novels. In 1874, he met his future wife Ellen, the daughter of Thomas French, who was the new rector of St Ebbe's Church, Oxford, opposite Christ Church. French had just returned from missionary work in India. According to Edmund's diary, he and Ellen were allowed to walk in the garden on their own and had 'a profitable talk in the summerhouse'. Thomas French approved of Edmund's preaching at a church in a run-down Oxford parish. The young couple had to wait four years, however, before they could get married, when Merton amended its statutes to abolish the celibacy rule.

Four children were born in Oxford, Ethel, Eddie, Winifred and Dilly, and with such a growing family, Edmund Knox was pleased, in 1885, to be offered the living of St Wilfred's at Kibworth in Leicestershire, which was under the ecclesiastical patronage of Merton. This was no casual college appointment, as for him heredity and motivation related whole-heartedly to the evangelical Church of England. When the children came to make the family tree there was a clergyman to be found on every line of both parents' genealogy, and they had been given a special ancestor to remember by the choice of one of their names. Dilly was named after his great-grandfather Peter Dillwyn French, vicar of Holy Trinity, Burton-on-Trent, the father of Thomas French, who had been 'called' back to India, this time as Bishop of Lahore.

The rectory at Kibworth was a paradise for the boys and their sisters Ethel and Winifred. Their father also remembered it with great affection in his *Reminiscences of an Octogenarian* as 'exactly the house that Jane Austen's Mrs Elton would have approved of with its lofty hall and reception rooms – its bay windows looking out on the rectory garden and fields'. There were strawberries, raspberries and Victoria plums for the picking, a snug rookery and rook pies in season, aconites, primroses and violets in the shrubbery and, as Edmund Knox said, 'like Herrick, our cows and a few sheep disporting themselves in our own field. What more could we wish?' In later years, the children used to say that they could cure sleeplessness simply by recalling Kibworth. The large nursery was at the top of the house, and for much of the time there they were taught at home with their father providing religious instruction and their mother, who had had a very sound literary education, reading to them by the hour. Dilly and Eddie later went to the village school. The great excitement was when their grandfather visited them from Lahore and took them all for holidays, telling them about his amazing missionary adventures. Just when everybody thought he had retired, he decided to set off again, this time to convert the Arab world, and there, after incredible hardships, he died and was buried under the cliffs in a cove on the Bay of Muscat. The children invented a new hiding game called the Caves of Arabia in remembrance.

Whether as missionaries or as clergymen, the Knoxes were brought up to pray for all relatives preaching the gospel at their family prayers. Soon their father, much as he enjoyed the rural parish of Kibworth and the family delights, knew he ought to be catering for the spiritual needs of industrial cities. Dilly was seven when, in 1891, they moved to their new life at Aston on the outskirts of Birmingham. Eddie and Dilly were now able to go to a day school, revelling in the trams that took them there. The vicarage was described by its new incumbent, who was concerned about his wife's health, as 'in a dark and narrow street set in a maze of smoke begrimed houses', but she, like her unworldly father, felt that sacrifices had to be made and that she was 'called' to brighten the lives of the industrial poor. Ellen Knox threw herself whole-heartedly into reading classes for adults, Sunday schools and the Ragged School for destitute children. Sadly at Christmas, deep in her charitable work, she caught influenza. For the next eight months she was sent to one nursing home after the other 'for the air', but in August 1892 she died.

The children were inconsolable, especially when they were separated. Only Eddie, who was then twelve, remained at Aston with his father. Dilly and the girls were sent to a widowed great-aunt in Eastbourne, and the younger boys, Wilfred and Ronnie, were packed off to their father's brother, the vicar of another Leicestershire village, Edmondthorpe. Dilly was utterly miserable and soon learned all they could teach him at the Eastbourne school. The only consolation was the occasional reunion at Aston when Eddie and Dilly were particularly pleased to be together again. Aunt Emily, who was in charge of the Bishop's household, had no ideas about what children needed and it was clear that family life could not be what it had been. In 1894, Edmund Knox was offered the vast parish of St Paul's, Birmingham, with the post of Bishop Suffragan of Coventry, and in his own words 'it became evident that I must marry again', and that his wife must be vicarage born and bred to be able to cope with his situation. Fortunately, Ethel Mary Newton, aged twenty-seven, was ideal. The children were to call her 'Mrs K', she said, which would not usurp their mother's memory, but they responded to her immediately. She wore Liberty gowns, introduced William Morris chintzes into the dark sitting rooms and called their father 'Bip', an affectionate shortening of 'Bishop'. She was as literary minded as their mother had been and had taught herself Greek and Latin. The entry in her diary for the wedding day, cherished by the family, read: 'Finished the Antigone. Married Bip.'

We have a first-hand account of what it was like to take on Bip's children in an article she was persuaded to write for the *Daily Chronicle* in 1930. When she first met them, she said, Eddie occupied the single shabby armchair, reading aloud with ribald comments Smiles's *Self Help*. Dillwyn sat lost in a Greek lexicon, Wilfred manipulated a toy train, the girls played a duet on the piano. Ronnie lay before the fire with Wylde's *Natural History*. They greeted her politely and continued with their pleasures. She withdrew and said to the Bishop: 'They really are clever children. They can occupy themselves.' Five minutes later, the scared face of Winifred appeared at the study door. 'You must come up. The boys are murdering one another.' She found the little boys cowering in corners; the furniture was overturned; *Self Help* had gone out of the window, and Eddie and Dillwyn were locked in what seemed a death grapple.

Something had got to be done to tame them. Edmund Knox was not in favour of boarding schools at their age, but everyone was aware that there was no money for public school education and that they would have to get scholarships. Eddie first went to a preparatory school at Hemel Hempstead and won a scholarship to Rugby in 1896, and Dilly went to Summer Fields in north Oxford, where he only needed a year's coaching to obtain his scholarship to Eton in 1897. Their step-mother organised the summer family reunions with great care. The location was discussed at Christmas and debated at Easter and every summer with their eight bicycles, golf clubs, book-boxes, fishing rods and tennis rackets they migrated for six weeks to some remote inexpensive house, usually a rectory. 'Everyone seemed in any holiday either to be reading for an examination or a scholarship,' Winifred remembered. For relaxation, the Bishop cheerfully spent hours playing cricket with the boys, Mrs K and the girls picking up the balls.

The brothers' reunions were eagerly anticipated at all stages in their lives and different careers. The shape of things to come began when Eddie, who would become a famous editor of *Punch*, produced a family magazine, *Bolliday Bango*, a parody of the popular weeklies of the day with gossip, news and jokes, in his school holidays. Ronnie, aged eight, wrote a Latin play for him, and Dilly, aged twelve, contributed a remarkably elaborate cipher. There was to have been a further instalment of Dilly's contribution, but the editor would have none of it. Rules for games and activities were essential, but any one of them who had a birthday was entitled to make his own rules for the day. One of Dilly's rules was 'nothing is impossible'.

In 1903, when Dilly was preparing to go up to King's College, Cambridge, the family underwent a great change when their father became Bishop of Manchester, and they moved to Bishopscourt, where the boys now had their own study on the ground floor. Ronnie, the youngest, was a precocious fifteen and many and varied were their amusements, solving problems being a particular fascination. They wrote a letter to Sir Arthur Conan Doyle pointing out errors in the Sherlock Holmes stories, enclosing four dried orange pips, an allusion to the letter in *The Sign of Four*. They were disappointed that he did not reply, but he did write to Ronnie when he published his *Studies in the Literature of Sherlock Holmes* in 1912. The brothers were fascinated by the arguments surrounding the controversial claims that Shakespeare's plays were in fact written by Francis Bacon, and Ronnie used Baconian reasoning to prove that Queen Victoria was the author of Tennyson's 'In Memoriam'.

The Knox brothers all had a great ability for words and were addicted to Carrollian 'chopped logic', the sort of nonsense based on the ambiguity of words as used by the Mad Hatter in *Alice's Adventures in Wonderland* or Humpty Dumpty's 'knock-down arguments'. Lewis Carroll liked to tease his child friends by leading them through the most complicated mazes of reasoning to the conclusion that they had meant exactly the opposite of what they had said, this also being a favourite Knoxian game. Carroll and the Knox brothers were devoted to *Punch*, which fostered similar humour. Apparent nonsense could always be unravelled by logic. Both Carroll and Ronnie Knox invented games for teaching logic and Dilly had a whole codebreaking career before him of making sense out of nonsense. I remember a Carrollian question he would ask us at Bletchley Park was: 'Which way does a clock go round?' and if you were stupid enough to say 'clockwise' he would answer: 'But not if you are the clock.' We had to think this way when dealing with the insides of the Enigma cipher machine.

Limericks and humorous verses were a speciality, such as this one from Ronnie on Bishop Berkeley's philosophy:

> *There was a young man who said: 'God*
> *Must think it exceedingly odd*
> *If he finds that this tree*
> *Continues to be*
> *When there's no one about in the Quad.'*

Reply:

Dear Sir, Your astonishment's odd.
I am always about in the Quad.
And that's why the tree
Will continue to be
Since observed by, Yours faithfully, God.

Rhyming and metre, which prompted trains of thought, were particularly important to Dilly, who would go on to produce his own types of acrostics and become an inspired unraveller of textual puzzles, ancient and modern.

In his *Reminiscences of an Octogenarian*, Bishop Knox comments how proud their mother would have been of their successes, and what pleasure it was to him to see that the output of his four sons and one daughter took up several pages of the British Museum catalogue. Much credit could also have been claimed by the Bishop for the upbringing of his remarkable, versatile family. Like John Bunyan's pilgrim, he was Valiant-for-Truth, preaching the gospel of truth, and had had a lifetime of coming to terms with challenges. When he took up his first incumbency at Kibworth he found that his church served two parishes, Kibworth Harcourt and Kibworth Beauchamp, the latter the home of radical 'Stockeners', who turned out hosiery on frames in their cottages. They were despised by Kibworth Harcourt, the home of the sporting squire-archy and retired businessmen of Leicestershire. Edmund Knox's heart was with the Stockeners, as he had witnessed his father's anguish arising out of the terrible agricultural depression of the late 1870s in his Rutland parish. At Merton College, with his evangelical convictions, Edmund had avoided being embroiled in the Oxford Movement – the group of high-church Anglicans also known as the Tractarians, who sought to show that the Church of England was the direct descendant of the apostles – but at Kibworth he had to replace a devout Tractarian, who had served the church for over thirty years.

He later wrote:

There are few people, certainly very few clergy, who doubt their competence to run a country parish. A nice little Church, not trying to the voice – a modest organ, which, at a pinch, the wife could play if necessary, a choir of boys from the Sunday school; backed by the gardener and a labourer or two – no week-night meetings worth mentioning, two of the old sermons cut down and simplified for village use each Sunday, no societies with tedious and tiresome accounts, no parish council likely to give difficulty, a good house, a delightful little garden with fresh-cut flowers and fresh vegetables – maybe a squire who will have to be placated, abundance of time for reading or learning the rudiments of horticulture. So it seems to the outsider. But the vicar who comes into the country with these impressions is not long in altering his mind, and usually arrives at the conclusion that his parish is a very exceptional parish.

I entered upon my work at Kibworth with very few of these illusions. Four years in an Oxford slum had taught me something about the difficulties of plain preaching and something too of the difficulties of wise almsgiving. Visits to my father's parish in Rutland had shown me that Joseph Arch's Agricultural Labourers' Union had created since 1874 a strong prejudice against the Church, and acted very unfavourably on the labourers' churchgoing. I had witnessed my father's perplexities arising out of the terrible agricultural depression of the later '70s. I knew also that my predecessor, a very devout and sincere Tractarian, had been Rector of Kibworth for over thirty years, and that a rumour had gone about that I was intending to wreck all his work, and to hand the parish over to the Dissenters. So I was not unprepared for difficulties.

The Kibworth Harcourt parishioners were happy enough with Anglo-Catholicism, but Beauchamp preferred to give it a miss. To satisfy his own evangelical conscience, Edmund Knox maintained only the ornaments and ritual he could live with, and gradually dispensed with those he could not; confession went by the board. It seemed to work and the Beauchamp poor were seen in the pews again. Little did he know then that he would later have to come to terms with religious controversy within his own family. During university vacations, Wilfred and Ronnie used to bicycle round Manchester to find a church which observed the Seven Points of Ritual, and their bewildered father said to his daughter: 'Between ourselves, Winnie, I cannot understand what it is that the dear boys see in the Blessed Virgin Mary.' He had become reconciled to Ronnie's rosary being produced at family prayers.

Ronnie would spell out his own soul-searching in his *A Spiritual Aeneid*, describing the period between 1910 and 1915, when he prepared to be ordained as a Roman Catholic priest. The Bishop's reply to the news of his son's final conversion in 1917 was typical of his ability to face facts and hope for the best. All he said in a letter to Ronnie was:

> *First, I must acknowledge gratefully the affectionate spirit in which your letter was written, and express my satisfaction that you will not be required to repudiate your baptism. Next, I will say what I said to both the Clergy in my diocese, that when the time came for their return, they might be sure of a most hearty welcome. I am enclosing a copy of the prayer which I have been offering and shall continue to offer on your behalf.*

Eddie managed to sit on the fence and to go through the motions of backing what the Church of England had to offer, but Dilly had clearly drifted away. He had done his best to conceal it from his father, but already when at Eton he had decided he was an agnostic. Dilly always maintained, however, that their father came to terms with his agnosticism more easily than with Ronnie going to Rome. All the boys continued to support the Bishop's humanitarian and reformist missions. Dilly refused an invitation to go to Brittany with his artist friend Henry Lamb in order to join his father's march to London in support of Church schools. The Bishop, a passionate advocate of free education, headed a procession a mile and a half long to a mass meeting in the Albert Hall singing 'Lead, Kindly Light, amidst th'encircling gloom'. Setting aside doctrinal beliefs, Dilly had been brought up in a world of active Christianity and charity which stood him in good stead, and he never forgot the resonance of the words of the daily Bible readings which seemed instinctively to come to mind for any situation.

Dilly had written two brilliant papers in his Cambridge entrance examination, one in maths and the other in Greek verse, but had left all the others unfinished. Nevertheless, such was the promise of his work that the King's admissions tutor in classics recommended him for a scholarship, believing him to be 'capable of indefinite improvement'. Dilly's friend from Eton, John Maynard Keynes, respected Dilly as a mathematician but said that he presented his work 'in a most loathsomely untidy, unintelligible, illegible condition', forgetting to write down the most necessary steps. As will be seen when Dilly later presented his brilliant codebreaking reports, they were incomprehensible to all but a few and his staff found his elliptic way of speaking challenging to say the least. Keynes, who had already been up a year, took Dilly in hand when he arrived at King's in 1903 and through him he met up with key members of the group of writers who would subsequently become known as the Bloomsbury Group. King's was a liberating experience for Dilly and he made friendships there that would last a lifetime.

The year 1903 was a defining moment for moral philosophy in Cambridge, when their own professor, George Edward Moore, published his *Principia Ethica*. Dilly was never one of the Cambridge Apostles, of whom Keynes was a leading light, although he had been proposed on more than one occasion. This exclusive intellectual society, officially called the Cambridge Conversazione Society, founded in 1820 for discussion, enthusiastically took up Moore's philosophy of open-mindedness and mutual criticism, which encouraged an unwillingness to let any statement go unquestioned. 'Why do you say that?' and 'What do you mean by that?' would frequently occur in Dilly conversations in the years to come.

Keynes was not the only Apostle to whom Dilly was close. His friends included the writers Lytton Strachey, E. M. Forster and Leonard Woolf, all later members of the Bloomsbury Group, of which Keynes would also be a prominent member. Strachey, who had initially disliked Dilly, would later fall deeply in love with him, an unrequited passion since Dilly was uninterested in the homosexuality then common at Cambridge. 'You must forgive me please if I can talk of nothing but Knox,' Strachey wrote to a friend. 'I came back from Cambridge having only seen him once –

but the impression was so wonderful! Oh dear! You needn't be jealous! I'm as far away from him as from you!'

In 1913, Ronnie Knox stepped in with his first serious book, *Some Loose Stones*, refuting Moore's idea of morality being self-evident common sense and truth intuitive, as opposed to the need for spiritual guidance. Dilly dismissed the whole subject as unnecessary by replying with *Some Floating Stones*, which he showed only to his King's friends. Dilly's father became alarmed at what he heard of Cambridge and Wilfred was sent to Oxford, where he, like Ronnie later, would begin a spiritual journey, which took him in a different direction from his father's Church of England. Wilfred became an Anglo-Catholic priest at the Oratory of the Good Shepherd and took a vow of celibacy, which the Bishop could not condone, but he whole-heartedly approved of his social welfare work in London's East End. Mrs K was a true Christian, keeping the family together as best she could.

Dilly left King's in 1907, having won the Chancellor's Classical Medal, but with only second-class honours in the second part of his Tripos, and, after a holiday with Eddie and Ronnie in Rome, he went to teach classics and ancient history at St Paul's, Hammersmith, where he made no attempt to keep order in class but was 'loved by all'.

For a short time, he tutored a young Harold Macmillan at his home for a Balliol scholarship, but was rejected as being 'too austere and uncongenial' and was replaced by Ronnie. It was a considerable relief when, in 1909, he was offered a fellowship at King's, where Keynes was now a lecturer in economics and engaged on an improving campaign, which necessitated getting rid of the bursar. Dilly helped him expose the bursar's incompetence, in a truly Knoxian way, by ridiculing the situation in the columns of *The Basileon*, the college magazine. He appealed to the bursar to inspect the rats in the fellows' bedrooms; then to come to the rats' rescue because the rooms were now so damp that they were being driven out by water-rats; lastly, to provide better care for the water-rats, whose nasty coughs kept the younger fellows awake at night. In 1911, he made a new friend, Frank Birch, a history scholar, who would remain close to him for the rest of his life. Frank, a born actor and brilliant talker, was much more amusing and relaxing than most of Dilly's Apostle friends, and he arranged for Dilly to have a part as Cecily in *The Importance of Being Earnest*.

Another new arrival in 1911, which greatly affected Dilly, was the scholar poet A. E. Housman, who became Kennedy Professor of Latin at Trinity College. Housman's poetry had been important to all the brothers, but particularly to Dilly, who revelled in the romantic pessimism of *A Shropshire Lad*, much of which he knew by heart. He counted himself lucky if he could exchange a few words with its author at the Classical Club. What Dilly admired most was Housman's skill with forceful simple metre. Dilly's fellowship dissertation had been on the prose rhythms of the Greek historian Thucydides; it was said that his argument was so clever that nobody could contradict it.

It was Dilly's tutor as an undergraduate, Walter Headlam, who originally inspired in him a passion for Greek literature and language. Headlam was a direct descendant of the great classical scholar Richard Bentley, the master of Trinity College, Cambridge. He was eccentric with little grasp of reality but a brilliant ability to understand the thoughts of the classical Greek writers and to work out, where passages were missing, what they would have contained. Headlam was greatly concerned with textual criticism and had read exceptionally widely in Greek texts. He had devoted much time to Aeschylus, the ancient Greek dramatist often seen as the father of Greek tragedies, but when Dilly knew him he was focused on producing an edition of the Mimes of Herodas, the classical Greek poet who flourished at the high point of Hellenistic poetry in the second and third centuries BC. The floor of Headlam's room in the Gibbs Building was notoriously untidy and stacked high with papers. The one thing Dilly wanted to do was to be of use to him in his project, and this he was unexpectedly able to do as a result of Headlam's tragically early death in 1908, at the age of forty-two. When Dilly returned to King's to take up his fellowship the following year, he inherited his former tutor's work on Herodas, whose *Mimiambi* or Mime Iambics, in the Ionic dialect, were short scenes of everyday life at the time, some very bawdy. The family knew that Dilly didn't admire Herodas as a writer but rather as a familiar foe, and the Mimes provided a difficult game in which nearly all the rules were missing, one which Dilly intended to win and arrive at the correct text. He commuted between Cambridge and the British Museum and corresponded with foreign scholars in Latin.

The Mimes papyrus, found in the excavations of the ancient Egyptian city of Oxyrhynchus, 100 miles south of Cairo, in 1889, was a little worm-eaten roll about 5 inches high, written out by a copyist around AD100 and preserved in the hot sands of the Sahara. They were transcribed in 1891 by the director of the British Museum, Dr F. H. Kenyon, an eminent palaeographer, but there had been a major problem when the charred fragments had originally been assembled as the papyrologist who had worked on the jigsaw puzzle had little knowledge of Greek letters. Dilly noticed something wrong with the strips that had been mounted and after some persuasion Dr Kenyon agreed to have the crumbling strips realigned. More literary papyri were being unearthed at Oxyrhynchus and Dilly was determined to find any in his anonymous scribe's handwriting which would throw light on the *Mimiambi*. Headlam had never worked on the puzzle aspect of the fragmented *Mimiambi*, although with his extensive knowledge of Greek literature he had detected quotes from them in other authors.

Dilly was now all set for working on the definitive text, which had eluded his tutor, although he knew it would take some time to achieve. He intended to be not only linguist, palaeographer and papyrologist but to understand the whole world of the ordinary Greek people depicted by Herodas. A scholar, particularly a Knox, must see things through. As the war clouds gathered in 1914, however, he knew Herodas and the Greeks would have to be put aside and he could not believe that his kind of erudition would be of any use in the years ahead. Having ridden one of the first motor bikes in Cambridge, he tried to enlist as a dispatch rider, but his poor eyesight and his erratic driving let him down. Fortunately, another fellow at King's was talent-spotting clever young men for the Naval Intelligence Division, which had set up a codebreaking section to be known as Room 40, after the room in the Admiralty in which it was housed. Dilly was duly recruited in early 1915 and would now find himself breaking enemy messages rather than attempting to deliver dispatches on a motor bike to British commanders in the field.

TWO

Room 40

The Admiralty had cut the German transatlantic underwater cables in the English Channel on the first day of the war, which meant that in future their communications overseas would mainly be through wireless telegraphy. As Morse messages could be intercepted, they would have to be encoded and new cryptographic bureaux set up to deal with them. In France and Germany they used servicemen, but in Britain it was wisely decided to search for candidates with wider experience and minds of their own, not intimidated by service hierarchy. Rear-Admiral Henry Oliver, the director of the Intelligence Division (DID), recommended that the man to recruit the right people for codebreaking and analysing the messages would be Sir Alfred Ewing, emeritus professor of engineering at King's College, Cambridge, who was no stranger to wireless. He had already patented an electro-magnetic wave detector some years earlier and addressed the Royal Society on the subject of identifying electric oscillations occurring during wireless transmission. Moreover, he had become interested in codes and ciphers when as director of Naval Education he had been consulted about the construction of secure codes for the navy. Breaking the enemy's coded wireless messages would have to be put on a secret service footing and the naval education department seemed a plausible temporary cover.

Ewing's first job in 1914 before looking for codebreakers was to set up a series of listening stations manned by the Post Office and the Marconi Wireless Telegraphy Company with the help of his friend William Russell Clarke, a barrister and radio enthusiast. As director of Naval Education, Ewing was also able to obtain the services of language teachers at the royal naval colleges and one of the first to be recruited was Alastair Denniston from Osborne College on the Isle of Wight, who was destined to become the first head of Bletchley Park in the Second World War. The new recruits were crammed into Ewing's room on a shift system, and, as Denniston said, all six of them were singularly ignorant of the process of breaking a code or cipher, which was like a foreign language, but they did make progress in distinguishing German naval messages and identifying call-signs. As yet the Admiralty had no inkling of what a revolution in naval intelligence they had on their hands; they were still in the days of patrolling vessels reporting movement intelligence to the fleets, but now minefields and submarines had to be contended with, and this sort of Nelson-like exercise had to be abandoned.

However, official attitudes to the possibility of breaking the enemy's coded signals changed after the German light cruiser *Magdeburg* was wrecked in the Baltic and the Russians captured two codebooks, one of which was duly delivered to the First Lord of the Admiralty, Winston Churchill, on 13 October 1914. Churchill was over the moon and, with some poetic licence, wrote the incident up in his *The World Crisis* in 1923, telling how he had personally received the precious *Signalbuch der Kaiserlichen Marine* (SKM) – the Signal Book of the Imperial Navy – a high-level 'flag code'. According to Churchill the 'sea-stained' codebook had been found on a German officer, 'clasped in his bosom by arms rigid in death'. It would not be long before Ewing received another maritime codebook, captured by the Australians from a merchant ship off Melbourne; this was the *Handelsverkehrbuch* (HVB) – merchant navy traffic book – used by the German Admiralty and warships for communication with merchantmen. The third stroke of luck would come when a British trawler in the Heligoland Bight found in its nets a lead-lined chest from a sunken German vessel containing a copy of the *Verkehrsbuch* (VB) – traffic book, the codebook used for routine message traffic. The delighted codebreakers called it 'The Miraculous Draught of Fishes' and Room 40 now had enough material to begin codebreaking in real earnest. There was then no copying gear available and as there was only one copy of the important SKM codebook, Russell Clarke turned himself into a photographer and laboured at home to produce three additional copies.

New premises were found in Room 40 of the Old Admiralty Buildings by the newly appointed DID in October. Captain Reginald 'Blinker' Hall was a much more dynamic leader than his predecessor, Admiral Oliver, and greatly improved the status of what was by now dubbed 'special intelligence'. Churchill then drafted in his own hand a charter for Room 40; it was headed 'Exclusively Secret' and called for a study of 'all the intercepts, not only current but past, and to compare them continually with what actually took place in order to penetrate the German mind and movements'. He expressed the wish that Ewing would 'associate himself continuously' with this work. A search would be made for what later became known as 'professor types'. However, this did not happen overnight, as although the Room 40 codebreakers had shown that they were capable of dealing with the messages encoded from the German navy codebooks, they had yet to convince some of the Admiralty's sea lords that the intelligence derived from the signals would be of any use to them.

Their Lordships were soon shocked into recognition of the value of special intelligence, when, on 14 December 1914, they received information from Room 40 of a planned bombardment by German vessels, possibly on towns along Britain's eastern coast. These towns proved to be Hartlepool, Whitby and Scarborough, but the navy was unable to get its act together in time to prevent the disaster. Churchill wrote in *The World Crisis*:

> *Although the bombarded towns, in which nearly 500 civilians had been killed or wounded, supported their ordeal with fortitude, dissatisfaction was widespread. However, we could not say a word in explanation. We had to bear in silence the censure of our countrymen. We could never admit for fear of compromising our secret information where our squadrons were or how near German raiding cruisers had been to their destruction. One comfort we had. The information on which we had acted had been confirmed by events. The sources of information on which we relied were evidently trustworthy.*

Trustworthy indeed! Room 40 was in business, and matters were very different when the Admiralty received information from Room 40 on 23 January 1915 that there was to be a second attack, with battle cruisers assembling at Dogger Bank. This time the navy was ready for them and inflicted considerable damage. Churchill was up at dawn on the next day with Admiral Fisher, when at 8 a.m. came the news that the enemy had been sighted. Churchill recalled in 1923, as though it were yesterday, the excitement and the tension in Room 40 as he watched the codebreakers at work on the *Magdeburg's* SKM codebook. The codebook had an accompanying grid chart for latitude and longitude, which made even routine messages important, since it allowed instructions about a ship's destination to be plotted. Churchill said:

There can be few purely mental experiences more charged with cold excitement than to follow, almost from minute to minute, the phases of a great naval action from the silent rooms of the Admiralty. Out on blue water in the fighting ships amid the stunning detonations of the cannonade, fractions of the event unfold themselves to the corporeal ear. There is the sense of action at its highest; there is the wrath of battle; there is the intense self-effacing, physical or mental toil. But in Whitehall only the clock ticks and quiet men enter with quick steps, laying strips of pencilled paper before other men, equally silent, who draw lines, and scribble calculations and point the finger or make brief subdued comments. Telegram succeeds telegram at a few minutes' interval as they are picked up and decoded, often in the wrong sequence, frequently of dubious import; and out of these a picture always flickering and changing, rises in the mind, and imagination strikes out around it at every stage flashes of hopes and fears.

Churchill was clearly hooked on special intelligence and laid down instructions for three copies of the message translations to be made, one for the chief of staff and his Operations Division, one for the DID and one to be retained in Room 40. He insisted during his two years in office that this should be done by 'logging' in true minute-by-minute ship's log style, which Room 40 always regarded as a useless burden. Denniston recalled wryly in his memoirs:

The Log became an object of hatred before long. The First Lord had called into being that particular kind of filing the current work and it was over two years when its originator was elsewhere, before a more labour-saving and less soul-destroying method was allowed to replace it. In the days when the watchkeeper averaged 12 messages it could be written up, though even then it was the fashion to let the messages accumulate and allow the new watch to write up the log and thus appreciate the situation. But it was beyond a joke when naval action was pending or Zepps [Zeppelin airships] fluttering and the watchkeeper had 12 to 20 pages of the book to write up.

Churchill's authority to increase the staff was another matter and when it came to intellectual capacity, Ewing naturally turned his attention to his old college, where he had already tentatively approached King's lay dean, the ancient historian Frank Adcock, the historian Frank Birch and the classical scholar Dilly Knox, who in addition to their research skills had the right 'ivory tower' approach that would allow them to focus exclusively on one subject and would be ideal for their secret work. Dilly was the first 'Kingsman' to find his way through the arches of the Admiralty Old Buildings early in 1915 to join Churchill's quiet men in Room 40, and it was not long before he would prove his skill as a codebreaker. Although Ewing was still nominally in charge of Room 40, when Dilly arrived at the beginning of 1915, in the aftermath of the Dogger Bank excitement, it was coming increasingly under 'Blinker' Hall's control, as Ewing had other activities to deal with, and it was Hall's name which in future would be associated with Room 40.

William Reginald Hall went to sea as a midshipman in 1884, aged fourteen, and became a commander in 1901, reaching the pinnacle of his sea-going career in 1913, when he was appointed commander of the new battle cruiser *Queen Mary*. He saw action at the Battle of the Heligoland Bight in 1914 before being recalled, by ill health, to the Admiralty to become DID, in place of Admiral Oliver. He was nicknamed 'Blinker' because of his frequent blinking mannerism. As well as supervising special intelligence, he operated as spymaster in traditional cloak-and-dagger work, which, like Churchill, he saw patriotically as part of Kim's 'Great Game', immortalised by Kipling.

Room 40's codebreakers were somewhat of a trial, as they never took to naval terminology and often failed to keep the right watches. However, just before Dilly arrived 'Blinker' Hall had had the good sense to appoint a real navy man to take charge, Commander (later Admiral) Herbert Hope, who would analyse the messages being broken every day by Room 40 and correct pitfalls, such as in one decoded German naval message, which had annoyed the Admiralty: 'One of our torpedo boats will be running out into square 7F at 8 p.m.' Ships do not 'run out', their Lordships complained, they 'proceed'. Hope knew little German and no codebreaking, but William 'Nobby' Clarke, another barrister, who worked under him, is on record as saying in a post-war archive account, 'Narrative of Captain Hope', that in spite of this 'his consummate seamanship and ability to read the enemy's mind made his election a stroke of genius'. Although 'Blinker' had had little experience of 'professor types', he admired their skills, but he wanted to widen the scope of Room 40's expertise. He brought in two personal assistants, Claud Serocold, a stockbroker, and Lord Herschell, a government whip in the House of Lords, plus 'Nobby' Clarke, and Nigel de Grey from the publishers Heinemann, who would soon prove an excellent choice.

Hall prided himself on finding the right slot for each of their different talents and capabilities and was a past master at delegation. In his biography, he wrote:

> *A Director of Intelligence who attempts to keep himself informed about every detail of the work being done cannot hope to succeed: but if he so arranges his organisation that he knows at once to which of his colleagues he must go for the information he requires, then he may expect good results. Such a system, moreover, has the inestimable advantage of bringing out the best of everyone working under it, for the head will not suggest every move: he will welcome and, indeed, insist on ideas from his staff. And so it was, from first to last, in the Intelligence Division.*

This was the advice he passed on to Rear-Admiral John Godfrey, the Second World War director of Naval Intelligence, when Godfrey was reorganising the Naval Intelligence Division in 1939 in preparation for the war.

Dilly was immediately put onto the small team dealing with codes and cipher keys. Messages were sent in groups of letters or figures. The operator would look up the relevant code-group for each word or figure in the message in a codebook. This would include code-groups that represented much-used terms such as '*Musterung auf der Gefechtsstation*' – muster at battle stations – and common syllables, so that unusual words which did not appear in the codebook could be encoded. Only low-grade messages such as weather reports were encoded directly from the codebooks; the code-groups for high-grade naval messages were given added security using a cipher. Simply put, codes replace single words, figures or phrases with a single code-group, while a cipher replaces each individual letter or figure with another letter or figure. Encoding the messages to form code-groups, which were then enciphered, in a process which came to be known as super-encipherment, was designed to make them harder for the British to break. The settings of a cipher are known as the 'key' in English or to the Germans as the '*Chi*', from the French *chiffre*. Room 40 referred to breaking these enciphered messages as solving the key. At the beginning of the war, the main key remained the same for three months, which gave the Room 40 codebreakers a good start in familiarising themselves with the message characteristics that provided the 'cribs' for key changes – pieces of known text that could be predicted to be used in certain situations and would therefore give the codebreakers a 'way in' to the cipher and the code that lay underneath it. At the beginning of 1915, when the key was changed, the messages began with an enciphered serial number, so that it was easy enough to see when a message was out of order and a change had occurred; it would then provide a way in to the new encipherment tables, which would not have been possible if the operators had given the serial number in clear.

It was Fleet Paymaster Charles Rotter, the principal expert on the Kaiser's navy in the Naval Intelligence Division, who had first understood that having the SKM codebook from the *Magdeburg* was not the end of the story, as there was a further process of encipherment to contend with. Dilly soon became involved in solving the first new *Chi* imposed on the SKM codebook soon after the Dogger Bank success. The cipher proved to be a letter-for-letter substitution where a vowel was replaced by a vowel in order to keep the code-group pronounceable. Churchill always felt that he was in on anything to do with signals intelligence derived from using the *Magdeburg's* codebook and immediately came in to congratulate Room

40 when he heard the overlying key to the SKM code-groups had been broken.

Dilly had taken to the deciphering side of signals intelligence like a duck to water and was the only member of Room 40 who had any experience of basic codebreaking, since similar attitudes and thought processes were needed for solving unreadable scripts and decoding messages. Both required inspired guesswork and this was Dilly's forte. Most of the other new recruits were fluent in German and were put to work on translating the decoded messages and analysing them, like Rev. William Montgomery, an authority on early church fathers, who had translated many German theological works and had been working in the censorship department. Dilly was obviously a godsend. He had not had much to do with secret writing, where the text is intentionally made unintelligible through encipherment, as he had dealt mainly with fragmented and damaged texts of literary papyri, which needed expert knowledge of the ancient language to unravel, but he must have been in his element when Room 40 received the charred remains of a codebook from a shot-down Zeppelin.

Dilly was also familiar with emblematic hieroglyphs, which served him well in attempting to reconstruct the 'telegraphese' in the German navy codebooks. This type of codebook had been in use for some time by commercial firms; provided you knew you were dealing with one for an oil company, say, the associated words of barrels and orders in the message were soon isolated and the repeated words guessed. A codebook needed two columns to serve sender and recipient in respective alphabetical or numerical order.

A new secret codebook would take a long time to compile but having the three naval books SKM, HVB and VB in its possession gave Room 40 a head start. Dilly had spent much time identifying the idiosyncrasies of Greek copyists on literary papyri and was well aware of how they made errors, so he was prepared for Morse operators making mistakes in the messages. He was also prepared for lazy operators taking short cuts in encoding telegrams, knowing this would provide a way in for him. A real bonus for Room 40 would be finding complete messages that had been decoded in one of the easy weather codes then repeated in the more difficult messages that had also been enciphered, giving the codebreakers the key to the cipher. Such repeated messages were the Rosetta stone of codebreaking and were later called 'kisses' at Bletchley Park as anybody who spotted one marked it XX.

Room 40's big moment would come at the beginning of 1916, when the first major encounter with the German High Fleet was being planned, which finally took place on 31 May. It is best described by Winston Churchill in *The World Crisis*, as Room 40's successes moved on from the Dogger Bank to Jutland:

> *Earlier in this account, I recorded the events which secured for the Admiralty the incomparable advantage of reading the plans and orders of the enemy before they were executed. Without the codebreakers' department there would have been no Battle of Jutland. But for that department the whole course of the naval war would have been different. The British Fleet could not have remained continuously at sea without wearing down its men and machinery. If it had remained almost continuously at sea the Germans would have been able to bombard two or three times a month all our East Coast towns.*

Speaking of the *Magdeburg*'s codebook as the triumph of signals intelligence, he continued:

> *These signal books and the charts associated with them were subjected to a study in Whitehall in which self-effacing industry and imaginative genius reached their highest degree … By the aid of these books and the deduction drawn from their use, the Admiralty acquired the power of reading a proportion of the German wireless messages … capable of presenting to the Fleet a stream of valuable information.*

Dilly was heavily involved and, like the other members of the team, frequently worked throughout the night on such messages with the windows blacked out against Zeppelin raids; by this time the key was changed every day at midnight and there was a rush to solve it before the morning. He managed to get his brother Ronnie recruited to join him and, as one of the codebreakers put it, a figure 'in clerical garb' now appeared in the Admiralty's Room 40. Ronnie mentioned mildly to one of the family that Dilly had never explained to him exactly what he was meant to be doing. As I was to discover myself, Dilly was never very good at explaining, always believing that people would rather work it out for themselves, as Ronnie did. After a short while, when the emergency was over, he was transferred to a branch of the War Office known as MI7, which studied the newspapers of neutral countries in order to trace the effect of enemy propaganda.

The Battle of Jutland under Admiral John Jellicoe was memorable as being the only occasion in the First World War when the rival fleets met and, although the outcome of the battle was not decisive, it left the British fleet the undisputed master of the seas. The undoubted important contribution made by signals intelligence led directly to administrative changes in Room 40. 'Nobby' Clarke, who was on duty analysing the traffic throughout the battle, recorded that the codebreakers had provided advance information about the exact composition of the German fleet and its movements through studying call-signs, transits in the Kiel canal and exercises in the Baltic, even before decoding the messages, but that the Operations Division had failed to make use of the information.

'Blinker' Hall was convinced that the failures during the Battle of Jutland would not have happened had Room 40 been allowed to submit full intelligence reports, based on their experience of German signals, instead of just passing on transcripts whose significance was not always grasped by the Operations Division. He was determined this would not happen again and began by setting up a war diary, but it would take his next move to achieve effective intelligence reorganisation. He decided the time had come to get in on strategic as well as tactical intelligence through setting up a new diplomatic unit under his own control. This began in the summer of 1915 when a diplomatic codebook was obtained from the Persian city of Bushehr on the Gulf. The German consul had left it behind when his consulate was hurriedly abandoned. Ben Faudel-Phillips, the Rev. Montgomery and Nigel de Grey would later join this diplomatic sub-section, headed by Sir George Young, himself an experienced diplomat. In order to conceal that they were engaged in reading diplomatic communications between neutral countries, they were referred to as the 'research party', rather than the diplomatic sub-section. In early 1917, they were dealt a diplomatic trump card which would greatly increase the reputation of Room 40. Dilly was also involved, and greatly admired the way Hall played his hand, particularly how he covered his tracks and protected the secret source of the intelligence provided.

On 16 January 1917, Arthur Zimmermann, the German Foreign Secretary, dispatched a long coded telegram to the German ambassador in Mexico, Heinrich von Eckhardt, which proved to be political dynamite. It had to be sent first by transatlantic cable to the German ambassador in Washington, Johann von Bernstorff, before retransmission. President Woodrow Wilson had granted German diplomats the privilege of sending their material under cover of US diplomatic traffic, hoping that this would enable Germany to keep in touch with the United States and further Wilson's aim of mediating an end to the war. The Zimmermann telegram to Washington was intercepted, as the cables touched on British soil at Porthcurno near Land's End, and was received in Room 40 soon after it was sent. The telegram was sent in the high-grade diplomatic code 7500, which Room 40 had only just begun to solve. Unlike the telegraphese of operational naval messages, diplomatic telegrams were formal and verbose, necessitating large codebooks.

When the encoded Zimmermann telegram first arrived down the pneumatic tube on the night watch, it seems it was taken first to Dilly. He could make out that it began with the alarming sentence 'We propose to begin on 1 February unrestrained submarine warfare', which of course would be of immediate concern to Admiralty Operations, but the gist of what followed sent Dilly scuttling over to de Grey. It turned out to be nothing less than a daring proposal that the Mexican government should form a military alliance with Germany against the United States in exchange for the return of Texas, New Mexico and Arizona, lost by Mexico to the US in the 1846–8 war between the two countries. The precise detail of the telegram was not immediately clear because so few of the 7500 code's groups had been recovered. De Grey was not only an expert German linguist but also a professional editor and as such was, like Dilly, very used to emending texts or in this case filling in gaps. Writing in 1945, de Grey recalled the moment as though it had occurred the previous day:

The telegram was first sorted to Knox, whose business it was to fill in any known groups. His knowledge of German was at that time too slender for him to tackle any difficult passages in telegrams. So that the procedure was that if the telegrams appeared from what could be read to have any interest he brought them to me for further study. We could at once read enough groups for Knox to see that the telegram was important. Together he and I worked solidly all the morning on it. With our crude methods and lack of staff, no elaborate indexing of groups had been developed, only constantly recurring groups were noted in the working copies of the code as our fancy dictated. Work therefore was slow and laborious, but by about midday we had a skeleton version, sweating with excitement as we went on, because neither of us doubted the importance of what we had in our hands.

It was then de Grey's responsibility to report to Hall all matters emanating from the diplomatic 'research party' in which Dilly had no official role.

As soon as I felt sufficiently secure in our version even with all its gaps I took it down to Admiral Hall … although Ewing was nominally our head, 'Blinker' Hall had made a compact with a few of us of the 'research party', that if we ever dug up anything of real importance we were to take it direct to him without showing it to Ewing, whom he distrusted as a chatter-box. Blinker was always accessible to the lads of Room 40, at least he was always to me at that time because I was getting him all the news from diplomatic Germany. I was young and excited and I ran all the way to his room, found Serocold alone and Blinker free. I burst out breathlessly: 'Do you want to bring America in the war, Sir?'

'Yes, why?' said Blinker Hall.

'I've got a telegram that will bring them in if you give it to them.'

Hall discussed it animatedly with Serocold and de Grey, but however important the message was, even in its incomplete form, he knew it would have to be handled very carefully diplomatically. He asked for the original telegraph in code, which he locked in his safe, and said that on no account was anything to be said about it to anyone and nothing was to be put on the files. First of all, he had to try and calculate the motives behind this extraordinary action by the Germans and the likely reaction of President Wilson. Secondly, as there was every chance that the Americans would declare war if they received the information, he had to weigh that against the great disadvantage of the Germans then finding out that we were reading their communications, just as Room 40 was providing good intelligence from Dilly about the movement of German ships and U-boats through breaking their naval codes. It was essential not to let the Americans know we had been intercepting neutral messages as well as preventing the Germans from discovering that we were breaking their codes. Hall's solution was nothing less than brilliant.

Hall rightly guessed that von Bernstorff would have to transmit the same message to Eckhardt in Mexico in a lower-grade code than the 7500 code. He also knew that the British embassy in Mexico had a source with access to the telegraph offices in Mexico City, whom he dubbed 'Mr T'. This was in fact Edward Thurstan, the British chargé d'affaires, who ran the embassy's source inside the telegraph office and was therefore able to obtain a complete copy of the encoded Zimmermann telegram as sent on by von Bernstorff to Mexico. It had been sent in diplomatic code 13040, an old code very similar to the one obtained at Bushehr, which Room 40 had been working on since 1915, with Montgomery in charge of trying to reconstruct its 11,000 groups. Although there were still a lot of unsolved groups in Room 40's reconstructed codebook, Montgomery and de Grey managed to use it to fill in the gaps in the Zimmermann telegram and were able to present Hall with the complete text. This was a triumph as Germany would think that the text of the telegram had been achieved by cloak-and-dagger work, which although regarded as dirty tricks was universally carried out, as indeed in part it had in this case, and would not reveal the interception and breaking of the secret diplomatic 7500 code, which had alerted Room 40 in the first place. However, when the moment came to reveal the content of the message, the doubtful US ambassador in London, Walter Page, wanted proof that it was not a fake and that they could in fact decode 13040 messages. De Grey obligingly went along to the US embassy with the codebook they had compiled, and to his great satisfaction the embassy secretary, Edward Bell, was able to decode a dozen groups of the Zimmermann telegram himself. But de Grey did the rest, and recalled having to bluff with some, as they weren't all written up in his version of the book:

Being in a hurry, I grabbed my own version of 13040 without thinking and went off to [Hall's] room. There Edward Bell produced a copy of the telegram and invited me to decipher it in his presence and to explain the system as I went along. I gaily proceeded and all went well with the first few groups but then on coming to the next I found my book blank and realised with horror that I hadn't done my homework. I had not written up my book and this was by way of being a demonstration to the Americans of the absolute cast iron certainty of our story, good enough to carry firm conviction to their hesitating hearts. If I stopped and fetched another book he would suspect at once that we had faked it up for his benefit. If I let him see that I was writing it down out of my head he would not believe me. If he did not believe me we should fail and have lost the greatest opportunity ever presented to us. Several seconds of bloody sweat. Then I bluffed. I showed him all the groups when they had been written in my book and passed quickly over those that were not, writing the words into the copy of the telegram by heart. Edward Bell, most charming man, was thoroughly convinced – the more easily I think in that he wanted to be convinced anyhow and regarded the whole thing as black magic.

Once persuaded by Bell that it was genuine, Page transmitted the content to President Wilson on February 23 and when it was released to the press, the ensuing outrage easily persuaded Congress to declare war on Germany.

Hall hushed everything up and destroyed the evidence, and it has been difficult to verify later stories from Room 40 insiders who were not actually there at the time. Dilly's family knew that he was frustrated by the secrecy imposed within the department. Penelope Knox, his niece, revealed in *The Knox Brothers* that the way in for the Zimmermann triumph had been through the second telegram obtained from the telegraph offices and that for its solution Dilly had felt 'professional admiration but also professional jealousy'. The latter was that he was not in at the kill as de

Grey and Montgomery had been with Hall. The 'professional admiration' was for Blinker's getting 13040 from the telegraph offices, which gave rise to Dilly's future plaintive murmurs of 'Can't we get something from the post office?' even in inappropriate situations.

After the great success of the Zimmermann telegram, Room 40 expanded into a set of rooms nearby to become known officially on 17 May 1917 as ID25, Section 25 of the Naval Intelligence Division, with small units dedicated to specialised tasks. In spite of its upgraded status, members preferred to continue to call themselves Room 40, as would happen at Bletchley Park when the staff of the iconic small Hut 6 and Hut 8 were moved to large blocks. Commander William James was now appointed as head to see that in future signals intelligence would be closely co-ordinated with the Operations Division. Hall sent de Grey out to Rome to liaise with Italian-based codebreakers and co-ordinate Mediterranean intelligence and Faudel-Phillips was then put in charge of the diplomatic section, now in Room 45. As the Germans had threatened in the Zimmermann telegram, unrestricted submarine warfare was now carried out and 835,000 tons of allied shipping were lost in the month after America declared war. A convoy system was set up and ID25's most important work would be concentrated on intelligence relating to the position of the U-boats. A submarine tracking room operated in the Admiralty under Fleet Paymaster Ernest Thring and was directly linked by pneumatic tube to the new direction-finding section Hall set up in ID25 under Frank Tiarks, whom he recruited from the City. The direction-finding network locked onto the signal from enemy wireless transmitters and took a bearing to their location. By using several direction-finding stations to track down the transmitters, a series of bearings could be traced on a map and where they met was the location of the enemy transmitter. The creation of the new sections to work on the codebreakers' material meant there was no longer any delay in it reaching the Operations Division, who could make immediate use of it, and there was soon a noticeable increase in the number of U-boats sunk.

There was great alarm when the SKM codebook, which had served Room 40 so well, was completely replaced by the new FFB book, at a time when it was essential to be able to read the flag code in order to track the submarines. This meant not just a key system that had to be deciphered, but a new codebook to be compiled from scratch without the benefit of a capture as hitherto. By the time the convoy system was set up in June, Dilly had made good headway with the new code and it became possible to divert convoys from dangerous areas. Renewed efforts were made to recover papers from any submarine sunk in water shallow enough for divers to operate. Dilly had acquired the small Room 53 in ID25 to work on the flag code. The room had its own bath, which was useful for Dilly since this was where he would do a lot of his thinking, whether on the mysteries of Greek papyri or German codes. He was also given a secretary, Miss Olive Roddam, the daughter of a Northumberland landowner, to help him. There was one problem, however, as he kept mostly night watches to be ready for the key change, but his secretary worked normal office hours and he had to rush to get out of his bath and into his uniform before she arrived. In common with all the other civilians in Room 40, Dilly was commissioned into the Royal Naval Volunteer Reserve in July 1917. Miss Roddam was the first woman outside his own family with whom Dilly had ever spent any time in close proximity. She meanwhile had come to London in the wake of the loss of her fiancé in France. It was perhaps inevitable that they would become close and once the war was over, and sights could be set on better times, Dilly would marry Miss Roddam.

There had been great celebrations when Dilly Knox found a way in to the new high-level SKM flag code and its key system. He had found a telegram which gave the notification that it was a practice message for the new code in the preamble. A practice message would come straight out of the operator's head and would almost certainly have a lot of words outside normal naval terminology so the operator would have to use code-groups representing syllables. Dilly noticed a pattern of a repeated syllable, which he assumed to be 'en', which – since in German many plurals and all the basic forms of verbs end in 'en' – is the most common German syllable; but there seemed to be rather a lot of them for such a short message and he soon detected that it was a poem with rhyming dactyls. Dilly believed that if the German operator had sent out a romantic poem, it was likely to include roses, which is rendered in German as *Rosen* and therefore also ends with the 'en' syllable, and in any case there would not be much opportunity to use naval telegraphese in a poem, whether or not it included roses. Normally, in the old SKM codebook, unusual words would have to be made up from relevant coded syllables and the inclusion of a large number of plurals and infinitives would account for the frequent syllable substitution of 'en' in the practice message. Even so, there were rather a lot of them for a short message. Dilly soon detected a pattern and tried out various syllabic metres, writing down examples of possible spaced syllables, with the repeated syllables he considered to be 'en' in what would have looked like this:

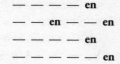

He then took his scribble along the corridor to the German scholars in the hope that they could piece it together through metre as he had done with his Herodas fragments. Dr Leonard Willoughby, the Oxford Taylorian lecturer, was an expert on the German Romantic movement and it did not take him long to identify a Schiller epigram, indeed with roses, heavenly ones at that, from Dilly's spaced out 'en' syllables:

Ehret die Frauen; sie flechten und weben
Himmlische Rosen ins irdische Leben
[Give reverence to women; they plait and weave
Heavenly roses in this earthly life]

This enabled Dilly to find the substitution 'key' and painstakingly work back to compiling the FFB code. Commander James, who was in charge of analysing the intelligence derived from the breaking of the U-boat code, remembered the little room where Dilly was 'labouring' over the apparently insoluble as one of the most 'astonishing sights' of his department.

Professor Walter Bruford, then the last surviving member of Room 40, himself a German scholar, was able to give this information about the break to Penelope Fitzgerald for her book. Hall felt personally involved and every time a submarine was sunk he said: 'Willoughby, go and fetch the rum.' Willoughby was in charge of writing up the translation of each message in the logbook; but doubtless he and Dilly and the other 'professor types' would have much preferred to celebrate with the Madeira or brandy they were accustomed to in their common rooms.

The Germans introduced many more different key systems which needed constant vigilance but, astonishingly, this small group of codebreakers in Room 40 had decoded and deciphered about 20,000 messages by the end of the war. The last of these messages was the thrilling climax, giving the news that Admiral Reinhard Scheer, the German chief of naval staff, hinted that the High Seas Fleet was to be scuttled. Alastair Denniston went out from ID25 to act as interpreter for Admiral Sir David Beatty, commander-in-chief of the Grand Fleet, at the surrender of the German fleet in Scapa Flow. Dilly Knox and Frank Birch thought that a suitable end-of-war celebration would be a pantomime parody of codebreaking to be performed at the Chelsea house they shared with a friend.

My interpretation of *Alice in ID25*, which follows, is from Dilly's own copy.

THREE

Alice in ID25

'I'm afraid it's all Greek to me'

Alice in ID25, written by Frank Birch with poems by Dilly Knox, both devoted Carrollians, is a brilliantly comic, but very authentic, skit of Room 40, following closely the pattern of Lewis Carroll's own *Alice's Adventures in Wonderland* and full of the Carrollian 'chopped logic' which Dilly loved so much. It was performed by the codebreakers as a pantomime for their own entertainment during a concert they held at the end of the First World War. Many of the characters would reappear at Bletchley Park. One of the songs performed at the concert makes reference to Dilly and Olive:

> *Peace, Peace, Oh for some peace!*
> *Miss Roddam says Knox does not please her*
> *When instead of a mat he makes use of her hat*
> *And knocks out his pipe on the geyser.*

But the *pièce de résistance* was Birch's skit, which begins at the time in May 1917 that William James, now promoted to captain, took over as head, when Room 40 became ID25, and carries on to demobilisation. It does include a backward look to the Battle of Jutland and the Zimmermann telegram and Dilly manages to get in a passing reference to his brother Ronnie, who had left before Room 40 became ID25.

The pantomime begins with Alice walking down Whitehall one day, when suddenly out of an upstairs window a sheet of paper fluttered down at her feet. She picked it up when her nurse was looking the other way, and written on it were the words: 'Ballybunion – Short begins- ud-sn-dd-um-um-vvv-depresses key-fierce x's and wipers.' Alice couldn't make a word of sense out of it. For members of Room 40, however, this was a recognisable preamble to an encoded message, giving the call-signs and chit-chat of the German station sending it out. Ballybunion was meant to be the British wireless interception station that had picked it up, which in the early days was Hunstanton. Without the intercept operators in what became known as the 'Y Service', the amount of material available to Room 40 to decode would have been considerably less; they became extraordinarily efficient in tracking down what was called the 'fist' of the individual German wireless operators. German wireless stations changed their call-signs frequently for security reasons so the 'fist', the idiosyncratic way in which individual operators tapped out their Morse messages, was a very good way of identifying stations – hence the note in the signal about the 'fierce' way in which the fictional operator intercepted at Ballybunion taps his Xs.

As soon as Alice touched the gobbledegook message a curious feeling of growing smaller came over her and the people in the street started to fade away. As in her previous adventures, the first person Alice met, fortuitously, was the White Rabbit. He was 'obviously very important' and, as always in the Lewis Carroll stories, in a great hurry.

He was dressed in his Sunday best – spats, spectacles, and a little black coat, and kept doing up and undoing its buttons with nervousness. 'Dear me, dear me,' Alice heard him say as he passed her, 'it's past ten. I shall be late for the DIND. I must be there when he comes round. I always am,' and with that he bustled out of earshot.

The White Rabbit was Birch's depiction of Frank Adcock, who was partly responsible for getting his fellow Kingsmen, Birch and Knox, into Room 40 and would play a similar role at the start of the Second World War. His friends describe him as a small round man with twinkling eyes behind thick glasses and that is how the Room 40 cartoonist, G. P. Mackeson, portrays him in the printed edition of the pantomime. The White Rabbit bustles off very disconcerted as he thought he was going to be late for the boss, who was of course the famous 'Blinker' Hall, the director of the Intelligence Division or DID, who for some reason the White Rabbit calls DIND.

Alice gave chase and, whereas in the previous adventures Lewis Carroll gave her she fell down a rabbit hole, in Birch's version she fell down a mysterious tube under an arch in the Admiralty Old Building. This was the pneumatic tube that delivered the messages to the codebreakers so instead of falling on leaves at the bottom, she ended up in a wire cage in a large room, Room 40, where there was someone waiting to extricate the shuttle full of gobbledegook messages that had preceded her in her fall.

She appeared to be in a sort of cage of golden wire, through which she could see into an immense room where there were many huge creatures. But Alice remembered that she herself had shrunk and supposed that they were all really only a normal size, except perhaps for one quite little man seated at a desk in the far corner of the window.

The 'Little Man' was Alastair Denniston, who was very small in real life, and Alice learned later that he never left his post and had a bed brought in beside his desk. He would see codes and ciphers through during the interwar years to become operational head of Bletchley Park, where he was still called 'the Little Man' by his old colleagues.

Alice was hoping to meet the boss, whom the White Rabbit had called the DIND and was so fussed about, but she would not do so until the end of the pantomime. She looked at all the rooms numbered along the passage, but the numbers appeared to have nothing to do with each other and they all said No Admittance.

At last, just as she turned the corner of a narrow dark passage, she ran into a large creature, who looked like a cross between a Labour member and Sir Francis Drake. He kept on turning out his pockets and poking into the dark corners.

'Mornin', Miss,' said this gentleman in a voice husky – with emotion, Alice thought. ''Ave you seen a bed anywhere?'

'No,' replied Alice, 'I haven't.'

'I've lost a bed,' he went on. 'I shouldn't be surprised if it weren't that hungry creature in 53. Very careless 'e is. Tried to bathe in it, I daresay, and swallowed it.'

The 'hungry creature' in room 53 who was inclined to bathe was, of course, Dilly. When Alice asked the husky-voiced creature the way to the DIND, she was told she ought first to see his deputy, Captain James. 'Nice chap, Captain James. Knows 'is place.' James was the only person who was actually named in the skit, all the others being given Carrollian guises. Dilly's poem, which Alice is later forced to recite, describes him thus:

The Captain in Room 54
Employs men and girls by the score.
But organisation
Leaves no occupation
For the Captain himself any more.

The occupation that had made poor James famous was blowing bubbles. He never lived down the portrait painted by his grandfather, Sir John Millais. It depicted the five-year-old James as an angelic small boy entranced with blowing bubbles. It was taken over by Pears as a soap advertisement and appeared on hundreds of hoardings. Inevitably he was nicknamed 'Bubbles' James.

Alice, by standing on tiptoe, could see one room marked 'The Mansion House' and underneath it the words 'This was the Lord Mayor's Show'. This was Room 45, Blinker Hall's successful diplomatic section, which he set up in 1915 under Sir George Young. Ben Faudel-Phillips was now in charge. Faudel-Phillips's father and grandfather had both been Lord Mayors of London and his colleagues said that he looked like one. He didn't appear to be on show at the moment; however, Dilly's poem, which Alice found herself reciting, claimed:

It is commonly thought we derive
Great blessing from Room 45.

Our courtly Lord Mayor,
By his policy there,
Has rescued the Empire alive.

Alice then met the Dormouse, Nigel de Grey, of Zimmermann telegram fame. The creatures were pushing and dragging him into a passage.

'What's the matter?' asked Alice, who felt sorry for the poor creature. Whereupon they all screamed: 'He does his own work and minds his own business. We don't want that sort of thing here,' and pushed him out of the room.

There was still resentment about the way in which, on Hall's strict orders, de Grey had to keep silent about Room 40 and the success of the Zimmermann telegram, which brought America into the war. He had been awarded the OBE, the first recognition ever to be given to a codebreaker, which clearly irked his colleagues. When Alice met him he was wearing a coronet.

Alice was about to meet the various types of intelligence officers who provided the back-up for the codebreakers. Leonard Willoughby, later a professor, an expert on German literature, was featured as 'the Grumbling Willow' because he resented having to log everything down in triplicate. 'Nobby' Clarke, depicted as the Chief Clerk in the pantomime, was the call-sign expert and always emphasised how much information could be obtained from messages even without decoding, by analysing the communications and the operator chatter, as he had done during the Battle of Jutland. As an experiment, probably set up by Frank Birch, Clarke had a special room set aside where the officers were given German signals as they arrived down the tube and told to interpret what they implied for the use of Operations, and then at the end of the day to examine the decodes to assess how they had fared. In Dilly's view, it seemed a rather pointless exercise, as he made clear in the poem which Alice recites:

Our minds are unable to fix
The uses of Room 56.

Yet they show no compunction
Concerning their function,
No scruple of conscience pricks.

After meeting a number of different members of Room 40, all disguised as 'huge creatures', it was time for Alice to see what codebreaking was all about and so she is sent to find Dilly Knox. Birch was really in his element when he came to caricature his friend and collaborator, now Room 40's chief cryptographer, whom he portrayed as the Dodo and had working in a room with the notice 'Mixed Bathing' on the door. Lewis Carroll had seen himself in that guise in *Alice's Adventures in Wonderland*.

'I'll just hand you over to Dilly the Dodo,' said the guide hoarsely, 'and then you won't want me any more, so I think I'll step out and see a man about a dog.'

'What, another friend?' ejaculated Alice.

'Yes, another one,' he replied shortly.

Alice was just wondering if he had a great many friends and if they all had dogs, when he opened the door, pushed Alice inside and, with a shout of 'Tea ready, Gentlemen, please' disappeared, slamming the door behind her.

The room was a very tiny one, 'no bigger than a bathing machine', Alice thought, and the table in the middle was so big that you could only just squeeze between it and the wall. Alice had plenty of time to take everything in because none of the creatures there took any notice of her. They were all scowling very hard at the table in front of them.

'Please can you tell me which is Dilly the Dodo?' Alice inquired politely after a minute or two.

'I am,' replied one of the creatures, jumping up.

Alice thought he was the queerest bird she had ever seen. He was so long and lean, and he had outgrown his clothes, and his face was like a pang of hunger.

Describing Alice's confrontation with the Dodo, Birch has fun with Dilly's dependence on his secretary, soon to be his wife, Olive Roddam, and his love of Greek. Dilly also managed to get a reference to his brother Ronnie converting to Roman Catholicism inserted into the pantomime, although Ronnie had left some time previously and was now in the throes of becoming a Roman Catholic priest. Perhaps the most important allusion is to the material the Dodo was working on. Dilly was rightly proud of having broken the German Imperial Navy's three-letter flag code and so the Dodo was anxious to explain this to Alice.

'I was told to come to you,' said Alice, rather disconcerted.

'You must ask the Secretary, ask the Secretary,' he answered with a wave of the paw. 'It is unconstitutional to approach me except through the Secretary,' and he sat down again.

Alice hesitated for a few seconds, but thought she would try again. 'Isn't it rather a small room?' she began.

'Not really,' said the Dodo huffily; 'not really a small room. It's just the right size, when you come to think. Of course, you know the Greek definition of the ideal room?'

'I'm afraid I don't,' Alice apologised.

'The ideal room is such', the Dodo quoted, 'that a man standing in the centre can touch floor, ceiling and all four walls.'

'Really?' said Alice, at a loss for anything better to say. Then she went on: 'But you can't stand in the middle of this room, because of the table.'

'I don't see the difficulty,' he snapped.

Alice thought the creature very hard to please, but she hastened to change the conversation. 'So you are very fond of Greek?' she inquired.

'Greek or Latin, Latin or Greek,' he replied. 'I love all the Classics. That's why I brought my brother here. He's a Roman, you know.'

Alice couldn't see how a Dodo could have a Roman brother, but, before she could ask for an explanation, he went on more kindly: 'Perhaps you would like to see some of my work,' and he handed her a sheet of very dirty paper on which a spider with inky feet appeared to have been crawling.

'It looks very clever,' Alice suggested politely, 'but I'm afraid it's all Greek to me.'

'That's why I like it so much,' the Dodo smiled. 'Let me explain it to you. It's three-letter stuff, you see, so we have one person for each letter.'

'But there are four of you,' countered Alice.

'You know the rule, don't you?' he said pityingly. 'One for each letter and one for the pot.'

Alice thought she had never heard such nonsense.

Alice in ID25 also refers of course to Dilly's bath in his 'very tiny room'. Room 53 had the only bath in the Admiralty, which is why Dilly had chosen it, as he was addicted to solving problems in a soapy, steamy atmosphere. As Alice says in the poem she recites:

The sailor in Room 53
Has never, it's true, been to sea,
But though not in a boat,
He has yet served afloat –
In a bath at the Admiralty.

Dilly could not be portrayed by Birch without some reference to his absent-mindedness so he has the Dodo fumbling in his pockets for something he appears to have lost.

'What's the matter?' asked Alice.

'I've lost my spectacles,' cried the Dodo angrily, as he turned up the chairs and table. 'Where are my spectacles?' and he glared angrily at the Secretary.

'I expect they are in that,' jerked the Secretary, pointing to a tobacco-pouch on the table.

'Of course, of course,' cried the Dodo foolishly. He opened the pouch and there, sure enough, were the spectacles.

Alice could not help asking the strange creature why he kept his glasses in a tobacco-pouch.

'A little idea of mine,' he smirked. 'Rather ingenious, don't you think? You see, by this means, when I find my spectacles I remember my tobacco.'

'But where is it?' asked Alice, puzzled.

'Well, if the spectacles are in the tobacco pouch, the tobacco must be in the spectacle case. It follows, you know, by logic,' and with that he took *his spectacle-case from his pocket and opened it. Inside was not tobacco at all, but a long and thin ham sandwich. Alice was about to ask for an explanation when the Dodo went on triumphantly: 'You see how it works? Now this serves to remind me that I am hungry.'*

Poor Alice was now completely bewildered, but she managed to ask: 'Can't you remember when you are hungry?'

'I'm always hungry,' he gobbled, 'but I can't always remember it. Being hungry', he went on with his mouth full, 'is like being in debt. You always are, but you sometimes need to be reminded of it. That's why I work at night. You see, you get more meals that way. The Night Watch', he murmured dreamily, 'is very generous. And that reminds me,' he suddenly shouted, 'it's tea-time. Come on!' And seizing Alice by the hand he ran with her out of the room.

The Dodo then takes Alice to Birch's equivalent of the Mad Hatter's tea party, although in a reference to the vital part of the codebreaking process, breaking the keys, this becomes a 'key party'. Alice is offered a few unappetising crumbs of cake.

Alice was thinking how she could refuse without giving offence, when the Dodo, who had been stuffing silently all this time, suddenly jumped up and doddered past her, crying: 'I must go to Room 40 and find fault with things. Come along.'

The director, Rear-Admiral 'Blinker' Hall, the DIND in Birch's parody, now occupied the original Room 40 and Dilly always found plenty to complain about. He was well known for his habit of sending in resignations, although he knew they could never be accepted. Finally Alice does get to meet the DIND and Alastair Denniston, the Little Man, explains the joke behind the 'N' inserted into Hall's pantomime title.

A trumpet sounded and the door flew open. At the same time all the creatures woke up and jumped to their feet. 'It's the DIND, the DIND,' they shouted in chorus.

'What does "the DIND" mean?' Alice asked the Little Man.

'Ssh!' he whispered. 'It's French, you know.'

Alice was a clever girl who knew French and it did not take her long to understand that Rear-Admiral Sir William Hall, who was so pleased with himself, was a *DIND-on*, a turkey cock. Birch also uses the Denniston character, the Little Man, to make a jibe at the wealth of Hall's two personal assistants, Lord Herschell and Claud Serocold.

> At this moment an imposing figure strutted into the room between two other creatures, scarcely less impressive.
> 'Who are his companions?' Alice asked in an undertone.
> 'They're his Banks,' answered the Little Man.
> 'Banks!' ejaculated Alice.
> 'Yes – he's always between them, you know – like a river.'
> 'Oh, I see. I thought you meant money banks.'
> 'I might have,' vaguely muttered the Little Man.

The announcement that the war was over had just come through and the DIND had a tray of flags to give out but not everyone was pleased with the distribution. When the creatures heard that some would have to be demobilised, there was a fierce argument and it was decided that Alice must be the first to go. By now she was understandably getting pretty fed up with them and, to their consternation, told them that, this being so, she would blow their cover. Birch, who was later appointed editor of the official history of signals intelligence, had the last laugh, however, as his pantomime was put on the secret list, although some copies were retained by those involved for private circulation. Denniston's copy is in Churchill College Archives Centre, Cambridge and the quotations in this article are from Dilly Knox's own copy of *Alice in ID25*.

FOUR

Between the wars

Demobilisation in 1919 meant a far-reaching decision for Dilly Knox. Like so many of his Room 40 colleagues, he had come to see the excitement of wartime codebreaking as a way of life; as he said at the end of *Alice in ID25*:

> *Oh, if a time should ever come when we're demobilised,*
> *How we shall miss the interests which once our life comprised!*

Dilly had every opportunity to return to King's and had even been appointed librarian fellow in his absence; there he could have accomplished the task of completing the Herodas text he was determined to do, in an academic environment. After careful consideration, however, he decided not to abandon cryptography, but to become part of the new Government Code and Cypher School (GC&CS), which the Cabinet Secret Service Committee decided to establish in 1919. Its public function was 'to advise as to the security of codes and ciphers used by all Government departments and to assist in their provision'; its secret directive was 'to study the methods of cipher communications used by foreign powers'. Dilly felt that a peacetime cryptographic unit, with normal working hours, would allow him to pursue his papyrus research with the British Museum to hand, and finish Herodas in the home he planned to set up with Olive Roddam.

Meanwhile, he and Frank Birch would keep on the shared house in Edith Grove, Chelsea. Birch, having achieved a double first in the Historical Tripos, was an accomplished historian and would return to King's as a history lecturer, but not until 1921. On leaving the Admiralty's service in 1919, he was awarded an OBE and was officially engaged to put Room 40's records in order and to write a comprehensive internal history, *A Contribution to the History of German Naval Warfare 1914–1918*, in collaboration with William 'Nobby' Clarke. After Clarke had finished his part of the historical research in 1921, he decided to abandon his legal career to join Dilly in the new GC&CS. At a salary of £500 a year he regarded himself a public benefactor, but for Dilly, like the rest of the Bishop's family, money was never a major consideration.

Although Dilly was not officially concerned with the history of Room 40, he clearly was involved with the discussions at Edith Grove on the implications of their wartime work. He is on record as saying that 'at the end of the last war, Birch, Clarke and I issued at great expense a report in which we were unanimous in denouncing the system of "working in Blinkers"'. Although Dilly whole-heartedly supported 'Blinker' Hall's achievements and his determination to keep their work out of the public domain, he felt secrecy about results within Room 40 had been counter-productive. He clearly still resented the Zimmermann telegram episode. Doubtless the paper would have included Dilly's perpetual grouse that a scholar could only operate if he could see his work through from start to finish.

Hall had left his post, however, and his dynamic energy was no longer officially available to the new organisation. His replacement, Admiral Hugh Sinclair, who held the new title of director of naval intelligence (DNI), was a bon viveur of some repute, known to his friends as 'Quex' from the title character in Arthur Pinero's popular play *The Gay Lord Quex*, who was supposedly 'the wickedest man in London'. Sinclair took on the task of forming the new GC&CS from the remnants of Room 40 and MI1b, the War Office cryptographic department, while still keeping it under Admiralty control. The navy's codebreakers had undoubtedly been a success but the Army's MI1b had also had considerable success against German military codes and ciphers. There had, however, been very little co-operation between the two, so that they were entering uncharted waters when they amalgamated. Sinclair moved the codebreakers out of the Admiralty and War Office and into new premises at Watergate House, on the Strand, a short distance from the Savoy Grill, his favourite eating place.

One person determined to see that the Admiralty would have a decisive input was Winston Churchill, who, although now Secretary of State for War, always associated himself with Room 40's activities and the importance of the intelligence derived from them. Before the meeting on the future GC&CS he wrote to Lord Drogheda at the Foreign Office setting out the unique skills they had acquired, which he had personally observed and which he almost seemed to be adopting as his own:

> *Our work has been done in the face of the enemy and always against time. The messages we have had to decipher were from ships at sea, engaged in actual operations, or from airships also operating. We have had to master a new key every morning before we could begin to read the messages, and sometimes we have had to grapple with two or three keys in one day! This has of necessity developed a kind of aptitude for the work, which depends on its success more on the study of the psychology of the persons sending out the messages and a sort of instinctive 'flair' for the kind of things they are saying, than upon careful study and analysis for which there is no time.*

Churchill made it quite clear that the Admiralty should consent to pool Room 40 staff with those in the War Office only on condition that Commander Alastair Denniston was in charge of the new department. This was agreed and the 'Little Man' was duly appointed. Oliver Strachey, brother of Lytton Strachey, had been chief cryptographer in MI1b and Dilly would work closely with him in the years ahead. It was, however, a very small organisation in 1919, for the Treasury had throughout the negotiations insisted on cutting expenses. Only one wireless intercept station was retained, on the grounds that only cable traffic would be dealt with in future. 'The inevitable had happened,' Clarke recalled later. 'There seemed no longer any need to study the communications of a naval or military nature. The navy and army of Germany had disappeared, never – it was supposed – to rise again, and the idea of watching those of Allied or friendly powers did not seem worthwhile.' On the other hand, the volume of diplomatic traffic grew steadily, as there were conferences still at work for some years settling the boundaries of Europe. Under a section added to the 1920 Official Secrets Act, the international cable companies were obliged to hand over copies of cables passing through the United Kingdom. Dilly and Oliver Strachey spent most of their time working on American traffic and a new US code in which messages were first encoded and the encoded message was then super-enciphered. The cipher tables changed quarterly. It took a year to compile the codebook as the code-groups were not in alphabetical order but 'hatted', that is to say presented at random or out of a hat, but the task was finished in time to provide intelligence on American policy during the Washington Naval Conference in 1922.

Dilly's domestic arrangements had changed. Birch married Vera Gage, daughter of Henry Charles, fifth Viscount Gage, in the autumn of 1919 and soon afterwards Dilly married Olive Roddam at her Northumberland home in 1920. Bishop Knox could not attend as he was in the thick of the Lambeth Conference, battling for the *Book of Common Prayer*. Olive was the daughter of Lieutenant-Colonel R. J. Roddam of the distinguished land-owning family the Roddams of Roddam Hall, and after a honeymoon in Scotland, the newly wed couple returned to Edith Grove, where it was thought they could set up home with the Birches. John Maynard Keynes had organised a generous gift from King's for both couples. Dilly enthusiastically bought a cookery book and opened an account with the Kensington Unique Laundry, but the housekeeping arrangement was not going to work the way Frank and Dilly had planned. Olive did not like living in Chelsea as her heart was in the country.

Fortunately, Dilly had recently found himself in a position to enter the housing market, with a legacy from the Bishop's first wife, Ellen French, the daughter of the unworldly missionary bishop, who had never spent a penny of his own family's accumulated wealth. A condition of the outstanding French family inheritance had been that the youngest Knox child should have turned thirty and at the end of the war Ronnie had done so. Most of the legacy was in Great Western Railway shares and, in 1921, with his portion, Dilly went house-hunting with Olive in the country, a place he had hitherto only thought of as suitable for holidaying in or enjoying in classical imagery or with 'the Shropshire lad'. He could not afford the upkeep of the kind of country house his wife was used to, but it would at least be a house in the country – albeit in the commutable

Home Counties. At the asking price of £1,900 they settled on Courns Wood in 40 acres of Chiltern woodland a few miles from High Wycombe. Dilly caused some consternation among the estate agents by sending a classics lecturer and an electrical outfitter to value the property.

There was no way that a Knox would become a country gentleman. Dilly took no part in country sports, nor did he feel at home in the trendy High Wycombe stockbroker belt, although he could occasionally be persuaded to join tennis parties. There were also a number of retired servicemen in the neighbourhood, whose wives Dilly seemed particularly allergic to. He kept a notebook of verse describing his neighbours and wondered at the prevalence of adultery when all the wives looked so much alike.

> *Sir John has bought an aeroplane*
> *Nor in his place would I refrain*
> *From scouring earth and sky and sea*
> *To get away from Lady D.*

He also identified his nouveau riche neighbours with characters in his favourite 'Just William' stories. Olive did do her best to provide him with the sort of peaceful background to continue his life's ambition to finish Walter Headlam's uncompleted Herodas. He used to travel up from High Wycombe to GC&CS by train spreading out photographs of the fragments of the mimes on his knees.

Dilly explained some of the problems he had to deal with in piecing together the Herodas in the introduction to the Headlam/Knox Herodas. The papyrus, written in the first century or the first half of the second, was not only fragmented with many pieces missing, it was a copy of Herodas's and the work of a basic copyist, not of a highly trained scribe. The copyist had miscopied and sometimes simply misread the material he was copying, Dilly said:

> *Not only was the writer constantly puzzled by the form of the letters which*
> *he was copying. Not only was he prone to all the common errors of copyists,*
> *but worst of all he suffered from a schoolboy-knowledge of Greek, and, where*
> *he followed the sense roughly, made, unconsciously, stupid alterations.*

The copyist's errors were 'those of a man following the sense of the passage, often at a considerable distance', Dilly said.

As well as using the metre, or the occasional lack of it, in the copyist's writing, to work out where things had gone wrong, Dilly used the better preserved portions of papyrus as a 'crib' which allowed him to become used both to the Herodas style and the copyist's handwriting, so he could better identify partial letters and work out where the copyist might have miscopied or misread the original text. But the problems were not simply caused by the copyist's errors or the deterioration of the papyrus. Herodas himself moved easily and deliberately between two different Greek dialects, Ionic and Attic.

> *Just as Herodas allows himself the frequent use of different word-forms, Attic as well as Ionic, so in grammar, vocabulary and style he varies between Attic and Ionic. Sometimes his piquancy comes from giving an Ionic cast to an Attic word; sometimes it is an Ionic word in an Attic sentence where one translates into Attic to arrive at the sense. The grammar, normally Attic, assumes an Ionic cast occasionally. The rule that style is Attic and forms are Ionic is true in a broad sense, not absolutely. The pleasing incongruity, at which Herodas aims, binds him to no hard and fast rule.*

Despite all these problems, Dilly succeeded in completing the Headlam/Knox Herodas, which finally appeared in 1922 and was lavishly praised by Professor W. G. Arnott as the restoration of an old master, 'a glowing achievement not merely for the text of Herodas but for the Greek language and literature in general'. The following year Dilly made another contribution to Greek scholarship when he published an elegant dissertation on Cercidas, the third-century BC poet and cynic. Dilly was fascinated by the way Greek dramatists and poets used metre to stress their themes. For some time he had been studying the Cercidas papyrus fragments from the excavations at Oxyrhynchus. The longest of these fragments contained a discourse on how the nature of gods and beliefs did not seem to match up to the facts of life. Dilly now identified in a new papyrus an introduction to a collection of poems collected and introduced by Cercidas and published it as *The First Greek Anthologist*.

Dilly was offered the professorship of Greek at Leeds University as a result. However tempting a professorship might be, it is doubtful whether Dilly gave it much consideration and in any case Leeds was out of the question for Olive, who was then expecting their second child. Their first son, Christopher Maynard, had been named after his godfather, John Maynard Keynes, with whom Dilly kept up a firm friendship. Now that he had no need to work on papyri on the train, Dilly bought a motor bike to get himself to London.

In 1922, the Foreign Office, having realised how useful the deciphering of diplomatic traffic under the Admiralty was to them, assumed control of GC&CS, which then had a largely civil role. In 1925, GC&CS moved to 54 Broadway Buildings, across the road from St James's Park Underground station. The DNI, Admiral Hugh Sinclair, had now become 'C', the head of the Secret Intelligence Service (SIS), in charge of foreign espionage, but had retained control of the codebreakers, whose 'special intelligence' would become known simply as a 'most secret source'. GC&CS was on the third floor of Broadway Buildings and SIS on the fifth; between them was a missionary society, which must have brought back memories to Dilly.

The main focus of the codebreakers soon became Bolshevik communications. GC&CS had enjoyed a great scoop for the team by acquiring Ernst Fetterlein, formerly the Tsar's leading codebreaker, and Dilly must have enjoyed working with such a character. Another of Dilly's colleagues, who also worked closely with Fetterlein, recalled that the Russian was a brilliant codebreaker.

Fetty, as we addressed him, would arrive precisely at 9.30 and read his Times until 10 when he would adjust a pair of thick-lensed glasses and look to us expecting work to be given to him. On book cipher and anything where insight was vital, he was quite the best. He was a fine linguist and he would usually get an answer no matter the language. When he deposited his first cheque at a London bank he was asked for his references, to which he replied: 'Pardon me? It's my money. Where are your references?'

When Winston Churchill became Chancellor of the Exchequer in 1924, he wanted to catch up with the backlog of Soviet intercepts. He told the new Foreign Secretary, Sir Austen Chamberlain, that 'I have studied this information over a longer period and more attentively than probably any other minister has done'. Speaking as one who had an intimate knowledge of Room 40's codebreaking and the intelligence derived from the messages, he added: 'I attach more importance to them as a means of forming a true judgement of public policy in these spheres than to any other source of knowledge at the disposal of the state.' Signals intelligence, or Sigint, as the produce of the codebreakers' work would become known, was a lifelong passion of Churchill's, which would serve Bletchley Park well during the Second World War.

At no time did the Knox family, apart of course from Olive, have any idea what Dilly did in the office. Dilly's niece Penelope Fitzgerald said the family thought his work might have something to do with the threat from Moscow, with anti-Bolshevik fever gripping the nation, especially after the publication in 1924 of the Zinoviev letter. The letter, supposedly written to the Communist Party of Great Britain by Grigory Zinoviev, the president of the Comintern, called for the mobilisation of sympathetic forces in the Labour Party and subversion of the British armed forces. It confirmed the widely held belief at the time that the Labour Party was soft on communism and in the middle of the 1924 election campaign was leaked to the *Daily Mail* by members and former members of the intelligence services, with both Sinclair and 'Blinker' Hall believed to have been involved. The newspaper put it on the front page with banner headlines, 'Civil War Plot By Soviet Masters, Moscow Orders To Our Reds', and Labour lost the election, although this was already a foregone conclusion. The General Strike in 1926 had also been seen by many to be part of the great Soviet plot to take over Britain.

Dilly's family were right to see a connection. In 1926, GC&CS received a new source of telegrams through the Peking post office, which must have pleased Dilly; a whole network of Russian intrigue was involved and these messages were also broken after discovering super-encipherments of the codebook that proved to be political dynamite. The Knox family knew that something had happened, as Dilly bought a new Burberry overcoat and took them all out to dinner at the Spread Eagle in Thame in January 1927; everybody knew that a celebration meant success in an enterprise of some kind, even though Dilly could not tell them what it was about. GC&CS had obtained the cables sent to the Soviet trade delegation based at the All-Russian Co-operative Society (ARCOS), which had been set up in London as a cover for their subversive activities. Dilly and his colleagues were able to read them, leading in May 1927 to a raid on the ARCOS premises and the decision to break off relations with Moscow. However, as it turned out, there was no cause for a celebration as, in order to justify the break with Moscow, the Prime Minister, Stanley Baldwin, and Chamberlain read out the text of some of the diplomatic telegrams in Parliament and the Russians lost no time in abandoning the cipher they had been using and substituting an unbreakable one-time pad system. Needless to say GC&CS was furious.

Dilly now concentrated on some lesser traffic from Austria, Hungary and the Balkans. His colleague Joshua Cooper, who had joined the section in 1925, felt that Dilly himself thought the intelligence derived from their work at that time was of little consequence. Cooper recalled:

Knox had a very powerful intellect but tended to be incomprehensible and intolerant of people who could not understand him. This was partly due to his background, which was classical rather than mathematical. He worked at one time on Hungarian and did not trouble to learn the language, treating the whole thing as an abstract problem. I remember him coming to me with a piece of paper covered with cipher groups with marks in coloured chalks over them. It was, he said, an account of an interview with an Italian diplomat. Did I have anything in Italian diplomatic ciphers on the same subject? 'This group taken with that one means that either Mussolini or Stalin did, or did not, say that the man named in this group, who may be Sir Samuel Hoare, is going to speak at the League of Nations,' he said. I could only say that I did not have anything to fit. 'Well, the Hungarian is probably lying anyway,' Dilly said, shuffling out of the room.

Nevertheless, a code was a code and was there to be broken, intelligence or no intelligence; as Alastair Denniston recorded in his own memoir of the period, 'Hungarian was successfully broken by

Knox, but it is doubtful if the results obtained at that time justified the enormous effort on his part.'

Although the Russian diplomatic material had dried up, an entirely new type of Russian traffic was emerging which would occupy Dilly more usefully than diplomatic Hungarian had done. Our wireless stations began to pick up a mass of secret radio transmissions all in cipher, except for the operators' chat, which was of the international amateur type. 'The analysis of this traffic was studied closely and from it emerged a worldwide network of clandestine stations controlled by a station near Moscow,' Denniston recalled. 'It turned out to be the Comintern network.' Its aim was the creation of a worldwide Soviet socialist republic. In 1929, John Tiltman, a former army officer, was recalled to England from India, where he had been reading Russian diplomatic traffic with Afghanistan and Turkestan, to head the new military section of GC&CS. He was a Russian expert and took over the new traffic, which he and Dilly soon broke into. Hundreds of the resulting decrypts, codenamed Mask, covering the period from 1930 to 1937, were released in 1997.

The Mask material produced by Dilly and Tiltman was of critical importance to Britain's intelligence war against the Soviet Union in this first Cold War. The attack by Dilly and Tiltman on the Mask ciphers met with 'complete success' and the material passed to SIS allowed Britain's spies to recruit a number of agents inside the Comintern in France, Holland, and Scandinavia and was a key factor in a number of major successes, most notably the dismantling of the Soviet networks in the Far East. It also provided further evidence of the links between Moscow and the Communist Party of Great Britain and led to the arrest of a number of Soviet agents in Britain.

Dilly and Tiltman would continue to collaborate into and during the Second World War. The military man with his highly efficient methods for getting into ciphers was never likely to be close to Dilly given the latter's penchant for Carrollian chopped logic, but despite their differences they worked well together, each respecting the other's strengths and spheres of responsibility, which is the way Dilly liked to operate. Tiltman, as a military man, remained in charge of the military section of GC&CS at Broadway and also at Bletchley Park, whereas Dilly, although turning his hand to any codebreaking problem, particularly relished any work associated with the naval section, which Sinclair had asked 'Nobby' Clarke to set up as early as 1924. Dilly always had a very easy relationship with 'Nobby'.

Dilly remained in touch with his brothers whenever he could and mostly with Ronnie, who was sometimes at a loose end when he was teaching at St Edmund's College in Hertfordshire, before he was given the Oxford chaplaincy in 1926. Whereas none of Dilly's literary efforts or puzzles were ever in print, Ronnie decided to publish his and earn an honest penny. Eddie had for some time been sending contributions to *Punch* and would become the magazine's editor in 1932. The Knox brothers had always enjoyed creating acrostics – poems where the first letters of each line spell out a word – and in 1924 Ronnie published *The Book of Acrostics* collected from periodicals. Needless to say one of their favourite acrostics was Lewis Carroll's *Golden Afternoon*, which begins:

A boat, beneath a summer sky
Lingering onwards dreamily
In an evening of July,
Children three that nestle near,
Eager eye and willing ear.

Dilly had another idea for a verse form which he called a 'pentelope', where each line must end with a word of the same form, but with a different vowel which must appear in the proper order, either in spelling or pronunciation. Perhaps there was a hint of a variation of a column of pronounceable code-groups in the pentelopes. These were never publicised but were piled into a tin. Dilly felt the day that the poet A. E. Housman died called for a pentelope:

Sad though the news, how sad [A]
Of thee, the poet, dead! [E]
But still, the poems abide [I]
There death, the unsparing god [O]
Himself dare not intrude [U]

Dilly's younger son, Oliver, particularly enjoyed his father's acrostics and pentelopes and memorable way of putting things. He would one day become an advertising executive and later worked for Margaret Thatcher's Centre for Policy Studies. His Knoxian advice to them was that 'government policies ought to be presented in an entertaining fashion. Limericks are remembered long after White Papers.' Oliver Knox worked on Japanese ciphers at Bletchley Park after his father's death and found his reputation thriving. This was the first time he understood what Dilly's wartime work had been. He told the story of early frustrations in trying to find out what his father did:

> *To his work he referred not at all, any enquiries in that respect being met with the dismaying device of total silence. Once at WH Smith's in High Wycombe, I bought a cheap primer about elementary codes. Perhaps by leaving it about casually on the dining room table, I might lure one of my parents to reveal just a glimpse or two about a world which seemed nearly as exciting as spying. I could promise my undying silence, of course. Ridiculous useless bait! The book was not even cleared from the table; there was silence over the sardines on toast.*

Although pentelopes never hit the headlines, there was one Knox pursuit in the twenties which did, and that was a new genre of whodunit detective stories with strict logical rules. In 1925, Ronnie published the first of six such novels, *The Viaduct Murder*, in which a clergyman, a don, someone from intelligence and a holidaymaker were playing golf together and hit a ball under a viaduct only to find a dead body; they try to solve the mystery in their own special ways with the clues given. Evelyn Waugh, Ronald Knox's literary executor and biographer, saw these detective novels as intellectual exercises, a game between the writer and the reader in which a problem was precisely stated and elaborately disguised. 'As his brother Dillwyn had systematised and regulated the haphazard games of the Birmingham schoolroom,' Waugh said, 'so Ronald observed and sought to impose a code of rules, which he later set out in his introduction to *The Best Detective Stories of the Year* in 1928. The criminal must be mentioned in the first five chapters and the reader must not be allowed to know his inner thoughts; no unknown poisons nor mysterious Chinamen; the detective must declare all the clues, as must the "Watson" or uncomprehending friend, were but a few.' These rules were adopted in 1929 as the Solemn Oath of the Writers' Detection Club, which included G. K. Chesterton, Agatha Christie and Dorothy Sayers. Dilly got to know and like Christie, who broke most of the rules and somehow managed to apologise for it.

The most entertaining of their father's friends, whom Christopher and Oliver were always glad to see at Courns Wood, was Frank Birch, who having resigned as a history don at King's had become a theatre producer and actor. A highlight in the children's life was when Dilly treated as many of the family as could be mustered to seats at the Lyric, Hammersmith to see Birch's splendid performance as the Widow Twankey in *Aladdin*. When the children saw another weekend visitor, the formidable Professor Edgar Lobel from Oxford, approaching they quickly disappeared as they knew he had come over to tell their father about the latest papyrus discoveries at Oxyrhynchus and attempt to reconstruct the ancient world with him. 'If Edgar Lobel was the most imposing of my father's friends, Frank Birch was the jolliest, most amusing and *mondain*,' recalled Oliver. 'When he came down to Courns Wood, I was slightly ashamed of the cold unworldliness of our home, and vaguely conscious that the half-bottle of Châteauneuf du Pape customarily provided for visitors was not enough.'

Dilly could not resist another return to Herodas and Cercidas for the 1929 Loeb Classical Edition, part of a series founded in 1911 to make classical authors accessible with Greek on one side of the page and English on the other. If the Herodas *Mimiambi* poems were good enough, Dilly translated them skilfully, reproducing the metre, as well as the sense of the Greek verse.

> *But now that there gleam on my head*
> *White hairs but a few at the edge*
> *Still does my summer*
> *Seek for the thing that is fair.*

However, there was now something at Courns Wood that did indeed make his summers fair. He had developed a passion for tree-planting and had even bought more adjacent land. He spent weekends happily in the woods with his two small sons making log cabins for them and a scaffold on wheels so that they could be at his height to watch him sawing the tops of trees. He liked to talk to the famous Chiltern bodgers in the beech woods, making chair legs for the High Wycombe furniture industry, and he learned a lot from them. In 1931, he had an accident on his motor cycle and his leg was badly broken, after which he always walked with a limp. He had to buy an Austin Seven to cover the five miles to get him to the station and the family wondered how long it would be before he had an accident in that, as he used to take his hands off the steering wheel when going downhill and recite his favourite poem *Lycidas* with its inspiring last lines 'tomorrow to fresh woods and pastures new'.

The artist Gilbert Spencer, whose portrait of Dilly appears on the cover, lived at the bottom of the road leading up to Courns Wood and Dilly always gave him a lift to the station in the morning. Dilly 'used to amuse himself by seeing how far he could go downhill with the engine off,' Spencer said. 'He also told me that our terminus (Marylebone) was so out of the way that he was pretty nearly the only passenger, which explained why he was so politely received by the station-master. But we thought it was his highly important position at the Foreign Office.'

Change was clearly being considered as, in 1934, Dilly wrote to John Maynard Keynes, as bursar of King's, with a proposal that the college should take responsibility for his now flourishing woodlands; that this was a part of a contemplated move back to Cambridge is confirmed by Oliver Knox's reminiscences of a conversation he overheard, when he was in the log cabin, about this time. What he heard, he said, was disturbing.

My father was talking of the frustrations of life in Whitehall and his yearning to resume his work on the obscurer corners of early Greek literature. My mother was reminding him, quietly but firmly, of his duty to educate his sons and of the national importance of his work, for good measure adding that she herself could not bear to return to the chill wastes of fenland and the inhospitable society of dons. I didn't dare to shuffle or in any way betray my presence but peeped through the cracks in the planks of the wall. My father was in his shirt sleeves, holding his saw. His pipe lay neglected on the makeshift window sill. For once he wasn't wearing his horn-rimmed spectacles, so that his eyes looked unfamiliarly naked. This was one of the very few times indeed that I ever saw him looking as though he was not in control of his destiny.

The 'obscurer corners of early Greek literature' which Dilly wanted to resume concerned his work on the metre of the Greek plays and poems. He had already published an article in 1925 and had been in contact with the German classical scholar Ulrich von Wilamowitz-Moellendorff over a highly technical point on the metre within classical Greek poetry and drama, which Dilly developed in another *Philologus* article in 1932 entitled 'The Early Iambers' and was anxious to pursue. Although Olive managed to persuade him that his codebreaking work was more important, he would earn his place as a scholar of classical Greek through his recent discovery of a key law governing the metre of Greek lyrical drama and poetry. This was Dilly's Greek swansong. It was fortunate that Olive prevailed as it would not be long before GC&CS presented him with a problem even more challenging than any he had ever encountered either in Room 40 or in the minds of Ionian dramatists and poets.

FIVE

Enigma

Cryptography, the art of secret communications, would be transformed by the advent of the cipher machine, particularly the Enigma, based by Arthur Scherbius on a secret writing machine invented by the Dutchman Hugo Alexander Koch. In 1923, Scherbius exhibited his machine with its striking art deco logo at the International Postal Union Congress and advertised it as a means of safeguarding the secrecy of cables and telegrams. What began life as a commercial enterprise was to end up as being a major influence on the outcome of battles. The businessmen of the world were slow in responding, however, but this was the year that British politicians had revealed how much wireless interception and Room 40's codebreaking had contributed to the allied victory in the First World War. Germany had found means of defying the Versailles treaty, which only allowed the defeated enemy to take measures for security and counter-espionage, by calling its growing army the Reichswehr and its secret service the Abwehr, both implying defence; it now needed a means of hiding its secret communications. Scherbius seemed to be the answer as his pamphlet claimed that there were so many millions of ways of setting the machine that it would be impossible to break the messages without knowing the key settings. Germany seized the opportunity to acquire commercial machines and adapt them for military purposes.

GC&CS appointed Edward Travis, Alastair Denniston's deputy, to take charge of all security aspects of British government communications and it therefore fell to him to investigate the commercial machine when the British patent was applied for in 1927. After an Enigma machine had been acquired for GC&CS, Travis asked Hugh Foss, who had joined GC&CS in 1924, to see if Scherbius's claims that it was unbreakable were true. The elaborate sales pamphlet, produced in English under the title of *The Glow-*

Lamp Ciphering and Deciphering Machine 'Enigma' showed that it looked like a typewriter in a wooden box with a standard keyboard (the continental QWERTZU instead of the British QWERTY) and above that a lampboard with a series of small light bulbs in the same order. The operator typed out the plain text message and the act of depressing the key sent an electrical impulse through the machine and the enciphered letter would show up on the lampboard, making commercial secrets safe for ever. Scherbius added in a non-committal way that 'decisive battles have been lost, by land and by water, in the air and in debating with each other, because the adversary had a better method of keeping his correspondence secret'.

The British patent specification no. 267,472, accepted on 11 August 1927, set out exactly how the electrical ciphering machine worked. Stress was laid on the importance of being able to change the order of the three wheels, that it was possible to acquire extra, differently wired, wheels, and that 'in the case of war' there was the further advantage 'that if surprised by the enemy it was only necessary to remove the wheels to render the machine useless'. The hint in the 1923 pamphlet had now turned into a bold statement about the importance of Enigma's use in war. Accompanying photographs showed how to set the machine, the interchangeable order of the wheels, the clip or *Ringstellung* which set the moveable rings on the wheels and the *Grundstellung*, the basic starting position in which the letters on the wheels were to appear in the windows before enciphering the message key. The operator positioned the three wheels in a pre-determined order. The Germans chose to set the rings to the agreed *Grundstellung* and then selected three letters at random as the message setting. These were encrypted twice to produce a six-letter message indicator. The operator then set the wheels to the message setting and enciphered the message, pressing the key for every letter of plain text and reading off the enciphered letter on the lampboard. He sent the enciphered indicators in the preamble to his message. Foss painstakingly got down to the problem he had been set and was able to produce his report in 1928.

Foss called the machine the Reciprocal Enigma, as a previous large typewriter enciphering machine described in a patent of 1924 had only been a one-way machine with no reflector (*Umkehrwalze*) and consequently was non-reciprocal. The electric signal set off by depressing the key travelled through wiring of the wheels to the reflector, which sent the signal back through the wheels a second time and the enciphered letter lit up on the lampboard. The action of depressing the key also moved the first, or right-hand, wheel one notch forward. Periodically, the movement of this first wheel led the other wheels to move forward. This was known as a 'turnover'. Foss considered that in spite of the high degree of security of the Scherbius Reciprocal Enigma, it could be broken, given certain conditions, if the codebreaker had obtained a piece of plain text or guessed it as a crib. If the wiring of the wheels was known, just fifteen letters were all that was needed to find the machine setting, but if the wheel wiring was unknown, at least 180 letters would be needed. It is uncertain whether, at this early stage, Dilly discussed the problem with Foss, who maintained that he was not making any attempt to provide a methodology for breaking an Enigma machine himself; that would be left to Dilly Knox to discover, but how much later is not clear. An unconfirmed statement quoted in Foss's 'Reminiscences on Enigma', written in 1949, says that Dilly Knox purchased an Enigma machine in Vienna in 1925, which seems odd. With two young toddlers, he and Olive are unlikely to have been visiting Austria on holiday, although perhaps there was an exhibition of the machine which led to him going on his own to gather intelligence on how it worked. However, there is no doubt that there was one in GC&CS available after Foss completed his work in 1929; that being so, there is no question that Dilly would not have wanted to investigate it, whether or not, with all his other pressing Russian cipher commitments, he was officially asked to do so.

Scherbius had never given any suggestions about indicating to the recipient how the machine had to be set up to decipher a message, with or without a codebook of settings. When first analysing the commercial machine, without having any enciphered messages and with no indicators to work on, Dilly would have to investigate the machine's characteristics and would soon discover that if the letter A was pressed and the light bulb showed K, in the same position K would light up as A; this reciprocal factor together with the fact that A could never produce A would be highly significant and would mean that initially he could approach the problem textually, as he was accustomed to doing. The first thing to do was to reproduce the action of the machine in a convenient manner to experiment on, as though it were a hand cipher; this he did by making lettered strips of cardboard, which he called rods, one for each wheel. He knew from testing the machine that what he called the 'diagonal', the wiring between the letter keys and the entry plate, was in the order of its keyboard, running from left to right, top to bottom, therefore beginning QWERTZU, the standard order of the German typewriter keyboard. This would figure largely in subsequent analysis of the machine.

Dilly could also observe from looking at the machine how the wheels turned over and deduced that it would be the right-hand one which, as the entry point for the current from the keyboard, would allow a stretch of up to twenty-five positions to work on the cipher text without a wheel turnover. Foss was quite specific that it was Dilly's invention of rods that had achieved the break into the commercial Enigma machine. In 'Reminiscences', he admitted that 'the methods I used were rather clumsy as they were geometrical rather than algebraical and, when Dilly Knox came to study the subject, he invented the "rods" and the process known as "buttoning-up", which used the same properties as I had done but did so in a more effective way'. (For a detailed explanation of 'buttoning-up' see Appendix 3.) Dilly's methods had nothing to do with algebra as such, of course; what Foss meant was that he had worked with diagrams and numbers and so missed out on all the linguistic potential that Dilly's lettered rods would bring to machine cryptography and make them such an effective tool, when there were real messages to work on. (For a detailed explanation of 'rodding' see Appendix 2.)

The first sign of wars and rumours of wars when the Enigma machine might be used militarily was with Mussolini's invasion of Abyssinia in 1935, which alarmed Britain and France and led to their co-operation in interception and other matters. Study of Italian naval traffic had already shown the growing interest of Italy in the Red Sea area and a jointly run wireless station was set up in southern France. Dilly joined 'Nobby' Clarke's naval section to work with him on breaking the messages. The need was now urgent as Mussolini's invasion threatened British-controlled Egypt and the route to India. In 1934, the Italian navy was still using super-enciphered codebooks and it was these that Dilly had to break to build up a background of naval vocabulary. The Italian naval attaché's method was by additives, where the operator had to put a long line of random numbers under the code-groups and add the two together in non-carrying arithmetic. Dilly's colleague Wilfred Bodsworth was impressed that Dilly was able to break the messages so effectively that, during the Abyssinian war, the Admiralty was kept fully informed of the strength and activities of the Italian navy.

The next threat imposed by the dictator Mussolini was even greater. He called the Mediterranean *mare nostrum*, as the Romans had done before him, and Gibraltar, Britain's key to dominating access to the Mediterranean, was at risk. This was in 1936, during the Spanish Civil War, when Mussolini backed General Franco's right-wing Nationalists against the left-wing Republicans. The Germans sold the Italians and Spanish a version of the commercial machine for their use and GC&CS could now receive the enciphered messages at the joint wireless intercept station in France. The first GC&CS break into Enigma would therefore be through Italian and not German traffic. The year 1936 was a watershed for Dilly as he was back into the excitement of Room 40 days with all the 'interests which once our life comprised' and he could now devote his time officially to breaking real operational Enigma messages, rather than ones he had concocted for himself in his spare time. It was that year that his family noted that something was afoot, as for the first time Dilly refused the invitation to the King's College Founder's Feast for fear of giving his new secret away over the port.

Dilly soon established that the Italian messages were not sent out on the commercial machine he knew; it was in fact an improved version of the commercial Enigma machine known as the 'K' model, in which the wheel turnover was attached to the alphabet ring and not to the wheel itself as in the 'A' model. The wirings of the wheels had been changed, making Dilly's task more difficult, as Scherbius had recommended for increased security in wartime use, but now that he had genuine messages he could undertake a preliminary exercise which would hold good for any Enigma encipherment whatever the wheel wirings or message settings. This exploited the characteristic that A could not encipher as A and so if the Italian messages had a standard opening, say *PER* (Italian for 'to)', these letters would not appear in the first three places of the cipher text. Dilly undertook what he called a 'boil', which became a standard procedure for investigating new traffic. He took a piece of squared paper with numbers across the top and letters down the left-hand side and a dot was then put for the cipher text letters in the appropriate square; if indeed *PER* was a standard opening over a period of time this would show up on the chart as empty spaces in the first three squares. Unfortunately, there were not enough messages to draw any conclusion on this occasion and the next step was to hope for procedural errors by the operators which would give him the way in. Dilly's work on Herodas meant he was used to slack Greek scribes and this approach was his forte in breaking Enigma messages.

Success came in April 1937 when twenty Italian naval messages were sent out on the same setting, contrary to strict training instructions given to operators; this meant that if the messages were written out under each other, each column of the resulting table would show plain text encipherment by a reciprocal simple substitution. It was an easy matter to start by letter frequencies and the guessing of probable words through repeated bigrams and trigrams or common opening words, provided the chosen letters did not 'crash' with the cipher text; that is to say that, since a letter cannot be enciphered as itself, if the message begins with the letter P, the message cannot have started with a word beginning with P. The guessed plain text was now written under the cipher text to produce 'pairs', each made up by the cipher letter followed by the plain text letter it represented as in the table below.

Cipher	R	T	F	B	R	X	E	Y	L	S	B	P	Y	S	P
Guess	P	E	R	X	C	O	M	A	N	D	A	N	T	E	X

Cipher	R	T	F	B	X	Q	C	R	L	Z	S	U
Guess	P	E	R	X	T	E	N	E	N	T	E	X

Cipher	P	S	R	F	C	Y	E	R	L	Z	P	U
Guess	R	I	F	E	R	I	M	E	N	T	O	X

Cipher	Y	F	N	F	C	X	G	H	M	O	X	X	S
Guess	N	U	M	E	R	O	X	C	I	N	Q	U	E

This produces the following resulting pairs in consecutive wheel positions: 1 = PR and YN; 2 = TE, SI and FU; 3 = FR and NM; 4 = BX and FE; 5 = CR and XT; 7 = XO, QE and VI; 8 = EM, CN and GX; 8 = YA, RE and HC. Using these pairs, Dilly could find the wheel wiring through the process he called 'buttoning-up', for which the rods, his outstanding contribution to machine cryptography, were made. Hugh Foss insisted that buttoning-up and the rods were Dilly's unaided inventions. Dilly had to break each message by rodding as no attempt was made to rewire machine wheels to assist the task even though our own Typex cipher machines were being manufactured at the time.

It was soon found that Franco's Enigma machine had the same wheel wirings, so that there could be communication with the Italians, which meant the same rods Dilly had made could be used for breaking Spanish messages. Wilfred Bodsworth, a Spanish expert, took over the task, employing Dilly's methodology. In Spain, the Enigma machine was now being used for operational purposes and for the first time it would be seen how it performed in the field. Franco needed to keep in touch with his generals to co-ordinate military attacks in different parts of Spain, keeping the Republican units in the dark about his plans. Commander Antonio Sarmiento, who was in charge of training the operators, assured Franco that 'to give you an idea of how secure these machines are, suffice to say that that the number of possible combinations is a remarkable 1,252,962,387,456'. He was unaware, however, in spite of his operator training, that this number could be considerably reduced through procedural errors, which were especially likely when a unit was on the move.

The Spanish Civil War gave Hitler insights into what modern warfare could now achieve, especially from the air. Although not officially backing Franco, under international law volunteers were allowed to give support in wars, as our volunteers to the International Red Brigade did to the Republicans. A volunteer unit of Luftwaffe pilots formed the 'Condor Legion' and were responsible for the bombing of Guernica, which alarmed the rest of Europe. They too used the type of commercial Enigma machine that Franco was using, which was broken thereby alerting Britain to Luftwaffe tactics and providing background knowledge for Dilly's attempts to break the German air force Enigma. Dilly's first break into an Enigma machine during the Spanish Civil War was an important cryptographical precedent for the Second World War, since it also ensured that, as war clouds gathered, the collection of intelligence from the deciphered messages was put on an operational basis.

Admiral Sinclair set up a committee to consider the implications of the Spanish Civil War, including the dreadful effects of mass bombing. Paymaster Lieutenant-Commander Norman Denning was appointed in 1937 to see what lessons were to be learned in linking cryptography and intelligence to best advantage. Mussolini had loaned four submarines manned by Italian crews to Franco to be used to blockade Republican ports and it was important for the Admiralty to establish the location of these 'pirate' submarines that were sinking merchant vessels and to keep track of any German or Italian ships in Spanish waters. Denning spent several weeks with Dilly and his colleagues following through interception and Italian and Spanish codebreaking and also made a detailed study of the First World War histories written by Birch and 'Nobby' Clarke in order to learn from Room 40's experiences. He soon learned of the disastrous consequences of the separation of intelligence and operations, most notably at Jutland, and he began to plan and organise an Operational Intelligence Centre (OIC), where the two functions would be totally integrated. He got the principle of a new centre accepted and the OIC, although small, was up and running in 1939. Meanwhile, the new director of naval intelligence, Rear-Admiral John Godfrey, recruited suitable outsiders, forming a brilliant team for the Second World War and housing them in the Admiralty Citadel under Horse Guards Parade.

Another most important advantage gained by Dilly's breaking of the Spanish and Italian Enigma was increased collaboration with the French Services de Renseignement, whose liveliest wire was the intelligence officer in charge of the cipher department, Gustave Bertrand. From 1926, when he first joined the service, Bertrand had received intelligence reports that the Germans had introduced an unbreakable Enigma cipher machine, first into their navy, then subsequently, in 1928, to the Reichswehr and, in 1934, to Göring's newly formed Luftwaffe. The idea of *Blitzkrieg*, a war of total mobility between the armed forces co-ordinated using wireless communications operated from the backs of army trucks, was being worked out by the German generals. In May 1933, when Britain was still treating Russia as its chief threat, Bertrand had joined the crowds saluting the new Chancellor Hitler in his first appearance wearing the Nazi uniform with a swastika badge. Bertrand returned to Paris and warned that he had witnessed the rebirth of German militarism, but did not get much backing for increasing intelligence funding for the schemes he had been trying to put in place.

Although the French military had been receiving intercepted German messages from stations close to the frontier, they had not had any success in breaking them and Bertrand had decided that espionage was the only way forward. Fate played into his hands when in 1931 an official from the German military cipher office, Hans Thilo Schmidt, called at the French embassy in Berlin and astounded officials by offering to sell top secret documents to the French government relating to German organisation and procedure for enciphering their signals; his purpose was purely mercenary. Schmidt was given the codename Asché and Bertrand agreed to pay him 10,000 marks. The German handed over the documents, which included two operators' manuals giving instructions on how to use the Engima machine and set the keys, at a rendezvous in a hotel in Verviers on the French–German border and Bertrand rushed upstairs, where there was a photographer waiting to copy them. Mission accomplished, Asché returned the precious documents to the secret safe from which they had come. Bertrand was greatly excited by the coup and bitterly disappointed when he was told by the head of the cipher department, a Colonel Bassières, that Asché's documents would be of little use to the codebreakers without the wiring of the wheels or the key setting. 'Impossible to get anything useful from your documents,' he said, 'too many things are lacking for us to produce the machine.'

A week later, Bertrand approached Wilfred 'Biffy' Dunderdale, the SIS station chief in Paris. Bertrand was the sole French liaison officer on intelligence matters and so had worked previously with Dunderdale, usually demanding payment for anything the French produced. Bertrand wanted a considerable sum for any more of Asché's secrets so Dunderdale had to seek permission from SIS headquarters. The request was turned down flat. It was a political matter of funding priorities and it seems that Denniston, Foss, Tiltman and Dilly were not consulted. Dunderdale did have the original batch of documents for three days and in all probability photographed them, allowing Dilly to analyse them later, but the ban on paying any money for them cut the British off from the rest of Asché's valuable secrets. Fortunately, when Bertrand turned to the Poles his reception was very different. The Nazi threat had become very disturbing for Poland, as there had been a tense relationship with Germany since the partitioning of Europe after the Versailles treaty. Hitler's threat in *Mein Kampf* in 1926 that the Germans should find *Lebensraum* on their eastern border made it worse. The Poles were able to intercept German wireless traffic, which was transmitted at low power on medium frequencies, difficult to intercept in the UK, and they were particularly eager to know what the Nazis were saying. The Asché documents were received by the Poles as 'manna in the desert', according to Bertrand, and produced 'an explosion of stupefaction and joy'.

One thing Dilly did learn at this time, although not having the advantage of the documents the Poles had received, was that the Germans had added a *Stecker*-board, similar to an old-fashioned telephone plugboard, to the commercial Enigma machine, which was clear from the photographs supplied by the French. This allowed many, many more different possibilities, thereby making the machine highly secure, if still vulnerable to the fact that no letter could ever be enciphered as itself. It would be another four years, however, before Dilly had any German service messages to work on and six years before he would finally receive Bertrand's 'manna in the desert'. The Polish codebreakers, meanwhile, had succeeded in breaking the German Enigma and were reading current messages by 1933, unbeknown to GC&CS. Bertrand was also ignorant of the Polish success, despite having contributed to it so much. Understandably, the Poles were anxious to conceal the break for security reasons, since if it reached German ears their ability to eavesdrop on their warlike intentions would have been lost. In retrospect, the early history of Enigma breaking and of appeasement might have been different if there had been co-operation between the wartime allies at this early stage. (The same security difficulty, concerning the secrecy over the breaking of Enigma, would later have to be weighed up by Winston Churchill in considering whether to share it with Americans before they came into the Second World War.)

Dilly first met up with the German Enigma messages during the Spanish Civil War, when their navy was on manoeuvres in Spanish waters; ominously by then they had renamed the navy Kriegsmarine, rather than retain its previous less offensive name, Reichsmarine. At this stage, Dilly was already aware of the introduction of the *Stecker* to the machine and, even before having any messages, he had worked out theoretically how they could be treated as a super-encipherment, which could be stripped off before applying his methodology for breaking un-*Stecker*ed machines. The Italians and the Spanish had used a separate codebook for the operators' indicators for all the machine's settings, but the Germans indicated the machine setting at the beginning of the message and this was for Dilly a new way in to codebreaking. Although the key setting of wheel order, *Ringstellung*, *Stecker* and *Grundstellung* was communicated in circulated German key lists, the operator chose his own setting, which he encoded on the basic *Grundstellung* and put the result at the beginning of the cipher text. If the indicator system could be unravelled it would mean that, when the machine was broken, a whole day's messages on a given network might then be read, whereas with the Italian and Spanish codebook instructions, each message had to be broken separately.

Wilfred Bodsworth was now in charge of the Italian and Spanish traffic, leaving Dilly free to concentrate on the German naval indicating system as a means of breaking the machine. Alastair Denniston wrote that 'Knox had made considerable progress in his diagnosis until April 1937', but the navy then introduced a new procedural complication of bigram tables for the indicators and Dilly concentrated on unchanged army and air force traffic. John Tiltman remained in charge of the GC&CS Army section and a new air section to advise the Air Ministry, headed by Josh Cooper, had been set up in 1936. The discriminants (the groups in the message preambles denoting the particular network cipher system) of the new army/air force traffic between Germany and Spain were isolated by Tiltman's deputy, Frederick Jacob, and its message indicators identified by Tiltman.

Hitler's first belligerent move had been undertaken in March 1936 when over 32,000 soldiers and armed police entered the Rhineland, which had been demilitarised under the Versailles treaty. Although it transpired that Hitler would have withdrawn if France had taken action, nothing was done by Britain and France in response to his violation of the treaty, but eavesdropping was stepped up. This was the period when Tiltman made a breakthrough identifying what he described as 'throw-on' message indicators used by the German operators when, for reasons of clarity, they were told to tap out the setting of the three wheels on the fixed message setting twice and put it at the beginning of their message. Tiltman swiftly realised this meant that this would be likely to produce repeat letters in the key-block, the set of indicators at the start of the message, at positions 1 and 4, 2 and 5, or 3 and 6. If, for instance, there was an M in the first position, invariably there would be a certain letter, say G, in the fourth position, and so on; this proved that the indicators were on the same setting and ripe for exploitation.

In the autumn of 1938, Admiral Sinclair, anxious to increase co-operation with France, authorised Denniston to invite Bertrand over for a council of war. Bertrand, the man whom Denniston later called 'a pedlar and purchaser of foreign government cribs', arrived on 2 November 1938 and handed over a large number of documents, including original German material relating to Enigma that had been obtained by Asché. The French material was so important that Denniston wrote to Sinclair the same day asking permission to hand over a significant amount of different material in return. 'We have received about 100 photographs of codes of which one might well have had great value in the event of war with Germany last month,' Denniston told Sinclair. The French also handed over a full description of the Germans' own communications intercept operations, some reconstructed German and Italian codebooks and a considerable amount of intercepted German and Italian telegrams. But the most prized documents were without doubt 'photographs of documents relating to the use of the Enigma machine, which did increase our knowledge of the machine and have greatly aided our researches', Denniston told Sinclair. 'Our main reason for seeking this liaison in the first place was the desire to leave no stone unturned which might lead to a solution of the Enigma machine as used by the various German services. This is of vital importance for us and the French have furnished us with documents which have assisted us but we are still doubtful if success can be obtained without further documents.' Sinclair immediately authorised the exchange.

The conference with Bertrand took place the following day and was held for security reasons at Sanctuary Buildings, Great Smith Street, a few hundred yards away from the Broadway headquarters. It was attended on the British side by Denniston himself, Oliver Strachey, as chief cryptographer, Tiltman and Dilly. The morning session began with a discussion of the various German armed forces Enigma material the French had produced, followed by a presentation by Tiltman on the British work on the indicators for the Enigma keys. After lunch at Simpsons in the Strand, Dilly explained the methods of breaking the latest commercial Enigma machines. The French were impressed. 'It appears to us that their cryptographic work is less ambitious than ours,' Denniston said. 'They have worked on the German and Italian unreciphered codes with success and on the German military [double transposition] hand cipher.'

Bertrand was subsequently given the opportunity to see the flourishing Italian and Spanish section and Dilly's methods of codebreaking and was promised a regular supply of decodes. 'I think he was impressed by our success and by the ability of certain officers and it might well be that this had an important bearing on his subsequent action,' Denniston later recalled. The whole Spanish situation was immediately apparent to the wily Bertrand, who understood that if Franco won his war against the Republican government and still used the same Enigma machine, France could keep an eye on its neighbour's relationship with Germany, through its intercepts; bearing that in mind, Bertrand 'salvaged five Spanish Republicans who had worked at Barcelona' and installed them in Paris as intelligence officers in his new Spanish party.

There was an urgent request from the British for more material from the French agent and before the end of the year Bertrand handed over the German users' manual for Enigma, which had been given to Rejewski in 1932. *Schlüsselanleitung für die Chiffriermaschine Enigma*, the directions for setting up the machine which, unbelievably, included a genuine example of a ninety-letter stream of text in both clear text and cipher, complete with key setting. This authentic example was soon replaced by a fictitious one in subsequent manuals, when someone in the German cipher authorities became aware of the blunder. The French material was passed over via 'Biffy' Dunderdale and arrived in GC&CS in the red-lined file covers in which SIS distributed its intelligence material, which we called 'Scarlet Pimpernels'. If only someone had recognised the value of Bertrand's version with its crib for GC&CS in 1932, Dilly might well have broken Enigma by 1938.

When Dilly finally received it six years later he immediately tried out his successful method for recovering wheel wiring, as he had done for the Italian and Spanish machines, but this time taking the German *Stecker* complication into account. Dilly had already decided that the *Stecker* merely added a substitution on the text letters entering the machine and the inverse substitution on the enciphered letters emerging. However, the way forward was not as easy as he thought. When Dilly was continually frustrated by not being able to recover the wirings by his well-tried crib methods, he feared that the diagonal, the entry connection from the keyboard to the wheels, was not QWERTZU, the typewriter order common to all the un-*Stecker*ed commercial machines he had worked on. QWERTZU was tried backwards to no avail and then came the awful thought that the Germans had achieved the ultimate Enigma machine complication – that of a random entry plate connection.

Bertrand set up a meeting with the Poles and the British in Paris in January 1939, which Denniston said was held in 'an atmosphere of secrecy and mystery'. The Poles were very suspicious since the Munich appeasement with Hitler in September 1938 and still not prepared to reveal their Enigma successes. Denniston and the three codebreakers Dilly, Foss and Tiltman attended on the British side but the Polish representatives did not include any of their real codebreakers, with whom Dilly could have had a meaningful discussion. Hugh Foss recalled how annoyed Dilly was that 'at these two interviews, the Poles were mainly silent but one of them gave a lengthy description in German of the recovery of "throw-on" indicators'. This was Major Maksymilian Ciężki of the Polish Cipher Bureau, who was in charge of the German section and had carried out the initial Polish work on the Enigma machine, before handing the material over to newly recruited mathematician codebreakers in 1932.

During Ciężki's exposition at Paris, Dilly kept muttering to Denniston 'but this is what Tiltman did', while Denniston 'hushed him' and told him to listen politely. Thinking that Ciężki must know how the machine worked, Dilly naturally asked him the burning question as to what the diagonal he had assumed to be QWERTZU was. Dilly soon realised that the Polish officer knew nothing about the actual breaking of the Enigma machine and it was all a waste of time. He frustratedly wrote in his assessment of the Polish work on Enigma: 'Practical knowledge of Qwertzu Enigma nil. Had succeeded in identifying indicators on precisely the methods always used here, but not till recently with success.' He [Ciężki] was enormously pleased with his success and declaimed a pamphlet, which contained nothing new to us.' It is clear that Dilly brought no information that would help him back from the Paris meeting with the Poles.

Dilly was also unimpressed by the French description of their attempts to solve Enigma, which they ended with a flourish and a dramatic '*Voici la méthode française*'. But he did strike up a lasting friendship with Bertrand's chief cryptographer, Henri Braquenié, at the meeting and according to Foss, who was present at the time, the French were delighted when Dilly demonstrated how to use his rods and by the next meeting had made a set of *reglettes* of their own.

Denniston rightly realised that the Poles had agreed to the Paris meeting because they had run into difficulties in April 1938 when the Germans changed the indicating system. Colonel Gwido Langer, head of the Polish Cipher Bureau, had been told by Bertrand of Dilly's progress in attempting to break Enigma and was anxious to seek his help. The minutes of the Paris meeting recorded frustration on both sides, Bertrand said, and 'it seemed that the work had arrived at an impasse out of which only information from an agent could provide a way. A technical questionnaire was drawn up, as simple as possible, to give to the agent.' Dilly asked Bertrand whether the agent could obtain sixteen alphabets enciphered on the Enigma machine for him, if he could not recover the wirings themselves, but any spy would be lucky to get away with half an hour's noisy clonking of the wheels and the idea was abandoned. However, Dilly never lost hope that his methodology would finally succeed in spite of the pessimistic belief elsewhere in GC&CS that Scherbius's claim that Enigma could be unbreakable if used properly was proving correct. 'Nothing is impossible' was after all Dilly's motto.

Up to this time, Dilly's only assistant on the German Enigma machine had been Tony Kendrick, but after the Paris meeting GC&CS decided to apply for a mathematician and appointed Peter Twinn from Brasenose College, Oxford. He recalled his first day at Broadway Buildings, where he found

> the people working on the Enigma were the celebrated Dilly Knox and a chap called Tony Kendrick, quite a character, who was once head boy at Eton. There was a slightly bizarre interview with Dilly who was himself a bit of a character to put it mildly. He didn't believe in wasting too much time in training his assistant, he gave me a five-minute talk and left me to get on with it.

Denniston now went further and made the rounds of the universities to bring in former colleagues and new talent, as Josh Cooper recalled:

> He dined at several high tables in Oxford and Cambridge and came home with promises from a number of dons to attend a territorial training course. It would be hard to exaggerate the importance of this course for the future development of GC&CS. Not only had Denniston brought in scholars of the humanities, of the type of many of his own permanent staff, but he had also invited mathematicians of a somewhat different type who were especially attracted by the Enigma problem.

Alan Turing, of King's College, Cambridge, went to one of the first of the training courses on codes and ciphers at Broadway Buildings; this was of a general nature and it is unlikely that Dilly was present, given his views on being thrown off at the deep end as far as breaking Enigma was concerned. However, Turing was put on Denniston's 'emergency list' for call up in event of war and was invited to look in on Dilly's small group to hear about progress with Enigma, which immediately interested him. Unusually, considering Denniston's paranoia about secrecy, it is said that Turing was even allowed to take the 'crib message' back to King's, and that 'he sported his oak', the then popular euphemism for working behind a closed door to discourage visitors, as well he might. They had begun to lose faith in Bertrand's miraculous operators' manual cipher and text crib and to think that what they were given to believe was an authentic example of cipher and plain text was after all fictitious. However, a meeting was arranged in Warsaw in July 1939, when the desperate Poles finally revealed, at the eleventh hour, how straightforward Dilly's QWERTZU problem was and how near he had been to winning the Enigma race.

SIX

The Warsaw conference

'Nous avons le QWERTZU – nous marchons ensemble'

Rumours of war had turned into the certainty of war by the time the tripartite conference of French, British and Polish codebreakers was called in Warsaw in July 1939. Hitler had demanded the return of Danzig and when the Poles refused tension reached breaking point, especially given that the Poles could read from the Enigma messages that tanks were about to assemble on their borders. Finally, when the Nazis marched on Prague in March, Britain gave an undertaking that the government would declare war on Germany if Poland were invaded. The situation was desperate when the Polish Cipher Bureau invited GC&CS to their war station at Pyry in the Kabackie woods near Warsaw. A decision had been taken at the highest level that, with the imminent threat of war, the time had come for their Enigma secrets to be handed over. A special request was made that Dilly Knox should be present. This was difficult. Dilly had been ill and the doctors had recently diagnosed lymphatic cancer. He had just had his first operation and was at the time suffering from influenza, but he insisted on accompanying Alastair Denniston. His family remember him staggering out of bed, ashen grey, but determined.

A fortnight before the departure, Rear-Admiral John Godfrey, the new director of naval intelligence, who was anxious to have personal contacts with GC&CS, had visited Courns Wood to renew an acquaintance made in the First World War. As a young officer on the staff of the Commander-in-Chief Mediterranean he had visited Room 40, where his brother Charles, headmaster of Osborne Royal Naval College, worked in the school holidays. Godfrey's mission at that time was to help organise intelligence for the Mediterranean fleet and he lectured to Greenwich Staff College on the contribution made by intelligence to naval operations. He would have met 'Blinker' Hall, Denniston, Birch and Dilly in Room 40. His objective in 1939 was to make sure that naval intelligence would make the utmost use of signals intelligence and he kept himself informed about the progress of the attempt to break Enigma. Learning about the forthcoming Polish conference he wanted to ensure he had an official representative. This was to be Commander Humphrey Sandwith, who was in charge of the Admiralty's network of intercept and direction-finding stations. The Knox boys were amazed to see an admiral in full dress uniform in their dining room, but it would not be for the last time.

Dilly and Denniston travelled by train on 24 July as they wanted to see Germany for the last time before all hell broke loose. They arrived in Warsaw the next day and were met by Colonel Gwido Langer, the head of the Polish Cipher Bureau, who took them to the Hotel Bristol, where they were to stay. Bertrand was the perfect host and took them out to dinner at the celebrated Restaurant Crystal, where they were joined by Commander Sandwith. Bertrand told Penelope Fitzgerald in 1974, when she was writing *The Knox Brothers*, that 'the naval commander ate and drank too much, Denniston remained discreet, and Dilly appeared *froid, nerveux, ascète*, scarcely touching any of the courses and concentrating only on the matter-in-hand.' In 1948, Denniston wrote a full report he called 'How News was brought from Warsaw at the end of July 1939'. Other first-hand accounts were also written by Bertrand and the Poles, but only thirty years later, and there is a discrepancy about the actual date of the two-day meeting. Denniston, however, had his pocket diary in front of him when he wrote and has the correct date. He records that 'the 26th (Wednesday) was THE day. The Poles called for us at 7am and we were driven out to a clearing in a forest about 20 kilometres from Warsaw.'

The 26th was not THE day for Dilly, however; it was in fact a disaster as all he wanted to do was to meet the cryptographers and sort out his QWERTZU problem, but if they were there they played no part as it turned out to be what Denniston called 'a prolonged full-dress conference' with Colonel Langer. All his life, Dilly had objected to what he called administrative 'window-dressing' and the 'prolonged full-dress conference' with senior officers who had no idea how to break Enigma doing all the talking was always going to bring out the worst in him. To make matters worse it was Maksymilian Ciężki, chiefly concerned with the wireless organisation, who was delegated to lecture on how the Cipher Bureau had broken the Enigma machine. Albeit a very pleasant man, it was Ciężki who had annoyed Dilly at the Paris meeting as his knowledge of the issues was limited and he did not understand Dilly's problem. However, be that as it may, there was no doubt that the Poles had somehow broken the German Enigma machine and it certainly made Denniston's day when they were shown an actual model they had made of it and the mechanical devices used to break messages.

But it did not make Dilly's day. Denniston subsequently described how he sat in 'stony silence' as Ciężki gave his lecture:

Knox, as our expert, was alongside Ciężki and in the best position to follow his explanation. He, however, reacted very badly to the explanation, which took about three hours with a break for a cup of tea. I confess I was unable to understand completely the lines of reasoning but when, as second part of the conference, we were taken down to an underground room full of electric equipment and introduced to the 'bombs' I did then grasp the results of their reasoning and their method of solving the daily key. Knox accompanied us throughout but maintained a stony silence and was obviously extremely angry about something. It was only when we got back into a car to drive away that he suddenly let himself go and, assuming that no one understood any English, raged and raved that they were lying to us now as in Paris. The whole thing was a fraud he kept on repeating – they never worked it out – they pinched it years ago and had followed developments as anyone else could but they must have bought it or pinched it.

The 'bombs' were an electro-mechanical machine which the Poles had devised as a means of breaking into Enigma. Dilly's anger was, in all probability, caused largely by the fact that he had yet to meet anyone on the Polish side who had the faintest idea how to break Enigma. The next day, Thursday 27 July, saw a complete turnaround to the point that

Dilly would never mention the previous day's unfortunate meeting again. The administrators were to meet and make arrangements for the Enigma treasure trove to be transported to Paris and London, which would ensure that GC&CS could take over where the Poles had left off, with the possibility of collaboration when war broke out. Meanwhile, Dilly and Henri Braquenié were taken to the cipher room itself to meet the people who had actually broken the Enigma machine. A worried Denniston managed to break away from the executive meeting to look in on Dilly and was mightily relieved to find that 'Knox was really his own bright self and won the hearts and admiration of the young men with whom he was in touch. If only that first day of formal disclosure could have been avoided and pompous declarations by senior officers had been omitted, Knox's mind and personality in touch with men who really knew their job would have made that visit a very real success.' The men Dilly met were Marian Rejewski and two younger colleagues, Jerzy Różycki and Henryk Zygalski.

Dilly's first question to Rejewski, who had broken Enigma theoretically as early as 1932, was, predictably, '*Quel est le QWERTZU?*', and one can only imagine poor Dilly's terrible shock when Rejewski told him that it was not random, as he feared, but just ABCDE. This was made worse by the fact that a certain 'Mrs B.B.', whose identity has not been traced, had actually suggested this possibility, but Dilly thought the Germans were not stupid enough to make it that easy! 'Had she worked on the crib we should be teaching them,' he lamented to Denniston that night in a letter written on the hotel notepaper. Dilly warned Denniston that although the Poles had done 'very well', changes to the German use of Enigma that took place in November 1938 had put an end to the Polish success, showing up the limitations of their system of breaking the messages. 'We should examine their system and statistics (if any) with considerable skepticism,' Dilly said. He clearly distrusted Ciężki but had the utmost respect for the three young mathematicians, Rejewski, Różycki and Zygalski, who had done the work. 'I am fairly clear that Ciężki knows very little about the machine and may try to conceal facts from us,' he told Denniston. 'The young men seem very capable and honest.'

The respect was reciprocated. Rejewski soon recognised Dilly Knox as an ace cryptographer. In an interview in 1978, he vividly recalled the meeting in the building in the woods at Pyry. 'Just how much Braquenié understood I don't know, but there is no question that Knox grasped everything very quickly, almost quick as lightning. It was evident that the British really had been working on Enigma ... They were specialists of a different kind – of a different class.' Rejewski also recalled the jubilation about their future co-operation and although alcohol was forbidden in the centre, a few bottles of beer were found and they drank to their joint success. Braquenié tells the story of going back to their hotel together with Dilly chanting: *'Nous avons le QWERTZU; nous marchons ensemble.'*

As soon as Dilly got home – having been delayed for a day in Poznan because his papers were not in order – he sent a letter of appreciation to his new Polish friends with his sincere thanks for their co-operation and patience. Rejewski gave a copy of the letter on Foreign Office notepaper to Władysław Kozaczuk, who published it in 1984 in his book *Enigma*. As Rejewski had been intrigued by Dilly's rods and the way they worked, Dilly sent him a set: the French had already made themselves a set of *'batons'*. Rejewski had never thought of this way of breaking Enigma, but in his interview he did not doubt that 'Knox's method' would have succeeded although 'unfortunately we got there first'. Despite his scepticism following the Ciężki lecture on the first day, having met Rejewski, Różycki and Zygalski and discussed their methods with them, Dilly had fully accepted that they 'got there first' and together with the rods he also sent three silk scarves showing a horse winning the Derby. The Poles treasured these souvenirs, one of which remained in the possession of Różycki's widow and, at Rejewski's centenary celebrations at the Foreign Office, Marian's daughter, Janina, told me that she had always known about the gift. It was indeed a nice gesture on Dilly's part to use the scarves to congratulate the Polish codebreakers on winning the race and must have made Denniston, who – in spite of frequent disagreements – always managed to remain on good terms with Dilly, feel better about the Warsaw visit.

In a memo written immediately after returning from the Warsaw conference, Dilly said:

At Warsaw, my French colleague and I were admitted into the Bureau itself and a course of lectures was arranged for us. After he had gathered the fact that 'le QWERTZU, c'est A, B, C', he took little interest and allowed the lectures to proceed. I tore up the programme and we proceeded by question and answer, writing these down in an odd variety of French. The expert staff of three were charming young men straight from the university. They had a good supply of mechanical gadgets. They were understaffed. They answered all my questions truthfully. What are the facts? When Major S [Ciężki] paraded before us in Paris his secrets de Polichinelle we took him for an ass; in fact he was bluffing. The Poles, getting in at the start had been reading the Enigma till 15th September 1938; at the time of arranging the Paris meeting they may have been in difficulties; at the actual time of that meeting things were going fairly well; they had got out the two new wheels and were reading SD [Sicherheitsdienst – the Nazi Party's own intelligence service] and military messages. In January, they ceased to be able, or had not enough staff, to read the latter; naval messages had not been read since May 1937. Discovery of le QWERTZU was effected (a) durch Verrat [through treachery], i.e. purchase of details of setting (? and the 'crib' message), (b) par hasard (they might have claimed par inspiration) … Doubtless they had also the 'key-block' and thus easily equalled the values; in which case it is just possible that they had enough. Anyhow inspiration served. Mr Twinn has just checked up on the genuineness of the crib. Such constatations are important as an answer to the question 'Is the Enigma safe?' The answer is that Enigmas of this pattern are definitely unsafe (since a thousand persons may handle the 'day-setting', memorise and betray the vital portions) unless the concealed and still more vital QWERTZU (diagonal) is such as cannot be guessed.

Dilly added that some of the Polish methods were 'neat' and tended to rely on the use of the 'bombs', which they called *bomby*. This had spawned in Dilly's mind the idea of a different type of electro-mechanical machine:

At the time of my visit I had ideas which seemed to be better, and I have since discussed them exhaustively with Mr Turing and Commander Travis and we believe that we could produce a really good alarm machine

– the Geschlechtzylinder. *This would give solutions for Army keys till (probably) March 21st: after that perhaps not. Almost all our guesses have been right except one of mine that there might be a naval book. I think we may hand some bouquets to the Poles for their lucky shot, but far more for their surmounting the difficulties after 15th September if only for two months. I could not possibly have finished the tasks I gave myself but for AGD's [Denniston's] help even in technical matters. I recommend strongly that if we have the Poles over here we ask AGD to invite one of the young men.*

How far Dilly had been from the winning post himself is shown by the fact that when he received the QWERTZU information, Peter Twinn was able to confirm within two hours that Bertrand's operators' manual crib was after all authentic; the wiring of the first two wheels could then be determined, using Dilly's 'buttoning-up' method, but now with an ABCDE diagonal. The way was now open to tackle another one of the 'Scarlet Pimpernels' from Bertrand that they had been given, described by Josh Cooper as practice messages 'made by an agent with access to an E machine' with no *Stecker* in place. Another three days' work produced these decodes, albeit trivial ones, and Cooper congratulated Twinn for being the first British codebreaker to read a German service Enigma message. Peter himself said modestly:

I hasten to say that this did me little if any credit, since with the information that Dilly had brought back from Poland, the job was little more than a routine operation. Indeed I had come out of my first few months at GC&CS extremely badly. If I had thought of making the guess, which in retrospect seems such a reasonable possibility, that QWERTZU was simply ABCDEFG, as Rejewski had done in 1933, I could have read a few messages within a fortnight of my arrival at GC&CS and made a debut of unparalleled brilliance. Alas! I failed to grasp my chance. I can only say in defence – and it is not much of a defence – that Dilly Knox, Alan Turing, and Tony Kendrick did no better, and none of that trio was known as an unimaginative dullard. Of course, reading a few scattered messages on a single day in 1938 was a whole universe away from the problems that lay

*ahead, but it would have been some encouragement; had we thought of it in
February 1939, we should have saved ourselves six valuable months.*

He seems to have forgotten the mysterious Mrs B.B.'s feminine
intuition! Although perhaps he never knew.

The Polish treasure trove, which included the replica Enigma machine,
arrived at Victoria station on the Golden Arrow on 16 August under
diplomatic seal, the arrangements having been made by 'Biffy' Dunderdale.
It was handed over by Bertrand to Colonel Stewart Menzies, the deputy
head of SIS, who was wearing the rosette of the Legion d'Honneur in
his buttonhole. '*Accueil triomphal*' was how Bertrand remembered it. As
soon as he returned from Warsaw, having thanked the Poles, Dilly's first
thought was to get in touch with Alan Turing to tell him how Rejewski
had originally solved the Enigma problem and for an inquest to be held
into their lack of success. Closeted in Dilly's study at Courns Wood, they
went over the whole story step by step. It is clear from the report he had
written on 4 August after Turing's weekend visit that what really bothered
Dilly was that Rejewski had, like Dilly, assumed that the diagonal was
as in the commercial machine QWERTZU, but when this would not
work on any of the messages he had, he guessed ABCDE as the entry
to the wheels. However, Dilly thought that the solution, which had so
held him up, could probably have been arrived at mathematically. Turing
recognised that Dilly had a good grasp of mathematics, albeit a disregard
for evaluating probabilities, and reassured him that this was very unlikely
with the limited amount of information GC&CS had. Rejewski himself
had never denied that the 'intelligence material furnished to us should be
regarded as having been decisive to the solution of the machine'.

It was Rejewski, however, who was the first to apply mathematics to
cryptology through permutation theory and it was Ciężki who recruited
him from Poznan University's Institute of Mathematics in 1932 to work
part time to seek a solution for Enigma. He seems to have produced
his theoretical result independently, a few months before the arrival of
Bertrand's intelligence material. Rejewski's permutation theory was not
published until 1979 but Gordon Welchman, a mathematician from
Sidney Sussex College, Cambridge, who joined Dilly Knox's section in

September 1939, was able to see the early history of Enigma breaking in perspective. When he came to write *The Hut Six Story* in 1982, having been its first head, he professed admiration for Rejewski's initial solution by permutation theory; however, he went on to say that the time required to turn this into codebreaking made his mathematical solution impractical and it was only when Bertrand's 'pinches' appeared on his desk that he was able 'to put this into practice', adding that 'it seems that Dilly Knox in England may well have arrived at a comparable theory, but he did not have access to the Asché documents'. Welchman dedicated his book to Rejewski and Knox, who had contributed so much to the early history of Hut 6. It appears then that Dilly's boast to Menzies that he believed himself to be 'the only man who can claim to have reconstituted with workable accuracy an Enigma machine without any purchase by Secret Service Funds' may well have been correct at that point. When Welchman came to recruit recently graduated Cambridge mathematicians for Hut 6 in 1940, he is on record as saying that the work they would be doing 'did not really need mathematics but mathematicians tended to be good at it'.

Before the release of certain classified material in 2001, a misconception had arisen among historians' interpretations of the information then available that although Dilly successfully broke un-*Stecker*ed machines he was 'defeated' by the German *Stecker*ed Enigma owing to his lack of mathematics and that success was only achieved with the advent of the mathematicians Turing and Welchman. Even Stuart Milner-Barry, a key Enigma player, who joined Hut 6 early in 1940, described the codebreakers at Bletchley Park as consisting of

> *a few old-time professionals who had worked in Room 40 at the Admiralty. Such for example as Dillwyn Knox, a Fellow of King's who died during the war ... and new recruits such as Welchman and Alan Turing. Knox had so, I understand, been defeated by the Enigma, and the main credit for solving the Enigma and subsequently exploiting its success should (subject to the Poles) probably go to the other two.*

This, as we now know, is simply not true. Defeat was not a word in Dilly's vocabulary and it was only those who actually knew Dilly's work on Enigma before the war and the setting up of the operational huts, notably Denniston, Tiltman, Foss, Bodsworth, Kendrick, Twinn, Cooper, 'Nobby' Clarke and Birch, who knew how much he had achieved. Dilly's early experimental methods for breaking Scherbius's original commercial machine had been a vital first step, allowing later complications to be dealt with as they arose.

Although Rejewski had been given a commercial machine soon after he arrived in the Cipher Bureau in September 1932, he went straight on to an analysis of the indicators on the German army messages enciphered on their *Stecker*ed machine, from which he would produce his mathematical theory; this would only hold good for the period of the fixed *Grundstellung*, when the six columns of repeated indicator letters for that particular setting, known collectively as a key-block, were in fact substitution ciphers. His detailed analysis of the indicators left him with six complex equations, each with three unknowns: the *Stecker*, the wiring to the entry plate and the wiring of the right-hand wheel (for the time being he could disregard the wiring of the other two, which only moved occasionally). Bertrand's gift of key settings for September and October 1932 revealed the *Stecker* for those months. Like Dilly, he too attacked the Wehrmacht machine on the basis that the diagonal was the same QWERTZU pattern used on the commercial machines. He was foiled for several weeks, but eventually tried the idea that it might be alphabetical. 'This time, luck smiled on me,' he said. 'The hypothesis proved correct.'

His correct guess that the diagonal was in alphabetical order meant Rejewski had solved the wiring of the right-hand wheel and because Bertrand had supplied the keys for two different months, using different wheels, he was quickly able to work out the wiring of the remaining wheels and the reflector. In an outstanding feat of cryptanalysis, Rejewski had worked out the wiring of the Wehrmacht Enigma by the end of 1932. Having obtained the details of the machine, and with only six possible wheel orders, the Poles were then able to read messages more or less currently using different methods, including 'grilles', a catalogue of patterns for the enciphered indicators (known at Bletchley as 'box-shapes'); 'perforated sheets', invented by Henryk Zygalski; and *bomby*.

Dilly also worked on 'boxing' the message key indicators (known as key-blocks). Unlike the Poles, Dilly did not use mathematics but a simple mixture of logic and guesswork with the key-block repeats and reciprocal characteristic of the machine. This of course meant a lot of hard slogging to get a sufficient number of 'alphabets', as Dilly called the clear and cipher pairs in the columns for the next stage of buttoning-up. Dilly was then concentrating on improving rodding techniques for the un-*Stecker*ed machines being used in the Spanish Civil War, which involved solving texts and not indicators and there is no working record of the 'comparable theory' that Welchman said Dilly had produced for developing his work on boxing. It was only when the new German indicators not enciphered on a *Grundstellung* appeared on Luftwaffe messages in November 1938 that Dilly's interest in indicators was rekindled and he produced what he called 'statistics' for a new line of attack even before the Warsaw meeting.

The Germans had perceived the folly of having a fixed *Grundstellung* for the indicators, which once discovered would render the system insecure, and had instructed operators henceforth to choose their own. Although this may seem less secure, as they were then forced to put the *Grundstellung* in clear in the preamble of the message, they had to set up their chosen indicator on the key setting given in their schedules and encipher it at the beginning of the message, thus removing the cryptographer's gift of a set of indicators on the same basic setting. However, the operators were still required to repeat the enciphered indicators, for the sake of Morse clarity, and Dilly now looked for remaining repeat characteristics. Like Rejewski, Dilly noticed that sometimes the repeat enciphered letter from positions 1 and 4, 2 and 5 or 3 and 6 of the indicator was the same, for instance AZN BZE, and these would only appear in a limited number of places. So if Z was not affected by *Stecker*, Dilly said (only six were in use in the early days), it would be 'possible to find the places on the cycle of keys'.

Unfortunately, at the same time the Germans had added two new wheels to their machines, but the Poles had a stroke of luck in September 1938 when the Sicherheitsdienst, originally set up by Heinrich Himmler as a secret police force for the Nazi Party, was made into a state intelligence organisation and provided with the armed forces Enigma machine. There was a delay before they changed to the new indicator procedure. When the new wheels were introduced two months later, the Poles were able to break them on the old method, thanks to the Sicherheitsdienst. GC&CS

was not able to intercept Sicherheitsdienst messages at that time and so Dilly lost the chance of continuing to work on boxing indicators when the change came and he was getting nowhere with Bertrand's 'crib message'.

Rejewski, however, with his colleagues, was able to work on known wheel wirings and had already produced a catalogue and a mechanical cyclometer to help break messages. At the time, Dilly did not know the wiring of the wheels, but proposed when he did to ascertain in the machine cycle where the same letters of the alphabet occurred at two places three positions apart; these he called 'females' and proposed to mark them on photographic film. He seems to have got some way with their production since in the memo he wrote after his visit to Warsaw, he says he 'could not possibly have finished the tasks I gave myself but for AGD's [Denniston's] help even in technical matters'. This would be referring largely to having to get permission for funding for every piece of equipment required. When Dilly discussed his method with the Pyry codebreakers, although he felt his method would work, he conceded that the Polish idea of stacking Zygalski's 'perforated sheets' was easier and cheaper. This would be his first task when war was declared and Bletchley Park, the war station for GC&CS, was established.

SEVEN

Bletchley Park as war station

Bletchley Park was up and running when war was declared on 3 September 1939, thanks to the foresight of the Head of SIS, Admiral Sinclair, who was also the overall director of GC&CS. He was known as 'C' to both organisations (so called after the initial of the first head of SIS, Commander Mansfield Cumming). Sinclair was increasingly aware of the destructive power of aerial bombing on cities, so dramatically demonstrated in the Spanish Civil War. Believing that war was now inevitable, he wanted to find a safe place in the country for his various secret intelligence departments away from Broadway Buildings in Westminster. Early in 1938, he asked the Foreign Office to provide the funds, but was told that it was the War Office which was responsible for war. The generals told him that as a former head of naval intelligence he should go to the Admiralty, who reminded him he was now part of the Foreign Office; exasperated, he paid the £7,500 asking price for Bletchley Park himself. If he had waited until the war started, the stately home could have been requisitioned by the government. It was, however, an excellent choice as Bletchley was ideally situated. By road it was on the A5, the old Watling Street, and more importantly it had good communications links with London and was a junction on the main-line train service between London, the north of England and Scotland; it was also midway between Oxford and Cambridge, from where Alastair Denniston's 'professor types' would be recruited, and the tree-studded lawns of a stately home would stand in for the groves of Academe.

Sir Herbert Leon, the builder of the flamboyant Victorian mansion, had himself chosen the site since, as a financier, company director and active Liberal MP, he needed easy access to London. He had a pathway made through his grand gardens with a special exit to the station. This proved very useful for us in wartime, as well as a pleasant walk, and had a sentry on guard during daylight hours. Leon had been determined to be upsides with his nearby fellow Jewish Liberal financier Lord Rothschild, in his splendid house and garden at Waddesdon. Bletchley Park was built in the eclectic 'Old English Revival' style with oriental additions, ending up a dizzy mixture of Gothic windows and a copper dome with very lavish Jacobean interiors. The Americans who arrived to work there in 1943 could hardly believe their eyes. It then suggested to one observer 'a 1920s movie palace', which, 'in coming to house the imaginative and mysterious activities of codebreaking, seemed at last to have acquired tenants to match its architecture'. They did, however, appreciate the ambience of the landscaped lake, although much of Leon's grand garden had been built on, with a naval hut in the rose garden and another hut in the maze. The stately home certainly contributed to the paradoxically relaxed atmosphere of Bletchley Park as a war station.

Sinclair was very aware of the need to upgrade security for SIS communications systems for both intelligence-gathering and dissemination of secret information. He recruited Richard Gambier-Parry from Philco Radio and put him in charge of a new division of SIS, known as Section VIII, to handle all its communications. Some of its representatives arrived on the site as soon as Sinclair purchased Bletchley Park for his overall organisation in March 1938. They were also present at the rehearsal in August 1938 to test Bletchley Park for all the SIS departments; called 'Captain Ridley's shooting party' to put the locals off the scent, it was organised by an SIS administrative officer, a real Captain W. H. W. Ridley. By all accounts it was a very pleasant occasion, Sinclair having brought his favourite chef from the Savoy Grill with him.

GC&CS was certainly not to be the only occupant of what was first called 'Station X', named after its wireless station. They returned to London in October 1938, after the Munich agreement, leaving Gambier-Parry's team in occupation. Staff from his Section VIII occupied the upper floor of the mansion and its engineers built a wireless telegraphy station in its tower. The Victorian grounds were full of mature conifers and the aerial was slung to the top of a *Sequoiadendron giganteum* on the front lawn. This was all part of the war station and intended to duplicate the existing SIS wireless 'Station X' at Barnes in west London. The plan was that the Barnes station would, like all SIS sections, be fully transferred to Bletchley Park in event of war. Some people, especially the Americans when they arrived in 1943, liked the cloak-and-dagger sound of 'Station X' and continued to refer to it as such during and after the war. However, almost everyone working there or connected with the place throughout the war referred to it as 'the Park' or more simply 'BP'.

In November 1939, the notorious 'Venlo incident', in which two SIS officers based in Holland, Major Richard Stevens and Sigismund Payne Best, were kidnapped by the Germans at Venlo on the Dutch border and taken into Germany, where they gave away a large amount of detail about British intelligence, led the new head of SIS, Colonel Stewart Menzies, to decide that having GC&CS on the same site as the SIS wireless communications centre was not a good idea. The SIS radio station and Section VIII of SIS, which in any case needed to expand, were soon transferred to nearby Whaddon Hall, along with the aerials and all the wireless gear needed for covert signals, leaving GC&CS as sole occupant of Bletchley Park. The capture of the two SIS officers at Venlo, one of them carrying a list of his agents, had sent shock waves through the Foreign Office and SIS. We are fully informed of quite how much Payne Best and Stevens had given away after the war by a remarkable Gestapo handbook by SS General Walter Schellenberg, who had been in on the Venlo incident. Its purpose was to give Hitler's staff planning the 1940 invasion a detailed analysis of the political and economic structure of the country. The chapter on British intelligence, operating from Broadway Buildings, provided largely by Stevens and Payne Best, was astonishingly accurate. The Germans positioned an agent, posing as a match seller, outside St James's Park Underground station opposite Broadway Buildings, to take photographs of the people going in and out. I worked there myself at the beginning of 1940 and would be intrigued to know whether I was in a Nazi file. A floor-by-floor breakdown of the departments was given, naming their heads. A special wanted list of those to be arrested even gave their home addresses and in some cases car registration numbers.

Sinclair was originally in charge, the handbook said, but on 4 November had been replaced by 'a Scotsman' called Colonel Stuart (*sic*)

Menzies, who was 'pronounced Mengis'. It referred to the administrative, military, naval and air sections. The head of the air section was said to be Wing Commander Winter-Bottom; the rank was right but his name was in fact Frederick Winterbotham. It also referred to the communications section, which Stevens claimed to know nothing about but which was allegedly headed by a 'Gambier Perry [*sic*], calls himself a Colonel but this seems to be untrue' and was 'reputed to have moved to Bletchley. Duties: wireless/radio communications, telephone, pigeon-post, etc.' A cipher section was mentioned somewhere else but its duties were said to be the preparation of our own codes and gave no Bletchley connection.

Mercifully the SIS policy of 'need to know' proved its worth. Even under torture Stevens could not have divulged the secrets of codebreaking, as he simply did not know it was being successfully undertaken. The information about Bletchley seems to have come from local fifth-column observation as there was a plaque on the gate saying 'Government Communications'. The term 'communications' is intentionally ambiguous, especially in translation, and gives no hint of codebreaking and there really were carrier pigeons in the stable-yard – SIS still used them at this stage – which provided a perfect alibi for what we were doing. It does not appear that Schellenberg's informative handbook was passed on to anyone else when the invasion was called off, otherwise the Luftwaffe would surely have dropped a bigger bomb on Bletchley Park than the half-hearted string of bomblets that was accidentally dropped on one occasion and did little damage.

The importance of GC&CS's activities had now risen considerably in the field of intelligence gathering. Signals intelligence, 'special intelligence' as it was then called, would for some considerable time have to take the place of agents. It was now imperative that Dilly and his team, installed in the Cottage, should be able to read current enemy traffic. A photograph of Captain Ridley's 1938 shooting party, taken by Barbara Abernethy, Alastair Denniston's secretary, shows Dilly in serious discussion with Oliver Strachey out of range of the main party. While the other chief players had been deciding on appropriate accommodation downstairs in the main part of the mansion, he had earmarked for himself a former groom's cottage in the stable-yard (where the pigeon loft was situated), well

1. The Knox family circa 1903: *standing, left to right* Wilfred, Dilly, Winnie, Eddie; *seated, left to right* Ethel, Bishop Knox, Ronnie.

2. The young Dilly Knox.

OUR NEW PLAY

[The world has been dredged by a certain well-known and talented author, to provide language in which he may exercise his dramatic skill. Our author, in endeavouring to find a new language in which he might express himself, met with the greatest difficulty, but at least he managed to rake up an old and long forgotten language from a distant quarter of the globe. In this he has written an entirely new and original play. Translation may be bought at the price of 5 guineas each at all well-known chemists.]*

$$] \sqrt{\%} = \therefore F$$

$\Delta = //\supset] \sqrt{5 + x}^2 \quad °H_2O \quad A \ltimes \% - \}$ R.S.V.P.^{g}

(dies)

(Exit)

$CxO_3{}^c] \perp [°^3 S.P.S.R \therefore \} F \prime ⊙^n \sqrt{-1+0} \} SD \blacksquare P$

(Intrat)

(Exit)

$\overline{HS} > \therefore] \quad HCl \quad °°° (\overline{}) \quad D.T.^2 \quad ⊙ > \circledA \{ F^3$

* It will be observed that stage directions are in English and Latin

20

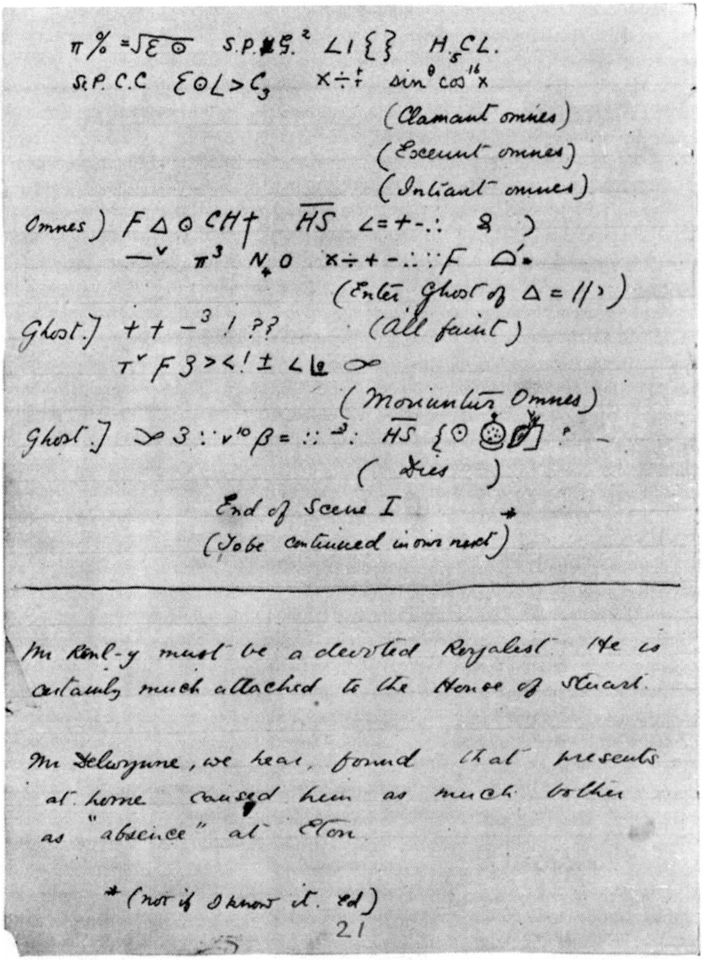

$\pi \% = \sqrt{\mathcal{E} \odot}$ S.P.#$5.^2$ $\angle I \{ \}$ $H_5CL.$
S.P.C.C $\mathcal{E} \odot L > C_3$ $x \div \div \sin^9 \cos^{16} x$

(*Clamant omnes*)
(*Exeunt omnes*)
(*Intiant omnes*)

Omnes) $F \triangle \odot CH\dagger$ $\overline{HS}$ $\angle = + - \therefore$ $\&$)
— ^{v} π^3 $N_4 0$ $x \div + - \therefore \therefore F$ $\triangle \cdot$
(*Enter Ghost of* $\triangle = //$)
Ghost.] $+ + -^3 ! ??$ (*all faint*)
$T^v F 3 > < ! \pm \angle \underline{\varrho} \infty$
(*Moriuntur Omnes*)
Ghost.] $> 3 \therefore v^{10} \beta = \therefore \overset{2}{\therefore} \overline{HS} \{ \odot \textcircled{\oplus} \}$: —
(*dies*)

End of Scene I
(*To be continued in our next*)

Mr Renl-y must be a devoted Royalist. He is
certainly much attached to the House of Stuart.

Mr Telwynne, we hear, found that presents
at home caused him as much bother
as "absence" at Eton.

* (not if I know it. Ed)

21

3. Dilly's schoolboy code for his brother Eddie's holiday magazine.

4. John Maynard Keynes, a close friend of Dilly's from Cambridge days. (Getty Images)

5. Frank Birch, Dilly's liveliest friend in Room 40, who went on to head Bletchley Park's Hut 4.

6. Cdr A. G. Denniston, who was in charge of GC&CS in the inter-war years and the early part of WWII.

7. Capt. Reginald 'Blinker' Hall, director of the Royal Navy Intelligence Division during WWI.

8. Courns Wood, the house Dilly bought in 1921.

9. Olive and the boys,
Christopher (*right*)
and Oliver.

A S 162 pr. 12. Januar 1917. p.m. 000001 Geheim

I

Berlin, den 13. Januar 1917.

A S 162

1. Gesandter von Eckardt

Mexico. Nr. 2.

Mit U-Boot am 15. d. M.

über Washington.

Chiffrierbureau: Ang. 1 ist mit Chiffre 13040 zu chiffrieren, die in Mexico vorhanden und soweit bekannt, nicht kompromittiert ist.

St. Sek. Montgelas z. g. Mtz

Bei Postziffern

Ganz geheim. Selbst entziffern.

[Wir beabsichtigen, am 1. Februar uneingeschränkten U-Boot Krieg zu beginnen. Es wird versucht werden, Amerika trotzdem neutral zu erhalten.

Für den Fall, daß dies nicht gelingen sollte, schlagen wir Mexico auf folgender Grundlage Bündnis vor: Gemeinsame Kriegführung. ~~und~~ Gemeinsamer Friedensschluß. Reichliche finanzielle Unterstützung und Einverständnis+ unsererseits, daß Mexico in Texas, Neu-Mexico, Arizona++ früher verlorenes Gebiet zurückerobert. Defensivbündnis nach Friedensschluß, wenn es Mexico gelingt, Japan in Bündnis einzubeziehen.

Zim

+ Eine Garantie wird darauf nicht zu geben sein.

++ Californien dürfte für Japan zu reservieren sein.

1020

1. } befördert 13/1.
2. } für U-boot

10. The Zimmermann telegram,
as prepared by the German foreign ministry.

11. Dilly planting in his Naphill woods.

12. Dilly and family on a picnic.

13. One of the damaged portions of the Herodas papyrus.

14. A clean portion of the Herodas papyrus that Dilly used as a 'crib'
to work out the text of the damaged portions.

15. Capt. Ridley's 'shooting party' arriving for the trial run at Bletchley Park in 1938. Dilly is on the far right, away from the main party, talking to Oliver Strachey.

16. The Cottage, where Dilly set up his Enigma research section in 1939.

17. John Tiltman, who worked with Dilly on the Mask ciphers.

18. Hugh Foss, who rejected the original commercial Enigma machine as too insecure for British use.

19. Alan Turing, Dilly's 'bombe-ish boy', who set up Bletchley Park's naval codebreaking secction, Hut 8.

20. Gordon Welchman, the head of Hut 6, which broke army and air force Enigma ciphers.

21. John Jeffreys, who worked in the Cottage, seen here with a colleague, Pam Hemsted.

22. The *bombes* being operated by Wrens.

23. Marian Rejewski, the young Polish mathematician who first broke the German armed forces Enigma.

24. *left to right* The head of the Polish Cipher Bureau, Gwido Langer; his French counterpart, Gustave Bertrand; the British representative at the French 'PC Bruno' code-breaking station, Kenneth Macfarlan.

25. The G312 Abwehr Enigma machine now on display at Bletchley Park.

26. Peter Twinn, who replaced Dilly as head of the Intelligence Services Knox (ISK) section.

27. Keith and Mavis Batey photographed soon after their wedding in November 1942.

28. Rear-Admiral John Godfrey, director of naval intelligence during the Second World War.

29. Admiral Sir Andrew Cunningham, Commander-in-Chief Mediterranean, who won at Matapan 'by the grace of God and Dilly'.

30. Sketch of Dilly by
Gilbert Spencer RA.

31. Dilly's gravestone
in his Naphill woods,
engraved by Eric Gill.

DILLWYN KNOX
C·M·G
1884 — 1943

away from any kind of administrative contact. Commander Denniston had chosen Lady Leon's morning room to the left of the mansion entrance as you looked at it from the circular driveway, so that he could keep an eye on everybody, just as 'the little man' had done in the *Alice in ID25* pantomime. 'Nobby' Clarke, the head of the naval section, settled for the library, John Tiltman's military section was assigned to the dining room and Josh Cooper, head of the air section, had his eye on the drawing room to the right of the entrance; he was still recovering from his journey from London. 'MI6 provided some cars for transport but many people used their own cars and gave lifts to others,' he recalled. 'It fell to my lot to be driven down by Knox, who had a remarkable theory that the best way to avoid accidents was to take every crossroad at maximum speed.'

After the war station was put into action in August 1939, Dilly immediately settled into his stable-yard cottage and made plans to receive his staff for his new Enigma research section when war broke out. He had always worked as a loner even when he had assistants and it would be a new experience to run a section, albeit initially a small one, with Tony Kendrick and Peter Twinn already part of the team. One career civil servant clerk, Joyce Fox-Mail, was allocated to him and Denniston sent along two new recruits, Elizabeth Granger and Claire Harding, the daughters of two members of his Ashtead Golf Club whom he knew well, to settle him in; they were reliably discreet and indispensable in getting things organised. The 'professor type' codebreakers, who had all been placed on the 'emergency list', then arrived on 3 September 1939 and Dilly was waiting to greet them. They included Alan Turing from King's College, Cambridge, Gordon Welchman from Sidney Sussex College, Cambridge, and John Jeffreys from Downing College, also Cambridge. They would all make significant contributions to the exploitations of the initial breaking of the Enigma machine.

Dilly's first task was to fulfil his promise of contacting and co-operating with the Poles. As the German armoured columns advanced on Warsaw, Rejewski, Zygalski and Różycki destroyed all their documents and equipment and managed to cross the Romanian frontier. In October, with the help of the French embassy, they reached Gustave Bertrand's wartime Cipher Bureau, codenamed PC Bruno, which he had set up in the

Château de Vignolles at Gretz-Armainvillers, near Paris. GC&CS made immediate contact with them and, urged on by Dilly, asked if Marian Rejewski and his colleagues could be allowed to join the codebreakers at Bletchley Park. However, it was made clear that 'the French government were paying for the Polish army and therefore the Poles must work in France'. Relations with Bertrand, however, were extremely good. Dilly was always at pains to see that he was kept informed of progress and approved of arrangements. In fact a permanent liaison officer, Captain Kenneth Macfarlan, called 'Pinky' because of his rosy complexion, operated at PC Bruno and through him Bertrand had a direct teleprinter service with Denniston at Bletchley Park.

Bertrand's chief cryptographer, Henri Braquenié, whom Dilly had first met at the Paris conference in January 1939, came over to work in the Cottage in September soon after war was declared. Dilly, having seized him by the arm and rejoiced '*Nous marchons ensemble*' at the Warsaw conference, was as good as his word. While he was at Bletchley Park, Braquenié stayed with Dilly at Courns Wood. On 29 September, Dilly wrote to Denniston: 'It has been a great pleasure to me, though somewhat testing of my French, to bear-lead Captain B from 8 a.m. to 10 p.m.' In a memo on 'Anglo-French Enigma Liaison', sub-titled 'Finance', Dilly pointed out:

> *I have taken the line, though he offered to pay generously, that entertainment is* une affaire de bureau; *that is from my angle, that I should get a billeting allowance from you and that you or he should deal with the French. Drinks and transport other than that to or from the office (for which I get an allowance) I treat as my private liability.*

Dilly was no wine connoisseur and one can only wonder how the *entente cordiale* survived, as Oliver Knox said that at Courns Wood even the odd admiral would be entertained with just a half-bottle of plonk.

The first task was to provide the quantities of Zygalski sheets for Bertrand's PC Bruno centre that Dilly's Polish friends needed. They had not had the resources to produce the number they needed after the Germans had added two extra wheels in autumn 1938. Jeffreys was put in charge of organising the 'sex statistics', as Dilly called the perforated sheets, tracking down 'female' positions in the machine cycle. A 'female' was a letter in the second group of a doubly enciphered Enigma message key which repeated a letter in the corresponding position in the first group, such as AFO, CFK.

A special machine was made for producing the *Netz*, as they were usually called, which was under Dilly's constant supervision. Denniston was invited over to the Cottage to punch the two-millionth hole and Harding and Grainger assisted Dilly in organising a 'punch' party; they said that he took endless pains to acquire the right ingredients for a wartime punch bowl. It was probably Braquenié who took the first batch of Zygalski sheets back to Bertrand's PC Bruno centre, where he worked side by side with the Poles until the fall of France. They were working day and night in the Cottage but Dilly was not satisfied that things were going fast enough at the administrative level. As usual, he had the highest praise for his underpaid 'girls', who, he said, worked long hours punching and never mentioned overtime. It was no small achievement by the Cottage team since sixty sets of twenty-six sheets had to be made, with many of the sheets containing 1,000 precisely cut holes. PC Bruno was also sent copies of the 'Jeffreys sheets', which were punched-sheet catalogues showing the effect of any two wheels and the *Umkehrwalze*, the Enigma machine's reflector. Pam Brewster, who had worked on perforating the sheets from the beginning and went on with the other girls to be a member of the teams who used the sheets in a process they called '*Netz* shoving', recalls the excitement when the light bulb revealed an alignment of holes and the testing for female positions could begin.

Although he had been anxious to supervise all that was going on, Dilly was not really any good at organisation. Welchman was just the man who was needed to come to grips with the as yet unsorted traffic networks through their call-signs and discriminants. As Welchman himself said, when he came to write *The Hut Six Story*, published in 1982: 'Dilly was neither an organisation man nor a technical man. He was essentially an idea-struck man.' Welchman and the old hand Tony Kendrick were dispatched to Elmer's School, which had just been acquired on the edge of Bletchley Park. As there were large empty tables there it was an ideal place for this essential task of sorting messages, given that every surface in the tiny cottage was taken up with the punching of the perforated sheets. Braquenié had provided sheaves of old French intercepted Enigma traffic and Dilly, through Tiltman, arranged for Welchman and Kendrick to visit the army intercept station at Fort Bridgewoods, Chatham, in Kent, to see how all the messages were received before they were sent to Bletchley Park.

Welchman's work was truly productive. In retrospect, he saw that it set the scene for Hut 6 when the Cottage research would turn into production. He recalled how Kendrick, having been with Dilly in the early stages, explained to him how far their Enigma research had got and had suggested how their present assignment should be approached:

> *Kendrick started to work on the large collection of material from Chatham, and set me a good example by beginning to analyse its characteristics in a methodical manner. His approach was reminiscent of the period some five or ten years earlier when I had been doing work on algebraic geometry and had often been faced with the problem of thinking of something to think about.*

Kendrick was dealing with the problem in the same way, he said, and 'I followed suit'.

Welchman made a thorough study of the traffic, taking note of the radio frequencies and times of origin as well as the discriminants, call-signs and messages sent in parts. He marked the different networks with red, blue and green crayons and when message-breaking for research purposes went into production in the huts in 1940 these colours were retained: red for the main Luftwaffe cipher, which was used widely for operational and administrative purposes, green for the cipher used by the German army's military districts, and blue for the Luftwaffe practice cipher. So far so good for Welchman's organisational skills, but he, like Dilly, was an ideas man and he mistakenly thought that Dilly had deliberately 'banished' him to Elmer's School away from the main cryptographic stream. 'During my first week or two at Bletchley, I got the impression that he didn't like me,' Welchman said. 'Very soon after my arrival I was turned out of the cottage and sent to Elmer's School.'

Welchman recalled having noticed the formation of the occasional repeat letters in the indicators at the beginning of the message, which both the Poles and Dilly had picked up and exploited in different ways, leading to the present all-out punching operation in the Cottage. Independently, he had come up with the same idea for what Dilly called 'females' in the machine cycle and rushed over from the School to the Cottage to tell Dilly about it. Dilly was furious, he said, and reminded him that he had been told to study discriminants and call-signs, not methods of breaking the Enigma.

The trouble with reminiscences forty years on is that while Welchman gives a very accurate account of his thought processes and technical achievements, his memory fails him on incidentally related matters and he did not have the benefit of being able to check them with the now released official records. From personal experience of my own Bletchley Park memories, I am painfully aware how essential that is, considering that our memories had to remain buried for over thirty years.

The records show that Welchman was not 'banished' to the School because, as he thought, Dilly did not like him. Where Dilly was concerned, lack of communication was not a sign of dislike but merely of total absorption in a project to the exclusion of all else. Penelope Fitzgerald, Dilly's niece, was told, very probably by Peter Twinn, who was aware of the situation, that when Dilly was told about Welchman's perception, he said apologetically: 'Hadn't one said the right thing?' The response was: 'You haven't said anything; you haven't spoken to him at all for two weeks.' Dilly was aware of how necessary and important the work of analysing the new wartime traffic would be and knew that Welchman had the right skills to do it; skills which would, thankfully, leave him to get on with the burden of all the tasks he had set himself. Nor was Welchman left without any explanation of what was going on in Dilly's Enigma research. Kendrick was no lightweight and it was he who normally gave fundamental explanations about the Enigma machine to newcomers, although he did not himself make any inspirational contribution to codebreaking. Hugh Alexander, the head of Hut 8, later commented that any new suggestion in the hut had already been proposed by Kendrick, who had worked for Dilly and knew all the answers. A confidential note of Dilly's in November 1939 says that Kendrick is 'quite admirable' and the 'obvious second-in-command' and it was a pity he was in Elmer's School. Welchman, he said in the same note, was 'doing well and is keen. I hope to get him back here to learn about the machines.' Several documents from 1 November 1939 onwards show that, although Welchman was not then actually working in the Cottage, he was considered to be part of Dilly's team as the documents are jointly signed by Knox, Twinn, Turing, Welchman and Jeffreys.

Dilly's relationship with Alan Turing was rather different. Turing arrived in the Cottage with a full understanding of the history of breaking the Enigma, having worked on it himself in the summer and having had the post-Warsaw discussions with Dilly. As soon as Turing arrived in the Cottage he wanted to tackle naval, which Dilly had put aside in 1937 to await a 'pinch' of bigram tables; this suited Turing as he could work on his own and he disappeared into the stable loft, away from the constant bustle of making the perforated sheets in the rooms below. He did not want coffee breaks or social meals in the mansion so Claire Harding and Elizabeth Grainger rigged up a pulley to send up coffee and sandwiches to him in a basket. As with Dilly, his ideas sparked off in all directions, which makes Dilly's confidential note on Turing a true case of the pot calling the kettle black:

> *Turing is very difficult to anchor down. He is very clever but quite irresponsible and throws out suggestions of all sorts of merit. I have just, but only just, enough authority and ability to keep his ideas in some sort of order and discipline. But he is very nice about it all.*

Ever since Room 40 days, Dilly's heart had been in naval intelligence and now that the U-boat war had started he was determined to do all he could to help Turing find a crib to solve the naval Enigma. His first opportunity came in November 1939, when he managed to be present at the interrogation of a recently captured naval prisoner of war, who might have had access to cipher material. Admiral Godfrey, the director of naval intelligence, thought it would be useful to have Dilly present at the interview. The information Dilly managed to extract from the sailor was indeed helpful. As there were no numbers on the Enigma keyboard, the German navy had hitherto used the letters QWERTZUIO for the figures 1 to 9, with Ys as separators, so that when a message was a continuation

(FORT) of a previous one, the time of origin at the beginning of the message, if 13.35, would appear in the format FORTYQEETY, where FORT for continuation, is followed by a space, indicated by a Y, followed by Q for 1, E (twice) for 3 and T for 5 followed by one more space. Now Dilly was told that the Enigma operators had in future to spell out numbers in full, which made for a much longer crib.

Turing was working on ideas for mechanised cryptography as well as attempting to solve the naval Enigma messages. Although his work was previously theoretical, he was mechanically apt and had once made an electric multiplier and later designed a mechanism for answering a problem dealing with prime numbers, cutting the gears himself. As soon as Dilly had got back from Warsaw, he wanted to tell Turing about the Polish idea, which was new to him. At Pyry, he had seen what the Poles called their *bomba* (*bomby* in the plural); this was an electro-mechanical device, superior to a cyclometer, based on the Polish Enigma models, given its name because the idea came to Marian Rejewski and his colleagues while eating an ice-cream dessert called a *bomba*. The *bombe*, as it was called in French, was made by the AVA Telecommunications factory in Warsaw in November 1938 to cope with the changes in the German Enigma service messages. Drawings and plans of it had arrived at Victoria station on 16 August 1939 and, along with the Zygalski sheets and the model of the Enigma machine, were now in the Cottage for Turing to study.

Before leaving Warsaw Dilly had commented that the Polish methods all depended on the double encipherment of the indicators, 'which may at any time be cancelled', as it indeed was in May 1940. Dilly had discussed his ideas for electro-mechanical machines similar to the Polish *bomby* on his return from Warsaw, telling Turing that they should be thinking of developing a *bombe* method to check for standard beginnings of cipher texts and indicators. A few weeks after setting up in the Cottage, Dilly obtained permission from Alastair Denniston to acquire the former plum store in the stable-yard as 'a small experimental workshop for trying out gadgets'. It was here that Turing's ideas took real shape. Dilly was well pleased with how Turing, whom he called 'my bombe-ish boy', developed the British *bombe*, an electro-mechanical machine which ran through all the various possibilities of wheel choice, order, ring position and machine settings at high speed to test whether favoured positions by the codebreakers worked. This would greatly speed up the breaking of Enigma messages and the intelligence derived from them.

A meeting on 1 November 1939, attended by Dilly, Twinn, Jeffreys, Turing and Welchman, set out their requirements; namely punches, cyclometers and a British variant of the Polish *bomby*. Denniston's deputy, Commander Edward Travis, liaised with the British Tabulating Company at Letchworth about ordering the machinery. Dilly's relationship with the bulldog-like Travis was hit-and-miss as both he and Denniston seem to have been paying unwelcome attention to the activities in the Cottage, which Dilly doubted they understood. The cyclometer was essential for testing female positions and consisted of two un-*Stecker*ed Enigmas wired together so that the output of each went straight into the input of the other. A Dilly memorandum stated:

> *What happened precisely was this. I found that the cyclometer was going very slowly and could not be speeded up to give more than four or five wheel orders. I told Jeffreys of my scheme and suggested that we should put on the best crew and get on with the scheme of check sheets. He demurred that it was against orders. I asked him what he thought of the scheme itself. He said it was the only sane thing to do. I threw about what little weight I have. I said I was his immediate superior; he was to keep the whole thing a secret; if AGD or Travis came in he was to conceal what we were doing as best he could. If God Almighty came in he was to report him to me.*

Travis also took active steps for the provision of huts for the increased staff that would be needed when current German Enigma messages were broken. His report to Denniston on 19 November 1939 shows he already had the structure of the research and production departments well in hand. Travis was on good terms with Welchman, who now had two staff working for him on traffic analysis in Elmer's School, allowing him to give much thought to how Hut 6, which he was destined to lead, could operate as the production line for the German army and Luftwaffe Enigma decodes. He estimated that it would be his red (Luftwaffe) traffic, which, owing to the increased number of intercepts, was likely to yield the first messages to be broken. As early as 29 October, Welchman had stipulated that the hut dealing with red would need a registration room, an intercept control room, a decoding room for the messages to be run off when the day's key setting was known, and the sheet-stacking *Netz* room. A plan he drew up for Travis was so detailed that it even showed where the light plugs should be placed in the skirting board for the bulbs under the glass-topped tables for inspecting the perforated sheets. As yet Turing's *bombes* were wishful thinking but the October plan showed where power plugs should be put in readiness. Dilly was preoccupied with other things at that stage and was happy to be left out of the production line discussions.

Thanks to Welchman's painstaking traffic registration, Dilly had been presented with many more cryptographical opportunities. 'Cillis' were one of Dilly's most important discoveries and would have far-reaching consequences. They resulted from a combination of two different mistakes made by some Enigma operators. While breaking pre-war traffic Dilly noticed that the operator often took the final position of the three wheels at the end of the preceding message as the setting for the next, thus saving himself the trouble of altering the wheels for the enciphering of the next message setting. This could be identified from the outside indicator in the message preamble. The first error the operator had to make for cillying to work was using a setting that could be guessed in the first message: the use of keyboard 'slides', where three letters next to each other on the keyboard were used – such as UJM or TGB – or 'pronounceables', the first three letters of a proper name, for example WALter, MARtha or CILli, in the first message; it was the discovery of an example of that last one in an early message that gave the name to the process. By subtracting from the outside indicator of the second message the number of letters in the preceding message it could be seen whether the first indicator had been cillied. The subtraction was done by sliding measuring strips, the number of units of length being the number of letters in the message, against a long strip consisting of the alphabet written out several times. Dilly in his playful way called these snakes. Other examples of this 'Dillyese' of the period include corsets, alligators, slugs, grass skirts, starfish and beetles.

Dennis Babbage arrived in the Cottage in December 1939 in time for the punch party and was present for the brilliant cilli discovery. He became an expert at cillying himself and found a new category where a lazy operator might even use the same three letters both for the indicator and the message setting, which was dubbed JABJAB. This all led on to the brilliant *Ringstellung* 'tip' by John Herivel in conjunction with cillis, where the lazy operator, having duly set up the clips on the wheels, when the key was changed at midnight shut the lid of the machine, allowing the letters to show in the windows, which he did not change when he came to send off his first message of the day. This became known as the 'Herivel tip'. Hugh Foss had invented sheets which would show any clusters of giveaway indicators in network settings. It was a simple sheet of squared paper with alphabets at the top and left-hand side. A three-letter indicator WER would have R written in the square marking W at the top and E at the side. Testing for self-*Stecker* and reciprocal pairings when the wheel order was known, by using an un-*Stecker*ed machine, was always a 'great thrill', Babbage recalled, all part of the 'magic' atmosphere of Dilly's early cilli handbreaks, the 'miracle' that became routine in Hut 6.

All the knowledge they had was based on pre-war information, however; it was not certain that the Germans had not changed the Enigma machine in readiness for the outbreak of war and there was in fact some indication that they had done so. Dilly carried on with the preparation of the Zygalski sheets, concealing from the exhausted staff that they might be useless for current traffic if the wheel wirings had changed. Fortunately, feeling so strongly about his promise to the Poles, he made one of his frequent threats to resign unless the final batch of Zygalski sheets was sent to Bruno.

The Cottage
7 January 1940

My dear Denniston,
As you remember on our Journey to Warsaw I promised to assist the Poles and the French in producing statistics. Actually we have produced these, or similar statistics, and in a third of the time that all three parties could have

been expected to produce them, but I hold, if only on personal grounds, that these statistics (under copy) must be handed over at once.

They were delayed for two reasons only:

1. *To devise a scheme of mechanical reproduction. This problem has been solved without using the Netz themselves.*
2. *In order to see whether the upper and under copies were needed at once. The answer here is 'No'.*

My personal feelings on the matter are so strong that unless they leave by Wednesday night I shall tender my resignation.

I do want to go to Paris but if you cannot secure another messenger I'm actually at the moment completely idle.

Yours ever
A. D. Knox

They were finally taken over by Turing on 17 January and given to Zygalski. Turing also met Marian Rejewski and told him of Dilly's recent successes but was evidently anxious not to discuss the *bombe*. Rejewski, ignorant of how much progress he had made, recalled that they treated Turing as 'a younger colleague who had specialised in mathematical logic and was just starting out on cryptology'. However, Rejewski was able to tell Turing why they had been unable to break wartime traffic with the Zygalski sheets and in his presence decoded a green message of October 28 with the new sheets Turing had brought over. Inadvertently, the Poles had given them some wrong information about the turnovers in the new wheels IV and V, which the Germans had introduced at the end of 1938. Dilly's cillis depended on wheel turnover matches, which accounts for his inability to make his crucial method work on the 1939 traffic. Immediately on Turing's return, the Cottage got to work on a green message for 25 October. Cillying had reduced the number of wheel orders for these messages to only three. This was the first wartime German Enigma message to be broken in this country and was received with shrieks of joy in the Cottage.

However, there was still the anxiety as to whether the Germans would make other changes in 1940 and it is best to let Babbage, who was there, describe the atmosphere in his own words:

We eagerly awaited the opportunity of finding the answer to the next great question. Had the Germans made a change in the machine at the New Year? While we awaited a suitable day, that is one with enough females for our purpose, several other 1939 keys were broken and we began to get evidence of the extent and nature of cillying. At last the favourable day arrived, and it had, besides the requisite number of females, several good cillies to cut down the wheel order. The sheets were laid, the stories tested and 'Red' of 6 January 1940 was out.

Up until now, a use for the Jeffreys sheets, as opposed to the Zygalski sheets, had not been found as they were designed to work with rodding, which was only possible with un-*Stecker*ed machines or on rare occasions where the *Stecker* were known and could be stripped off, as with the Enigma manual with its genuine crib. Dilly's next observation detecting such a situation is a splendid example of his long experience in being prepared for anything, however unexpected, in the way of procedural errors which would give a way in. He had observed a simple meteorological telegram transmitted at midnight from German airfield radio stations in three letter groups, presumably taken from a codebook, which did not take him long to compile. Before long it appeared that someone had had the bright idea of adding a layer of cipher for increased security and Dilly noticed at once that this was an unusual reciprocal substitution, which suggested possible *Stecker* connections that the operator could have obtained from the daily Enigma settings.

Colonel Gwido Langer visited Dilly's section in December 1939 to sort out arrangements for liaison with Bruno and the new discovery was soon shared with the Poles. As the weather messages were always transmitted at midnight, knowing the *Stecker* for a given day was appreciated as an early start to finding the Enigma settings. With the *Stecker* removed, Dilly's rodding was possible and the Jeffreys sheets came into their own. If there was a crib guess of cipher and text involving rod couplings on the right-hand wheel, those sheets were superimposed and any hole alignment would indicate a possible combination and position of the first two wheels for which all these couplings were valid.

Dilly's tour de force did not appear in any British official history as he kept no records himself; at best F. H. Hinsley referred to it in a footnote as 'short-lived'. But Rejewski took a different view of its significance. 'We had the English to thank for yet another observation,' he wrote in a reference to the weather messages' important give-away of the *Stecker* setting. 'Every day they changed the letters in the code in a way that betrayed the plug links. This was a cardinal error on the part of the Germans since in this way there was no need to even solve the code to find the plug links every day without difficulty.'

Hut 6 Production had now taken over from Research with Gordon Welchman as its first head. The Cottage was shut down for security reasons and for a time Dilly was left like a fish out of water until new arrangements could be made. He made sure that the contact with PC Bruno continued and, according to Rejewski, flourished. 'In the framework of the co-operation with the British,' he said, 'there was also regular liaison about the machine keys of the day. Whoever was the first in the possession of the keys for the given day would immediately notify their Allied counterparts. Thanks to this, during the whole Norwegian campaign there was, I believe, not one cryptogram that was not read by us or the British.' To begin with there was the problem of how we could be in secret communication. Obviously we both needed the same cipher machine, but the French did not have one of their own and we could not have our Typex machine put at risk. However, we both had the Polish models of the German Enigma machine and that proved to be the answer. Bletchley and Bruno audaciously exchanged Enigma secrets on the Germans' own machine, ending the messages '*Heil Hitler!*'

Babbage, a key player in the new Hut 6, leaves us in no doubt of the vital role that Dilly Knox had played in what is referred to in the official histories as the 'Pre-history of Enigma':

> *Knox had been the pioneer worker on Enigma in this country and his energy*
> *and enthusiasm had been an inspiration to all in the early months. When the*

Enigma had disclosed its secrets and Hut 6, under Welchman, was firmly on its feet, Knox and his Cottage party turned their attention to new problems.

For Dilly this called for a Carrollian celebration, not a full-scale Alice pantomime with Birch, as in the final Room 40 days, but a throwaway imitation of Lewis Carroll's poem *Jabberwocky* and its famous whimsical beginning.

> *'Twas brillig, and the slithy toves*
> *Did gyre and gimble in the wabe;*
> *All mimsy were the borogoves*
> *And the mome raths outgrabe.*

In the Knox version, Carroll's 'borogoves' become the 'wranglercoves' newly recruited from Cambridge by Welchman for Hut 6, one of whom was my husband-to-be. The point at which "twas brillig' in the Knox version can be dated to February 1940, when Hut 6 was first up and running. The *Ringstellung* problem had been solved and they were profitably busy with Dilly's cyclometer (abbreviated to 'cyc'), and the *Netz* and Jeffreys sheets, but there is a warning in Dilly's parody that the females and the *Netz* might be in trouble in the future or there might be a new seventh wheel introduced. Although he was in charge of 'the Cottage crowd', Dilly acknowledges his need of Welchman and his team of 'registrators'. Babbage was shrieking with joy at his cillying but Foss sheets do not appear to be popular with the girls who had to deal with them. Dilly had shown everyone how to look for 'confirmations' and 'contradictions' in the *Stecker* knock-out. Alan Turing broke the blue traffic, whose discriminant had been identified by Welchman, on 29 January 1940, and Dilly's 'bombe-ish boy' was all set to slay 'the Jabberwock' with his equivalent of Carroll's 'vorpal blade'. The Cottage had been shut down, leaving Dilly only a small haven in the plum store, no longer being used, where Turing could visit him away from the bustle of Hut 6.

> *'Twas HUTSIX, and the WRANGLERCOVES*
> *Did twist and twiddle at the CYC;*
> *All grimset were the JEFFREYBROWS*
> *And the BABBAGE outschreik.*

'Beware the SEVENTHWHEEL, my son!
The pale FULLHOUSE, the NETZ that fail!
Move not the UMKEHRWALZE, and shun
The UNCONFIRMED FEMALE!'

He took the COTTAGECROWD in HAND:
Oft times the REGISTRATORS sought –
Then midst his CILLIS, SLUGS and SNAKES,
He sat awhile in thought.

And as they over FOSSSHEETS groan,
A REDHOTTIP (with wheels to name)
Came TURING through the telephone
And DILLIED as it came!

4, 5 and 2! No more ado –
The RINGSTELLUNG. Turn wheels about
Still doubt appal, but STECKER fall
Uncontradicted out.

'And hast thou truly BROKE the BLUE?
Come to the STORE, my BOMBE-ISH boy!
Fetch JOSH, KITS, BOLS, AARD, CERA, WALTZ!'
He LUFTGAUED in his joy.

'Twas HUTSIX, and the WRANGLERCOVES
Did twist and twiddle at the CYC;
All grimset were the JEFFREYBROWS
And the BABBAGE outschreik.

At the end of the real *Alice's Adventures in Wonderland,* the first of Carroll's two Alice books, Alice and the King of Hearts discussed the frustration of trying to make sense of all the lines of gibberish spouted by Carroll's Knave of Hearts.

'I don't believe there is an atom of meaning in it,' said Alice.

'If there is no meaning in it,' said the King, 'that saves us a world of trouble, you know, as we needn't try to find any … and, yet I don't know … I seem to see some meaning in them after all.'

EIGHT

Dilly's girls

We're breaking machines. Have you got a pencil?

Admiral Sinclair's concept of a country house with landscaped grounds for the secret work required was preserved even when expansion was urgently needed and the hut system put in place. The ground floor of the mansion with its stately rooms was kept intact for administrative and recreational purposes and, until a canteen was built, meals were also served there. The first small hut had been built in the early days near to the wireless tower and a discreet one which became Frank Birch's naval Hut 4 was put up on the south side of the mansion in the former rose gardens. Hut 6, for decoding messages, and Hut 3, for processing the intelligence from the decoded messages, were built in readiness for the Enigma machine break. Many wartime hand ciphers, particularly those used in the Italian naval messages examined by 'Nobby' Clarke's section, were already being broken and accommodation was needed for their staff. The *bombe* hut with blast-proof walls would be built in the old maze, leaving the tennis courts intact. Although the ha-ha was filled in as a danger to those crossing in the blackout from the huts to the mansion, the landscaped lake was protected and much appreciated for skating in the icy winter of 1939–40.

Dilly's cottage in the stable-yard, known as Cottage 3, was shut down after the first Enigma break; it was at the eastern end of a row of three cottages. Cottage 1 was internally separate but the lofts of Cottage 2 and 3 were joined and considered to be insecure as Cottage 2 was then inhabited by an estate worker, who, although having signed the Official Secrets Act, was unconnected with codebreaking. Although Dilly was intensely interested and involved in the activities of Hut 6, he bitterly resented not having his own accommodation, however small, and having to hand his work over to others before completion, which he said was 'impossible for a scholar'. He was extremely allergic to what would now be called flow-charts. He was particularly incensed when Alan Turing was put 'under Mr Birch', which he thought to be 'so absurd and unworkable'. To him Frank was best friend, good historian, but no cryptographer. Dilly refused to be pinned down, complaining that research was being downgraded in the rush for production. Another resignation letter, which Dilly knew could not be accepted, was dispatched.

Alastair Denniston, who always did his best to humour him, recalled Dilly's anger over the issue when answering a later outburst protesting about the treatment of scholars.

My dear Dilly,

Thank you for your letter. I am glad that you are frank and open with me. I know we disagree fundamentally as to how this show should be run but I am convinced that my way is better than yours and likely to have wider and more effective results. If you do design a super Rolls-Royce that is no reason why you should yourself drive the thing up to the house, especially if you are not a very good driver ... Do you want to be the inventor and the car-driver? You are Knox, a scholar with a European reputation, who knows more about the inside of a machine than anybody else. The exigencies of war need that latter gift of yours, though few people are aware of it. The exploitation of your results can be left to others so long as there are new fields for you to explore.

New fields there certainly were for Dilly to explore. He had been made chief assistant in January 1940, effectively giving him back the title of chief cryptographer that he had enjoyed in Room 40 but lost on the creation of GC&CS. The accommodation problem was settled in March as it was obvious Dilly could not be left as a cog in the hut system. Denniston and Edward Travis arranged for Dilly to return to a reorganised and enlarged stable-yard cottage which was made secure by joining Cottages 2 and 3. Dilly insisted that his new research unit should be entirely female and I was fortunate enough to be one of them. We became known even in high places in Whitehall as 'Dilly's girls'. A myth has arisen that he went round Bletchley Park picking the most attractive girls he spotted to work in the Cottage, whereas in fact we were selected solely from notes supplied by the formidable Miss Moore, who had interviewed us all at the Foreign Office. Dilly had made it clear that he did not want any debutantes whose daddies had got them into Bletchley through knowing someone in the Foreign Office, nor, he said, a 'yard of Wrens' among whom you couldn't tell one from the other; he wanted to know our qualifications. He did now appreciate the mathematical input to cryptography and was pleased to be able to recruit Margaret Rock, a mathematician from Bedford College, London, who was older than most of the 'girls'. She was a great asset to the Cottage and a great support for Dilly. I was initially sent to work for GC&CS at Broadway Buildings in January 1940, before Dilly's new section was set up, and did not arrive until April.

I am often asked what skills had to be shown at an interview for selecting codebreakers. We certainly weren't given any crossword puzzles. I suppose Miss Moore was satisfied with my CV from University College, London (UCL), and my spell at Zurich University, as linguists were obviously needed. I had been booked into a German university but, when Hitler annexed Prague in March 1939, I was sent to the German-speaking University of Zurich instead, where I stayed for the summer and had to beat a hasty retreat when it was said the Siegfried line was being manned. Miss Moore seemed to approve of my reason for curtailing my university German studies. UCL was evacuating to Aberystwyth and I thought I ought to do something better for the war effort than reading German poetry in Wales, especially as the Nazi Propaganda Minister, Joseph Goebbels, had got his doctorate on German Romanticism, the very subject on which I was proposing to embark. I said I would train to be a nurse, but was told I should use my German and was sent to the Foreign Office. That was all right by Miss Moore, who clearly did not wish to prolong the conversation; the next interviewee was called in. Strangely enough it was in fact the romantic Dr Goebbels who had really got me into Bletchley Park. When Hitler's troops occupied the Rhineland in 1936, he sent brochures over here offering bargain tickets, so that we could see for ourselves what a peaceful idyllic place Rhineland Germany was and that we had nothing to fear.

My family only went on holidays to Bournemouth but I persuaded my parents that a Rhine holiday would be just the thing and that my recently acquired equivalent of O-level German would see us through any problems. I got my way and we bought cheap roving tickets for a brand new steamer trip along the scenic parts of the Rhine. We joined crowds of happy German workers with free tickets, all part of Goebbels's 'Strength through Joy' campaign. They were to be indoctrinated in the myths and legends of German heroes as part of the Nazi philosophy of Aryan superiority, preparing them for the Third Reich, which was going to last a thousand years. Wagner's blonde Rhine maidens were with us constantly and the band struck up as we passed Die Lorelei. I lapped it all up and when I got back decided to opt for German literature in the sixth form, where I managed to win a copy of *The Romantic Movement in Germany* by Leonard Willoughby, Dilly's old Room 40 colleague, as a prize. My future was then decided but not in the way that I could have foreseen.

My professor of German literature at University College turned out to be none other than Leonard Willoughby, who had appeared as 'the Grumbling Willow' in the pantomime *Alice in ID25*. It was he who had identified Schiller's '*himmlische Rosen*' crib for Dilly's U-boat break, but of course I was unaware of that at the time. UCL was quite revolutionary in 1938, inspired by the dynamic Marxist professor J. B. S. Haldane. The Spanish Civil War was at its height and we starved for Republican Spain on a Tuesday, which was a bit confusing for me as I had just come from a convent school where we had prayed for General Franco at morning assemblies. However, I was soon into sewing red flags for the young men going off to join the International Brigade and waving farewell to them.

Kristallnacht soon followed in November and we marched on the German embassy, bearing our mascot Phineas, but it had little effect on the fate of the Jews. The German department encouraged students to befriend the influx of refugees and try and find jobs for them. I went through all the situations-vacant columns with my pair and finally found an advertisement for a couple needed in a country house in Kent and took them down to settle them in. Unfortunately, Hitler had found the Jewish exodus a perfect opportunity to infiltrate fifth columnists and it was my bad luck to have been given two of them. Perhaps I should have been suspicious that they were so keen on Kent as they were subsequently caught photographing military installations along the coast and gave my name as sponsor when they were arrested. This was at the time that my application to the Foreign Office was being processed, but it took me some time to find out that the reason for the delay, from the interview in November 1939 until being summoned to Broadway Buildings in January 1940, was that MI5 had been investigating my blameless past with the local Croydon police.

Broadway Buildings, opposite St James's Park Underground station, where the German spy match seller was watching us, housed 'C', the chief of SIS, which those of us working for GC&CS on the floor beneath called 'the other side' in hushed tones. Being put onto commercial codes seems pretty trivial compared with what was going on upstairs but in fact it was considered very important in the phoney war. I now know that we were supplying industrial intelligence for the Ministry of Economic Warfare (MEW), whose mission was 'comparable to the operations of the three Services in that its object is the defeat of the enemy and complementary to them in that its function is to deprive the enemy of the material means of resistance'. My section's task was to blacklist firms in neutral countries supplying Germany with the essential goods they needed through scrutinising the codebooks they used to order them.

Commercial telegraphic codes sent in Morse were internationally available on the market and easily mastered; there was no super-encipherment as with secret codes. The codebooks were look-up tables for code and decode and the code-groups could represent a whole sentence. When the Government Code and Cypher School was set up it firmly implied in its title that codes and ciphers were two different things but nowadays the term 'codebreaking' is commonly used for both. Scherbius was quite clear that he had not invented a codebreaking machine but a 'ciphering and deciphering' machine, whereby one letter was encrypted into another mechanically. The important thing for the MEW was that we should identify the neutral country that was providing the illegal commodity. One miscreant from a place called St Goch, which could not be found in the gazetteer, had foxed them, and the problem was given casually to me.

After a time, I realised that the issue might be being confused by the capital letter and that perhaps it was not necessary to chase a saint around the world. There is much of Wonderland in cryptography and it often pays to be like Alice and ask disconcertingly innocent questions. I simply asked how they knew when there was a capital letter in Morse code and they had to confess they didn't as there was no provision for them. I then tried changing the capital letter and looking for an abbreviation and, when I got to StgoCh, I thought it might be Santiago, Chile; it worked and the culprit was tracked down. This seemed to impress somebody and, aged not quite nineteen, I was given a railway ticket to Bletchley and told which train to get and that I would be met there. At least I knew where I was going and could tell my family, but I met up with a new recruit, Joyce Mitchell, who had merely been told to be at Euston at a certain time, where she would be met and given a ticket, but when she left home she did not know whether her destination was Watford or Scotland. Having arrived at Bletchley and reported to Commander Denniston, I was taken across to the Cottage by his secretary, Barbara Abernethy, and introduced to Dilly Knox.

When Penelope Fitzgerald came to see me, when writing her book *The Knox Brothers,* she asked me if I could remember my actual first meeting with her uncle. I described the cottage room where he was sitting by the window in wreaths of smoke and, taking his pipe out of his mouth, he looked up and said: 'We're breaking machines. Have you got a pencil?' I knew nothing about the existence of the Enigma machine, only having seen commercial book codes at Broadway, as he knew, so that did not get me very far. He then handed me a bunch of gobbledegook messages made worse by his purple inky scrawls over them and said: 'Here, have a go.' My code-groups had been neat and tidy and although not comprehensible were at least pronounceable or even in clear. 'But I am afraid it's all Greek to me,' I said in despair, at which he burst into delighted laughter and said: 'I wish it were.' I felt very embarrassed when I discovered that he was a distinguished Greek scholar.

I couldn't understand what Penelope meant when she said: 'Half a moment, you know what you are saying, don't you? That is exactly what Alice said to Dilly the Dodo when she met him for the first time in Room 40.' She then produced a copy of *Alice in ID25*, which I have treasured ever since. His appearance, as I remembered him, was still as in Frank Birch's skit, when 'Alice thought that he was the queerest bird she had ever seen. He was so long and lean and he had outgrown his clothes and his face was like a pang of hunger.' Alice also noted that he was very shortsighted and that his spectacles were kept in his tobacco pouch. I was reminded of the amount of time we spent searching for his spectacles and his tobacco tin buried under stacks of messages and how often when preoccupied he mistook the cupboard door for the exit. By one of those inexplicable coincidences, Penelope and I were sitting in my husband's rooms at Christ Church overlooking Alice's garden and I was writing a book on Lewis Carroll. I have always felt a bond with Dilly, who was for me Alice's White Knight, endearingly eccentric and concerned about my welfare.

There were only about eight girls in the Cottage when I arrived. Their work was devoted to 'retrieving the misses by Hut 6 and to discovering new lines of attack', according to a Dilly memorandum. For new girls, this meant endlessly putting dots in squares for frequency counts. There were catalogues called 'corsets' attempting to locate the word EINS in the text. There was also something in Hut 6 called Dillyismus, being a method for determining *Stecker* when the rest of the message setting was known, but it meant nothing to us then. Claire Harding was in charge of the allocation of work and for relief we sometimes made snake alphabets for cillis. It was hardly stimulating but everything changed when the phoney war ended in May, followed by Dunkirk. It was brought home to us starkly when the trains taking exhausted troops north stopped at Bletchley. A cry went up for help at the forces canteen and we rushed down in between shifts. The fierce woman in charge ordained that the young girls should be confined to the kitchen out of sight and that only the godly matrons would take out the tea and chips to the troops on the train. We thought they would have preferred it the other way round; we certainly would have done. Dilly answered the call for the Home

Guard, which practised in the stable-yard. When I told Penelope that we were glad that they only had broomsticks and not rifles she said that we need not have worried as her uncle was rather a good shot in spite of his poor eyesight.

It was now imperative, with U-boats on the rampage in the Atlantic, to break the German wartime naval Enigma traffic, as Alan Turing had not yet solved the additional indicator bigram problem. Admiral Godfrey was very conscious of how much Room 40 had done to beat the U-boats and he wrote to Frank Birch, now head of the naval section, to say that he was now setting up an organisation to arrange 'pinches', thefts of original German codebooks, or cipher material. 'I think the solution will be found in a combined committee of talent in your department and mine who can think up cunning schemes,' Godfrey said. Who better to dream up such schemes than his personal assistant, Ian Fleming, and who better to send him to than Dilly Knox, the ace cryptographer who had broken the First World War U-boat code? Dilly was not lost for bright ideas and Birch records: 'When talking to Lt-Cdr Fleming the other day Mr Knox put forward the following suggestion. The Enigma key for one day might be obtained by asking for it in a bogus signal.' Dilly would have explained to Fleming that it was not the actual Enigma machine that was needed, as was often thought. We already had a working model of it, but that was useless by itself as there were millions of possible settings; it was the key to these that was needed. James Bond's creator had a much more bloodthirsty suggestion: to obtain the keys from a German naval vessel in the Channel. He sketched out Operation Ruthless, involving a captured German bomber and a participant who could have been the model for his own fictional hero and 'should be tough, a bachelor, able to swim'. The tough bachelor would be part of a crew of five who would dress up as Luftwaffe crew trying to fly a damaged German bomber back from a raid on the UK. They would ditch in the Channel near a German ship and once rescued kill the crew and sail the German ship with the vital Enigma keys back to Britain. Fleming pencilled his name in as a possible participant although he knew full well that anyone who had knowledge of what went on at Bletchley Park was forbidden to put himself in a dangerous situation where he might be taken a prisoner and interrogated.

The circumstances were never right for Operation Ruthless to be activated, causing immense disappointment at Bletchley, and Birch, who had given enthusiastic backing to the 'very ingenious plot', gave a flavour of the dismay of Dilly and the other codebreakers over the lack of 'pinches' in a memo to Fleming. 'Turing and Twinn came to me like undertakers cheated of a nice corpse yesterday, all in a stew about the cancellation of Ruthless,' Birch said. 'The burden of their song was the importance of the pinch. Did the authorities realise that there was very little hope, if any, of deciphering current, or even approximately current, [naval] Enigma at all.' During the Fleming centenary year in 2008, I was frequently asked if I had met the creator of James Bond. I certainly met Godfrey, on whom Fleming modelled Bond's 'M', but I feel sure that if Dilly had become aware of the Fleming lifestyle he would not have let him near his girls.

Life had changed for us in the Cottage when Italy declared war in June and instead of being at the bottom of the pile doing unconnected things for Dilly to pass on to Hut 6 we were now put on to breaking the Italian naval Enigma in the Cottage. Denniston's 'new fields to explore' revived Dilly's spirits. He had of course already broken the machine the Italians had used in the Spanish Civil War, which only ended in March 1939. There was great excitement when the first wartime Italian naval messages were intercepted but there was only a slim chance that their naval high command (Supermarina as we would learn it was called) was using the 'K' Enigma for which Dilly had worked out the rodding solution. Naturally the first thing to do was to try out the existing crib charts, such as PERXCOMANDANTE ['For Commandant', the X representing the space between the two words], but this yielded nothing as the traffic we had was from Rome to stations in the colonies, which did not use any known cribs. Dilly's girls then had to resort to rodding likely beginners, such as '*destinario*' or '*per*', where the guessed letter and the cipher text did not 'crash'; that is to say when hunting for '*per*' we would disregard a message beginning with P as P cannot be enciphered as P and likewise with the other crib letters.

Rodding was a great improvement on dots in squares. The important thing about it was that Dilly had made it into a kind of word game which even a beginner could do without knowing how the machine worked, rather like driving a car without knowing what goes on under the bonnet. Few of Dilly's girls ever grasped the mechanics of the machine but became skilful rodders. It was, however, a very laborious task requiring infinite patience as there were seventy-eight different rod trials to make in order to cover all twenty-six positions of each of the three wheels. Finally in September 1940, after many frustrating weeks of rodding, when it was feared that the wheel wiring had indeed been changed, success came. When I rodded PERX for the right-hand wheel, as instructed, in one position the first three rod pairings necessary for the cipher and clear texts produced good letters in other positions on the rod but instead of X in the required place the letter S appeared of its own accord from the last rod coupling. My lucky guess was that the message might begin PERSONALE, rather than PERX, and I then had five other couplings to work on and my Italian crossword puzzling was looking good. Of course it all depended where the turnover would be and gibberish could then be expected. When that happened I was meant to hand the message over to Dilly, but it was the evening shift and he was at home and I was determined to get over the turnover on the right-hand wheel and on to the middle wheel.

Dilly's advice was always to use pencil for guesses in rodding and ink for 'clicks', confirmations of probable cribs of individual letters. There were two kinds of clicks. The most important were what Dilly called 'beetles'. These were direct clicks in which both letters of the crib occurred side by side on the same rod. Dilly called the other kind 'starfish'. This was a cross-click where one of the crib letters was on one rod and the other on the second rod. A starfish click came as an effortless bonus, as mine did in PERSONALE, but beetles were very important. If one occurred in, say, positions 24 and 25 on the rod, then one of the remaining bigrams in the same column on the rod square would have to be used and most of them would be impossible combinations that could not be parts of real words such as WJ, QB, KP and so on. When I came to my beetle in the text there was a limited range to choose from as I had already used up so many of the rods. I tried NO, which produced the making of SIGNOR, and then, having put up the rods a gobbledegook man's name appeared, which caused me a lot of trouble. However, I had got enough couplings on the other side of the turnover to know that I must try and find somewhere on one of the other rod squares where these would not only comfortably lie side by side but produce sense when the missing rod couplings were supplied for the previous stretch of the message before the turnover. I then struggled with the rest of the text with my pocket Italian dictionary and it was well after midnight when the task was completed.

Dilly couldn't believe his eyes when I handed him the deciphered message the next morning. He took me out to dinner in the evening to the Fountain Inn at Stony Stratford. It was my first experience of being driven in Dilly's Baby Austin. As Denniston said, he was not a good driver, especially in the blackout. Preparations for a possible German invasion were already in place but he somehow managed to evade the tank traps along Watling Street. We had a very relaxed dinner and he was anxious to know what I wanted to do when the war was over. I hadn't given it much thought, with the Germans poised at the other side of the Channel, and, having abandoned all idea of an academic career with the German Romantics, I said I might try for journalism. He promised to introduce me to his brother Evoe, who would get me started. More helpfully, he managed to get me put up a grade, which was a great relief as I was only earning 35 shillings a week and having to pay a guinea for my billet. I was also promoted from a backroom girl to the front room as a machine cryptographer.

By this time, Alan Turing had written a manual for newcomers to Huts 6 and 8, which became known as 'Prof's Treatise on Enigma'; it covered Dilly's breaking of the un-*Stecker*ed Enigma, leading on to the *Stecker*ed German armed forces machine they would be dealing with. Examples were given of the breaking of the 'K' model railway Enigma machine by Turing and Twinn in 1940, using Dilly's rodding methods and depth-reading of messages by John Tiltman. There was no necessity for providing the history of Enigma-breaking so that Dilly's name does not appear and consequently it has often been assumed that the methods given for solving un-*Stecker*ed Enigma were Turing's own work, although he never claimed them to be so himself. Needless to say, Prof's manual was never used in the Cottage and the first time I heard of it was when it was released as a national archive in 1998. Dilly's rodding technique looked strangely different without his whimsical nomenclature. Beetles and starfish had become direct and cross-clicks and buttoning-up adding-up. Probability had replaced serendipity and it all seemed very heavy going compared with our treatment of Enigma linguistic puzzles.

The good thing was the psychological effect of knowing that we were no longer working in the dark and that we were dealing with the 'K' machine, whose wheel wirings Dilly had broken in the Spanish Civil War. Each message had to be broken separately, however, as the indicating system was never solved, presumably having been taken from a codebook. Moreover, since no real values for the settings were ever available, the wheel turnovers were never known. Consequently each message had to be broken independently of any other on the same key. To standardise the volume of traffic the Italians used to send out dummy messages, usually of two kinds. Fortunately these were easily recognisable, otherwise it would have been infuriating to have spent days working on a dummy or worse still to have broken a real language message only to find it was a passage from Dante's *Inferno*.

One dummy occurred when a series of unenciphered groups were tapped out and transmitted with the usual type indicator, where the groups always formed patterns from the German keyboard such as QWEAS PYXCF. The second kind was extremely useful, since it was thirty or more groups of solid crib and the first time one was sent enabled a new wheel wiring to be broken. As soon as I picked the long message up, I saw it had no Ls in it and realised that this operator must just have pressed the last letter of his keyboard, probably relaxing with a fag in his mouth. Dilly's usual method of 'buttoning-up' on the QWERTZU diagonal was proving very difficult owing to the repetitive nature of the crib. Once again I was alone in the Cottage on the evening shift and this time I sought the help of someone on Hut 6 watch. As luck would have it, it was Keith Batey. We put our heads together and in the calmer light of logic and much ersatz coffee, the problem was solved.

After the Italian break, the good thing was we could not expect many L duds but the biggest gift the Italians gave us was that they insisted on their operators spelling out full stops as XALTX, and in order to keep the message in five-letter groups, the end one would have Xs added, so that there might be an eight-letter crib XALTXXXX right at the end of the message. Dilly's XALTX charts, also known as 'click charts', were not confined to locating adjacent starfish and beetle clicks, they showed all possible clicks of the X to A, L, T and X; of the A to L, T, X and so on; the clicks were all reduced to the rod position of the original X, so that a click between X and T in positions 1 and 4 and A and L in positions 2 and 3 would appear in the chart as a double click in 1. Little did Mussolini know that a humble full stop would be responsible for the defeat of his navy in the Mediterranean.

NINE

The Battle of Matapan

Tell Dilly we have had a great victory in the Mediterranean.

The Battle of Matapan was Britain's first major naval victory during the Second World War and coming at a bleak time in 1941 it was a real morale booster. A naval victory was traditionally encouraging to the British public, especially as it could now be seen in newsreels with guns blazing and the dashing Admiral Sir Andrew Cunningham on the bridge of his flagship HMS *Warspite*. Prime Minister Winston Churchill hailed it as 'the greatest fight since Trafalgar' and Cunningham was acclaimed as a second Nelson. It was a fortnight before the Admiralty received the news of Nelson's victory but almost before the last shot was fired at Matapan, in the early hours of 29 March, Admiral Godfrey rang through to Bletchley Park with the message 'Tell Dilly we have had a great victory in the Mediterranean and it is entirely due to him and his girls'. All very heady stuff for Dilly's girls and we only wished we could have told our families that we had had a hand in it.

For Dilly it was a twofold triumph, not only for breaking the Matapan messages in the Cottage but also for the special procedure by which Cunningham had received the intelligence derived from them, known as ULTRA. This was the brainchild of Wing Commander Frederick Winterbotham, the head of the SIS air intelligence section, who superintended the setting up of Hut 3 in 1939 in readiness for Hut 6's production line of German air force and army traffic. Winterbotham was an old hand, having been sent to Germany in the early 1930s to monitor the expansion of the Luftwaffe and appeared (misspelt) on the Gestapo wanted list. He put up a plan to Stewart Menzies to ensure that the intelligence derived from Hut 3 messages would be disseminated in a way which was both operationally effective and secure.

In the normal course of events, information from a secret source would be passed only to the directors of intelligence of the service ministries and it was up to them to distribute it as they saw fit. This would work quite well with the small number of messages then in circulation but when it came to thousands, not only might the translations and interpretation differ with so many people handling them, but information might be transmitted to commanders in the field in several different ciphers, which Winterbotham had learned from the codebreakers was a dangerous practice. He also knew that those commanders in the field could be lax about security and had been known to leave secret documents in their shaving mugs. He set up Special Liaison Units to deliver ULTRA messages to commanders under constant surveillance. By 1942, after America had come into the war, ULTRA became the standard designation for intelligence derived from all decrypts of high-level messages, but at the time of Matapan it was only used as Winterbotham originally defined it.

Since the red Luftwaffe signals were the first to be broken in Hut 6, Winterbotham got permission to send three or four German-speaking RAF officers to Hut 3. The Hut 6 codebreakers would pass the decoded signals to them for translation and assessing for priority, whether for distribution to the Prime Minister, the chiefs of staff, directors of intelligence or commanders in the field. Very soon a joint RAF and Army section was put in place, but the sea lords were adamant that decoded naval signals should be sent direct to the operation intelligence centre at the Admiralty verbatim for them to take the necessary action. When it came to Dilly's turn to learn how GC&CS was to deal with the naval intelligence following the break of the Italian Enigma machine messages in September 1940, he was determined that the material we were working on in the Cottage should receive the same treatment as the ULTRA intelligence put out by Hut 3. He angrily claimed that he had been tricked into allowing the Cottage to become 'an obscure subsidiary' of 'Nobby' Clarke's Italian naval section. 'This Italian business has now reached large proportions and takes up almost all our time in the cottage and very much work is done in the hut,' Dilly told Alastair Denniston, while 'the Enigma results are of an order of certainty differing wholly from the products of most other intelligence sections. On personal grounds, I find that I have been tricked by your arrangement of 5 December. Had I appreciated at the time the sense in which you now take it I should have gone to any lengths to oppose it. I must ask you to deal at once with the question. I have no intention of continuing to work as an obscure subsidiary of Commander Clarke.'

As ever, Denniston attempted to mollify Dilly, pointing out that the arrangement of 5 December merely reinforced the GC&CS tradition that the various specialist sections processed the decodes for their own areas. Hut 3 processed German air force and army Enigma; the Spanish naval attaché messages originally broken in the Cottage were processed by the Spanish naval section; the small amounts of German naval Enigma that had been broken so far had been processed by Frank Birch's German naval section. None of them could have done anything without the work put in by the codebreakers led by Dilly's research section in the Cottage.

So far as the Italian Naval Enigma is concerned, I cannot understand why you should wish for an alteration of the practice. Clarke deals with the circulation of all this [Italian] traffic of which the Enigma forms a part. He dealt with it in pre-war days when you first broke into the machine. If the duty were given to Hut 3, it would be necessary to find Italian speaking staff to work there and to study the contents, in fact to duplicate the work which Clarke's section already does. So far as the personal side is concerned I hope you do not underrate your own position. It is obvious that the Research side of Enigma, which, you direct, has met with very considerable success, and it must be perfectly clear to you, to all those concerned in GC&CS and to the recipients of the decodes that without the Cottage and Huts 6 and 8 there would be no Enigma traffic. This is my view; I cannot, therefore, see any reason why the existing methods of circulation should be changed.

But Denniston's insistence on the status quo did not suit Dilly, who wanted to have a finger in the intelligence pie, his permanent complaint being that 'there is no proper distinction between research cryptography and cipher and intelligence work'. By January 1941, a solution had been found and it may be one of the occasions Clarke had in mind when he said that

> *Dilly was a genius in cryptography as well as in other matters but he was very temperamental and had to be handled tactfully or else he refused to play; I happened to be one of the few people who understood how to manage him and when these clashes occurred I was called in to restore peace and ward off the resignation which he threatened.*

Clarke was able to cope tactfully with the Italian crisis in a way which suited all parties. His intelligence officer, Commander Charles O'Callaghan, who had been with him in the Italian naval sub-section for some time, had been transferred to the Admiralty. Clarke now managed to get him back as an Italian expert and made him liaison officer to Hut 3. Intelligence derived from codebooks and hand ciphers would be passed to Hut 4 as usual but Italian Enigma intelligence would go straight from the Cottage to Hut 3, where Dilly would have direct access to O'Callaghan. There were very few Italian naval Enigma messages for the Cottage to deal with for the first few weeks to enable us to produce crib charts to speed up the rodding technique. However, submarines seemed to be the order of the day and a 'sommergibili chart' was made for all possible clicks, *sommergibili* being Italian for 'submarines'. We pronounced *sommergibili* in a very English way with the emphasis all in the wrong place. No doubt Dilly knew what it was all about but his belief that there was intelligence he did 'need to know' did not naturally extend to his staff and I have only found in recent records that we were dealing with the Italian invention of the midget submarine on which two sailors had to sit in divers' suits. The first use of them was when two attacked Gibraltar in October 1940 and our messages gave the first knowledge of them. They were carried on the exterior of a full-size submarine or vessel and launched near the target. Having now seen photographs of them it is small wonder that the poor sailors forced to sit astride them detested them and called them 'swine'.

The Italian fleet itself seemed reluctant to make an appearance, but in early March 1941 the Germans made it clear that something was expected of the Italians in the way of hindering what we called Operation Lustre.

British and Australian troops were being sent to our ally Greece from north Africa at regular intervals after the failure of the Italian invasion and Admiral Cunningham, as Commander-in-Chief Mediterranean, was given the additional task of taking charge of the convoys. Hut 3 received a decoded Afrika Korps Luftwaffe message of 21 March 1941 revealing that German fighters were being flown to Palermo to provide cover for a special action and immediately alerted Dilly to be on the lookout. It was essential for Cunningham to know where and when this was to take place; with the fleet stationed in different places he needed ample warning to overcome the distances in the Mediterranean. Knowing the day the operation would start was essential and the Cottage, which was on red alert, soon discovered it for him.

Fortunately, we had broken the new wheels the Italians had introduced and, although there were now six possibilities for rodding and charting for the right-hand wheel, it did not take us long. Dilly had rounded up all those members of the Cottage staff who had been seconded to Hut 6 and Hut 8 during the slack period and on 25 March we broke a signal which said quite simply, with the minimum of topping and tailing, 'Today is X-3,' but even in such a short message the operator had inserted three full stops. Our XALTX charts were put to good use and, as Dilly quipped, success added a new meaning to the word exaltation. We went round chanting: 'Today's the day minus three.' We waited anxiously all night for the dispatch rider from the 'Y' intercept station and stayed at our posts for the days leading up to the Italian intervention. Finally, in the late evening when we could do no more, I made my way down to the station in the hope of getting a train to Leighton Buzzard, where I was billeted. I found the Royal Scot taking on water and went up to the driver and asked him if he could give me a lift. 'I'd do anything for you, Missie,' he said, 'but I'm afraid the train can't get into Leighton Buzzard.' I think I fell asleep on Bletchley station until the milk train came through. Dilly made sure that I was moved to a local billet in readiness for the next crisis.

It had indeed been a marathon. Each day had a different key setting and each message had to be broken separately. XALTX could not always be relied on to produce clicks but we also had crib charts for *Supermarina*,

Inglese, and *incrociatore* (cruiser). Claire Harding was responsible for organising the shifts and seeing that all possibilities were covered and that the rods were not left lying on desks but put back in the right jam jars. Although it was unlikely that Bletchley Park received any of the instructions sent direct to the Italian fleet, *Supermarina* repeated them to the commander in Rhodes on the Enigma machine, and these were intercepted. EGEOMIL, the official title of the commander on Rhodes, became a good friend and a very useful crib. The Rhodes messages that reached Cunningham enabled him to make his battle plan in good time but in his *Sailor's Odyssey,* which he published in 1951, he was not able to disclose any secret sources. That the important one was given special ULTRA treatment, thanks to Dilly, was vividly described by his flag officer, Captain Hugh Lee, in 2001:

I was working in my tiny cabin in HMS Warspite, *the Fleet Flagship, on 27 March 1941, when the Royal Marine orderly told me I was required in the Admiral's Staff Office, only a few yards away. On arrival, I was handed a signal by the Staff Officer Operations and told to put the positions given in the signal on the strategic chart, which I kept in the Admiral's dining cabin, and as soon as I had done this to bring the signal straight back to him 'under pain of death'. Naturally I did as I was told! I did notice that the signal was marked ULTRA but I did not have the faintest idea what it meant. Security and secrecy were paramount. At 11 am a meeting of the Commander-in-Chief's operational staff was called in the cabin and Admiral Sir Andrew Cunningham explained to the Staff that 'reconnaissance' had sighted a strong force of the Italian Navy, including Mussolini's pride and joy, the battleship* Vittorio Veneto, *steering towards the Eastern Mediterranean. He suggested that they might have one of three aims and he asked the staff to return at 2 pm and give him a consensus of what they thought was the aim of the Italian Force. At 2 pm (the timing had been carefully worked out by those in the know) the staff returned and their unanimous opinion was that an attack was planned on the British military convoys carrying troops from Alexandria to Piraeus in Greece. The Commander-in-Chief concurred in their judgement and ordered the Fleet to prepare to sail at 7 pm that evening and the aircraft-carrier HMS*

Formidable *to embark torpedo-carrying aircraft. He then said: 'I am going ashore for a game of golf,' and I went with him. After the game, making sure that the local spy, the Japanese consul, was in earshot, the Admiral discussed with me the details of a mythical dinner party ashore that evening, put the empty suitcases in the car and went to have a cup of tea with Lady Cunningham at the Residency, which he had been lent to live in. At 6.30 pm as darkness fell the Admiral and I returned to HMS* Warspite *and the Fleet sailed at 7 pm.*

As soon as Cunningham had received the first X-3 message, on 25 March, giving notification of 28 March as D-day for the Italian operation, he cancelled the Royal Navy convoy from Piraeus and instructed the Alexandria convoy to continue northwards as planned, but to turn round at dusk on 27 March, so as not to arouse suspicions. He then ordered his 'B Force', based at Piraeus under Vice-Admiral Henry Pridham-Wippell, and the 'C Force' at Alexandria to the points where the convoys would have been at dawn as calculated by the Italians, and thereby 'endeavour to make the enemy strike into thin air whilst taking all action possible while he is doing so'. It was only shortly after midday on 27 March, when he received the ULTRA message on X-1 giving the first intimation that there was a possibility of a naval engagement rather than just protection of the convoys, that he signalled to the Admiralty: 'I have now decided to take 1st BS [first battleship, i.e. HMS *Warspite*] and HMS *Formidable* to sea after dark tonight.' Cunningham was duly carrying out all the instructions that Wing Commander Winterbotham had laid down for a commander receiving an ULTRA message: never refer to the secret source which promoted the action but make it sound like his own impromptu decision and make sure that a cover-up was in place, in Cunningham's case aerial reconnaissance. Doubtless the Special Liaison Unit officer who delivered the ULTRA message would have, according to the instructions, destroyed it after perusal. Fortunately, in early March 1941, a special signals link had been set up between the SIS communications base at Whaddon and Alexandria to pass the Bletchley intelligence on to senior British commanders in Egypt.

Dilly's girls knew that he was delighted about what he called the 'cottage aeroplane', but not knowing the ULTRA deception, they thought it related to the official story of reconnaissance in all the newspapers, when an airman got a much-publicised award for spotting the Italians. In fact, when I was asked to do the entry on Dilly for the *Dictionary of National Biography*'s Missing Persons volume in 1992, I still thought the cover-up was for the deliberately misleading press release. The official history in 1979 had hardly been informative about Cunningham's plan and it is only revealed as an afterthought, in a footnote which says that 'the conclusion that he decided to sail only after receiving the aircraft sighting at 12.30 on 27 March is incorrect'. Italian records on what they called Operation Gaudo indicate that Admiral Angelo Iachino had a cryptographer on board who broke the signal, as Cunningham knew they might well do, but the RAF Sunderland from Malta gave pre-arranged false information, so from our point of view no harm was done. However, it now appears that, throughout the night battle, the Italians continued to intercept many of the signals passed between Cunningham and Pridham-Wippell, which must have caused Cunningham problems. At this stage of course there could be no help from ULTRA; our advance intelligence could only influence strategy, tactics were lonely on-the-spot decisions for the admiral and by all accounts the night action was brilliant. On the night of 28 March, the Royal Navy crushed its Italian counterpart with three British battleships sinking an entire Italian cruiser squadron of three heavy cruisers and two destroyers, with the loss of 3,000 Italian sailors. The Italians had no radar so the British caught them completely by surprise. The Italian navy never challenged the Royal Navy in the Mediterranean again.

It was in the early hours of 29 March that 'Nobby' Clarke's son Edward received the news of the victory in the Bletchley Park naval hut from Admiral Godfrey. By the following day Dilly was ready with a poem called 'Swollen Heads' to celebrate the occasion, naming every one of his Cottage girls who had taken part, including the tea lady, who had been brought in so that we should not have to waste time wrestling with a cantankerous urn; so Mrs Balance, the tea lady, who was the mother of one of the Cottage girls, had duly signed the Official Secrets Act. Each verse began with the words 'When Cunningham won at Matapan by the grace of God and…', taking it in turns to mention each girl with a rhyming tribute; the rhyme for Mavis conveniently being *rara avis*. All very flattering for a nineteen-year-old. Dilly was considered by some to see cryptography only as a theoretical problem unrelated to real events; but that was a mistake. Undoubtedly aerial reconnaissance played an important part in allowing Cunningham to draw up his battle plan, but it was Dilly who rang the Admiralty immediately to make sure that when the battle was reported in the press its success would be attributed entirely to air reconnaissance to cover the real source. He chuckled in his poem when he referred to the reconnaissance 'Cottage aeroplane'.

When Cunningham won at Matapan
By the grace of God and Claire,
For she pilots well the aeroplane
That spotted their fleet from the air.

When Cunningham won at Matapan
By the grace of God and Jane,
For she was the girl who spotted the Wops
From the Cottage aeroplane.

When Cunningham won at Matapan
By the grace of God and Nancy,
Now she is a girl, the Admiral said,
That might take anyone's fancy.

When Cunningham won at Matapan
By the grace of God and Mavis,
Nigro simillima cygno est, praise Heaven,
A very rara avis.

When Cunningham won at Matapan
By the grace of God and Margaret,
It was thanks to that girl, the Admiral said,
That our aeroplanes straddled their target.

When Cunningham won at Matapan
By the grace of God and Phyllida,
And made that impossibly self-willed girl
If possible self-willeder.

When Cunningham won at Matapan
By the grace of God and Hilda,
And sank the Vittorio Veneto
Or at least they can't rebuild her.

When Cunningham won at Matapan
By the grace of God and Jean,
And if Jean Harvie had been there too,
Hoots man, what might na ha been?

When Cunningham won at Matapan
By the grace of God and Mrs Balance,
Indeed, he said, the Cottage team
Is a team of all the talents.

When Cunningham won at Matapan
By the grace of God and Elisabeth,
The credit was almost entirely ours
But possibly God did his a bit.

Dilly then added a tribute to the two people who had made the ULTRA treatment possible, 'Nobby' Clarke and Admiral Godfrey, the DNI.

When Cunningham won at Matapan
By the grace of Godfrey and Nobby,
Though not of our outer or inner rooms
They're allowed sometimes in the lobby.

Clarke added his own, much to the point, verse later:

127

When Cunningham won at Matapan
By the grace of God and Dilly,
He was the brains behind them all
And should ne'er be forgotten. Will he?

When we suddenly heard later that Cunningham was coming down with Godfrey to congratulate us in person, we rushed down to the Eight Bells at the end of the road to get some bottles of wine and if it was not up to the standard the Commander-in-Chief Mediterranean was used to he didn't show it. The Cottage wall had just been whitewashed. Someone enticed the admiral to lean against it and we tried not to giggle when he left. He had shaken us all warmly by the hand and we thought that was the end of Matapan. It was in fact practically the last we would hear of the Italian fleet, which only made one more appearance before surrendering to Cunningham in 1943.

For Dilly's girls, as for the rest of Bletchley Park, we were Churchill's 'geese who laid the golden eggs and never cackled'. Most of us were grandmothers by the time Frederick Winterbotham's book *The ULTRA Secret* appeared in 1974, with an illustration of Bletchley Park on the cover; we were horrified. Could we now tell our families why we were so good at anagrams and Scrabble and crossword puzzles then? We eagerly looked in the index for Dilly Knox and thoroughly approved that it said he was 'the mastermind behind the Enigma affair'; but there was not a mention of the Cottage and Matapan was wrongly credited to the Luftwaffe break in Hut 6 since Winterbotham only knew about the German air force ULTRA intelligence and nothing about the Italian. What about the rods and X-3 and the drink with Cunningham and Dilly's poem? Maybe Dilly's mentor Lewis Carroll was right after all and life was but a dream.

Fortunately, it was the Italians who came to the rescue and proved that it was real after all. The Germans had always accused the Italians of having traitors in their midst, which was made worse when, in 1966, H. Montgomery Hyde published the story of the beautiful spy Cynthia, who was alleged to have seduced the Italian naval attaché in Washington and obtained the codebook from him which resulted in the defeat at Matapan:

Cynthia's first major assignment, in which she won her spurs during the winter of 1940–41, was to obtain the Italian naval ciphers from the Italian embassy in Washington. She began by securing an introduction to the naval attaché, Admiral Alberto Lais, whom she lost no time in cultivating assiduously. He responded to her charms in the manner she desired, and soon within a few weeks of their first meeting he imagined himself deeply in love with her. As a result she was able to do with him virtually what she pleased. In retrospect, it seems almost incredible that a man of his experience and seniority, who was by instinct, training and conviction, a patriotic officer, should have become so enfeebled by passion as to be willing to work against the interests of his own country to win a woman's favours. But that is what happened. As soon as she had him where she wanted, Cynthia came straight to the point. She told the admiral that she wished to have copies of the naval cipher. Astounding as it may appear, he agreed without apparent demur to assist her.

As one reviewer observed, 'treason in bed and death at sea made a libretto which sold well' and the admiral's family felt obliged to take out a libel action, such a course being permitted in Italy on behalf of the dead. Montgomery Hyde was found guilty but the real evidence to clear the admiral was not then available. All went quiet until Winterbotham's book appeared in 1974. The Italians were delighted as it paid off an old score by proving, as they thought, that it was the German and not the Italian signals which had forewarned Cunningham about *Operazione Gaudo*. They wanted to have *The ULTRA Secret* translated and published at once. However, Dr Giulio Di Vita, a fellow of Clare College, Cambridge, who was asked to edit the book, was determined to investigate the matter more thoroughly than Winterbotham, who was no historian. When records were released in 1978, Di Vita found plenty of evidence that it was in fact Italian and not German messages that had given the game away, but was forbidden to publish his findings. However, he became aware that Ronald Lewin had also seen the public records and was writing a book on ULTRA in 1978, which for the first time would show the part played by Dilly's section in the Battle of Matapan from declassified records, which had not been available to Winterbotham.

Now it was official that the Italian ciphers had been broken, but when the BBC ran a series of TV programmes called *Spy!* in 1980, the story of Cynthia was rehashed. After all, they alleged, it was she who sent the codebooks to the Admiralty, which allowed the signals to be read. Di Vita was incensed and wrote to *The Times* about the misrepresentation of the facts, having by then decided to track down the real Bletchley Cynthia, or at least one of them. I was sent a glowing account of the interview in an Italian newspaper referring to me as an *'affascinante signora, il tipo Penelope Keith'* in her *'bella casa di Oxford'*. At least I was able to scupper the idea that we had been given codebooks by Cynthia or anybody else; if we had had such books, machinists would merely have had to put the key settings on the simulated Enigma machine without any need of codebreakers. It was then, having seen the letter in *The Times*, that 'Nobby' Clarke's son wrote in to say that he had been on duty the night the message was received: 'Tell Dilly we have had a great victory in the Mediterranean and it is entirely due to him and his girls'.

Unfortunately, the secretary of His Honour Judge Edward Clarke (as Nobby's son now was) had typed 'guts' for 'girls' and an urgent note followed, 'for guts, please read girls'. Dilly would have loved it. At last, the evidence was available for the courts to exonerate poor Admiral Lais and I was asked whether, if they brought the Matapan messages, I could testify that they had been broken cryptographically. I warned them that as it was forty years ago there wasn't much chance of my remembering the actual break. Nevertheless, losing no time, Di Vita brought the admiral in charge of naval history over from Rome and, when I picked up the first long message headed SUPERMARINA, it seemed that time had stood still and I was nineteen again and wearing a green jumper. It had been raining all day and it was still pelting down when I rushed it over to the hut, where Dilly, as I now know, was securing ULTRA treatment for its transmission. Cynthia was finally put to bed; no seduction and no codebooks but just hard cryptographic slogging by Dilly's girls. On his return to Supermarina, my new admiral friend wrote a charming letter of thanks, but with the lesson of Cynthia still in mind, he ended on a cautious note: 'Hoping to be given the opportunity of meeting you again on work matters.' Perhaps Dilly should have the last word on Matapan in his epitaph to Mussolini:

These have knelled your fall and ruin, but your ears were far away
English lassies rustling papers through the sodden Bletchley day.

TEN

Dilly and the Spy Enigma

Dilly's greatest triumph in cryptography and intelligence, which for him were always inseparable, was the breaking in October 1941 of the Enigma machine used by the German military intelligence service, the Abwehr. Little was known about the Abwehr organisation before the war. In March 1940, two members of the Radio Security Service (RSS), charged with intercepting illicit wireless in the UK, broke some simple hand ciphers from a Hamburg-controlled station, which at first aroused little interest. Finally Hugh Trevor-Roper and E. W. Gill, the latter a leading member of the Army's First World War codebreaking organisation, had succeeded in attracting Bletchley Park's attention and Oliver Strachey was asked to set up a section to be called Illicit Services Oliver Strachey (ISOS) in Elmer's School to research this traffic. By December, Strachey had broken the main hand cipher, enabling Bletchley to give MI5 advance warning of the arrival of German spies. These individuals were rather different from the disorganised refugee fifth columnists I had inadvertently befriended in 1938, when there was still free access across the Channel. It was now apparent that the Abwehr was operating a considerable professional espionage network across Europe.

After the fall of France and Hitler's plans to invade Britain, Operation Sea Lion, were drawn up, the agents being infiltrated were meant to be an advance guard to wait for the arrival of German troops and to report on morale. However, in 1941, when the threat had receded, there was a reorganisation of our security and the RSS (largely still amateur 'ham' wireless enthusiasts) was put under direct control of SIS. Dick White, a future head of both SIS and MI5, covering both espionage and counter-espionage, suggested that captured agents should be left in place and 'turned' to work as double agents. Camp 020 was set up for interrogation at Latchmere House, Ham Common, Richmond, to identify suitable double agents who could send back false information to their unsuspecting controllers.

MI5 managed the controlled agents and a London clearing house was set up to co-ordinate operational activities; it was known as the Twenty (XX) Committee, hence Double Cross, under John Masterman, a future vice-chancellor of Oxford University. The double agent was to send out his false information on his wireless transmitter as directed by his case officer, using his own hand cipher given to him by the Germans. Their controllers in neutral capitals, mainly Lisbon and Madrid, would receive and analyse the messages before transmitting the information to Berlin on the Abwehr Enigma machine.

Before this high-grade Enigma traffic was recognised for what it was and thought to be on the services machine, it was sent to Gordon Welchman in Hut 6 but he could make no headway and it was given to Dilly as unknown Enigma research. After Matapan the Italians mostly used their Hagelin machine; the Enigma machine traffic was infrequent and was turned over to routine production outside the Cottage, so that Dilly was able to give the Abwehr material his undivided attention. The Knox family had always been fascinated by spies and Kim's 'Great Game'. Dilly spent some time over at the School with his friend Oliver Strachey (the brother of his good Cambridge days friend Lytton) learning about the organisation of the Abwehr. First of all the many different spy networks had to be sorted out covering Spain, Portugal, the Balkans and Turkey to see how the ISOS hand-ciphered messages related to Dilly's Enigma messages sent on from the neutral capitals to Berlin after December 1939. It was hoped that there would be good cribs from the previous hand-cipher traffic, which Dilly studied carefully. One member of Strachey's section, who was proving to be very skilled at breaking ISOS hand ciphers, was Denys Page, a kindred spirit for Dilly as he was also a scholar of Greek poetry and interested in the Oxyrhynchus papyrus texts. Page would succeed Strachey as head of ISOS in 1942 and would collaborate with Dilly's friend Edgar Lobel in publishing literary papyri after the war.

At this stage, however, Dilly's easy-going relationship with ISOS had not been officially approved. Dilly kept Denniston informed of his progress on the Abwehr Enigma machine but Denniston, with his obsession for secrecy, seemingly disapproved of the way he was going about things. Denniston's success about keeping secret his own activities in signals intelligence is shown by the Venlo incident. The Schellenberg document on the British secret service following the interrogation of Richard Stevens states that the head of the cipher and decipher section is unknown and implies that he ran a code-making and not a code-breaking department. Denniston knew how essential it was not to let the Germans know that their messages were being broken as the whole signals intelligence system which had been gradually built up would be lost. 'Need to know' restrictions were strictly enforced, but it is difficult to understand why Denniston considered that Dilly had no 'need to know' about ISOS, which was obviously so relevant to his work. Infuriated, Dilly sent Denniston a fierce note, again threatening resignation over what he saw as a ridiculous 'hush-hush' policy imposed by Denniston – almost certainly on the insistence of SIS – that prevented him seeing material which would help him break the Abwehr machine.

My dear Denniston,

As you, I think, are aware I have decided to attempt a scheme for the reconstitution of one or more outlying German Enigmas. Before proceeding further in the matter there are one or two points, relevant either to the matter itself or to my examination of points of attack, on which I must press for your assurances, and failing these, for your acceptance of my resignation …

In the event of success the whole traffic must be handled in 'The Cottage' or our nominees. This is a fundamental point in all research of an academic nature. Research, in fact, does not end till the person responsible has affixed his imprimatur on the last proof sheet …

We still have far too many intelligence sections, appearing to the casual observer, as mangy curs fighting over whatever bones are tossed to them, and (as far as circulation goes) burying their booty in grimy and schismatic indexes. Yet what they get is the material which assists the cryptographer in his researches and this he is wholly unable to see. Occasionally someone may hand him a slip of paper with references to a buried file, but this is not wanted. As in Broadway, he wants the document, all the documents, and nothing but the documents …

These burials of essential documents are, I believe, made in accordance with your policy of 'hush-hush' or concealment from workers in Bletchley Park of the results of their colleagues. Against this I protest on several grounds ... Such action cripples the activities of the cryptographer who depends on 'cribs' ... Such action wholly destroys any liaison or pride in the successes of colleagues ...

I would urge with the utmost assurance that your action in directing any acts of concealment in Bletchley Park is wholly unconstitutional and ultra vires. Under the Official Secrets Act, I may discuss my work with anyone in the course of my duty. Of this I am the only judge, but it may perhaps be limited to the time of my arrival at, and departure from Bletchley Park. Outside Bletchley Park you may authorise me to discuss with anyone or refuse such authorisation. That is your constitutional prerogative.

When Dilly knew that he was near to a successful break, he wanted to know how the intelligence from the messages would be dealt with before the inevitable flow-chart appeared indicating who was in charge of what. Another letter to Denniston, a mixture of under- and overstatement says it all. He speaks of a 'minor ailment', which is why he is away for a few days; it was in fact a secondary cancer but few people were aware how ill he was. He wants to know where he stands and to try to 'establish an independent line as I nearly secured at Matapan'. He tells Denniston: 'I am almost despairing of making you see reason on the major issues. You owe the present solution, for it is near to that, to my interest in enemy intelligence as a whole.' Now apparently Denniston has a 'monstrous theory' that when the messages are broken they are to be handed over to ISOS as the operative unit and it will 'now be possible for Strachey to prevent my free inspection of his other material and use of the new', Dilly complains.

As a scholar, for of all Bletchley Park I am by breeding, education, profession and general recognition almost the foremost scholar, to concede your monstrous theory of collecting material for others is impossible. By profession in all his contacts a scholar is bound to see his research through from the raw material to the final text. From 1920–1936 I was always able to proceed as a scholar, and I simply cannot understand, nor I imagine can the many other scholars at BP understand, your grocer's theories of 'window dressing'. Had these been applied to art scholarship, science, and philosophy, had the inventor no right to the development and publication of his discourses, we would still be in the Dark Ages.

The inevitable threat of resignation unless things improved follows and the letter ends, 'a small grouse … Yours ever, A. D. Knox.'

Dilly's irritation at the way in which his material was handled by intelligence officers writing reports to be passed on to the various services and government departments was a recurrent theme in his complaints. In a letter to Menzies, he insisted that the material should be passed on in its original format. 'In my opinion, Bletchley Park should be a cryptographical bureau supplying its results straight and unadorned to intelligence sections at the various ministries,' he said. 'At present we are encumbered with "Intelligence Officers" who maul and conceal our results yet make no effort to check up on their arbitrary corrections.'

Above all, Dilly wanted to be in on the overall intelligence and suggested that heads of sections should be issued with regular bulletins with headings 'Enemy Operations, Enemy Intelligence, Enemy Codes'. In anticipation of his wish being carried out, he went over to see his old friend Professor Edgar Lobel to discuss whether he was free to leave Oxford. As a former keeper of Western manuscripts in the Bodleian library, and as editor of the Oxyrhynchus papyrus texts, Lobel was renowned for his critical intelligence and concise abstracts. For good measure his wife, who was an editor of the Victoria County History, impeccable on sources, could accompany him. 'She is a very nice and remarkable woman of the donness class,' Dilly told Denniston. Although the double Lobel scoop did not materialise, Dilly must have been satisfied with Denniston's circulation arrangements as the next communication with him was the report on the breaking of the Abwehr machine, dated 28 October 1941, and a request for the increase of Cottage staff.

Hopes of reliable cribs from ISOS messages, given that the messages encoded on the Enigma machine were a version of the actual text dictated to the double agent by the British case officer, had soon been dashed; but it was not immediately clear to Dilly why. However, once the various networks and their message indicators had been sorted out Dilly found the successful way in to breaking this unknown Enigma variation without textual cribs. Fortunately, nobody seemed to have told the Abwehr of the danger of having repeat indicators on a fixed *Grundstellung*, which the services had abandoned as long ago as 1938. Instead of three-letter indicators as in the services Enigma, Abwehr was seen to have four, the same number as the 'K' Enigma, which meant that there was a settable *Umkehrwalze*. When Dilly embarked on making key-blocks he found that the number of messages on any one day in a network was insufficient for evaluation and the boxing chains were too fragmentary to be of use. He decided, therefore, that if he could find two days where the same wheel order was used, and in such a way that the *Grundstellung* from one day could be got from rotating each wheel and the *Umkehrwalze* through the same number of places, he would be able to double the number of indicators on the key-block. This would be observed because the cipher pairings at each position of the *Grundstellung* would have a QWERTZU substitution relationship, if indeed the diagonal was, as in the commercial machine, his old friend QWERTZU.

Dilly accordingly went off to Hut 7 to enlist the help of Frederic Freeborn's Hollerith card-sorting and tabulation section in searching for two such days. Then followed a true example of serendipity, as defined by Horace Walpole: 'making discoveries by accident and Sagacity of things they were not in quest of '. Freeborn had been unable to find the two QWERTZU-related days' settings required but when Dilly studied the results 'he found what was wanting standing, like the abomination of desolation, precisely where it should not – on a single setting'. Then he had one of his 'quick as lightning' inspirations that he was dealing with a multi-turnover machine and that in one day's key-block all three wheels and the *Umkehrwalze* had turned over between the first two letters of the indicator and again in its repeat position, i.e. (1) ABCD (2) BCDE (3) BCDF (4) BCDG (5) BCDH (6) CDEI. This phenomenon he called a 'crab', which he deemed to be useless for his purposes, but if there were four-wheel turnovers on both sides of the throw-on indicator key-block there would probably be many more cases of such turnovers on one side of the key-block alone and this possibility he called a 'lobster'; this indeed was the brilliant idea which would break the Abwehr machine, thereafter always called the 'Lobster Enigma'.

Dilly worked on far into the night but we always made sure that there was someone on in the backroom to make black coffee and find lost things for him; there was no filing system as such. It was Phyllida Cross who was there on this momentous lobster occasion and she tried her best to come to grips with it when he rushed through to tell her but she admitted that she didn't understand a word. The next day, he excitedly instigated a lobster hunt. The method involved his well-tried boxing or 'saga' method for breaking key-blocks of indicators on the same *Grundstellung* with the additional QWERTZU bonus of the lobster turnover. Chains were made for positions 1–5, 2–6 and so on; if a cipher letter pairing was assumed in position 1, the chains gave deductions about other pairings in 1 and 5 and, if a lobster turnover existed between 1 and 2, there would be several pairings implied for 6; it was then easy to see whether these were consistent with the implications for the chain 2–6. Having confirmed the position for the lobster, the fun could begin guessing the indicators.

Dilly's report to Denniston says: 'The hunt was up and scent was good. One very fine Lobster among others was caught and after two days Miss Lever by very good and careful work, succeeded in an evaluation which contained sufficient non-carry units to ascertain the green wheel.' It was obvious by the repeat patterns that many operators were choosing pronounceable indicators such as WEIN, DEIN, NEUN. In one column of a key-block there was an indicator cipher bigram of the order TR, NB or WQ in the third and fourth place, which meant that if there had been a lobster four-wheel turnover at that point the clear text would also have to be a bigram reverse on the QWERTZU keyboard and if it were pronounceable then SA was just about the only choice. My lucky guess was that an operator on the Balkan network had a girlfriend called Rosa, who really did have a lobster on her in the required place. Having hopefully fixed ROSA in the position on the indicator key-block, as it was all on the same setting, reciprocal values could be filled in and in the repeated ROSA indicator on the other side of the key-block and continuing backwards and forwards with evaluations from one side of the key-block to the other. The generated alphabets of text and cipher could then be 'buttoned up' and Dilly's normal saga methods applied as there were 'sufficient non-carrying units' (positions without turnovers) to find the wheel wiring.

After Margaret Rock and I had evaluated a number of key-blocks, it became possible for Dilly to discover how many turnovers each of the wheels had. Each evaluation produced seven consecutive places at which it was shown whether the wheel had a turnover or not: if a turnover the position was marked by +, if not by -, so that the turnovers produced by an evaluation would be shown by a sequence such as + - + + - + +. With evaluations for several days, these sequences could be fitted together – in a process akin to dendrochronology, the ring-dating of trees by overlapping sequences – to give the complete sequence of turnovers, which became known as the wheel track. The wheel we called green had 11 turnovers, blue had 15 and red 17. It was now clear why there had been no success for Dilly in trying to get cribs from ISOS messages for rodding, which needed a good run on the right-hand wheel; the most one could hope for on the Abwehr machine was a run of four in two places on the green wheel. Dilly's invention of the lobster process meant that a long crib was no longer necessary but having discovered the wheel wiring and wheel tracks through 'lobstering' the key-block, it still remained to discover how the letters on the wheel rings related to the turnovers and that would take longer, as it necessitated the breaking of a message.

The first message was actually broken on 8 December 1941. As usual Dilly gave credit to his girls and when Denniston told Menzies of the success, he wrote:

Knox has again justified his reputation as our most original investigator of Enigma problems. He has started on the reconstruction of the machine used by the German agents and possibly other German authorities. He read one message on December 8th. He attributes the success to two young girl members of his staff, Miss Rock and Miss Lever, and he gives them all the credit. He is of course the leader, but no doubt has selected and trained his staff to assist him in his somewhat unusual methods. You should understand that it will be some weeks, possibly months, before there will be a regular stream of these ISOS machine telegrams.

It was again an obligingly positioned lobster, as in the key-block break, which provided the break for the first Enigma Abwehr message. When Dilly first analysed the traffic, it was found through a 'boil' that it was possible that most of the messages began NRX (number–space), but, owing to the multi-turnover nature of the machine, guessed numbers yielded nothing. Then one day, a possible lobster was noted in the second and third position of the number following NRX and if there had actually been a four-wheel turnover at that point the only number with a lobster in the right place could be dREi (three). As luck would have it, we had actually hit the 300s serial number in the relevant month and so there were several possible lobsters to choose from in that position; for good measure now that the rods were made from the known wheel wiring a click was found somewhere in NRXDREI (Number–space–three) and there was a run on, which threw up right letters for the two other numbers in the 300 series. We did, as Denniston said, indeed employ 'somewhat unusual methods' in the Cottage and it was a real Wonderland situation when lobsters, starfish and beetles could all be coaxed to join in the dance.

Denniston must have found Dilly's Carrollian logic particularly difficult to cope with. Lewis Carroll's *Sylvie and Bruno* was a favourite book, especially the Professor's seemingly inconsequential lecture beginning:

> *In Science ... in fact in most things, it is usually best to begin at the beginning. In some things, of course, it's better to begin at the end. For instance, if you wanted to paint a dog green, it might be better to begin with the tail, as it doesn't bite that end.*

Carroll had actually heard a child in a train make a similar remark when warned about pulling a dog's tail. Dilly frequently left bits of his reasoning out in the same way, which we had to try and fill in for ourselves. Completing Dilly's ellipses was a good training for cryptographic puzzle-solving.

Dilly's original report to Denniston on the breaking of the Lobster Enigma machine told him that 'the solution was based on a theory and observation and a procedure devised by the head of the section who had decided that as everything that has a middle has also a beginning and an end'. After the long night when he had the lobster inspiration, he was waiting for Margaret and myself in the morning at the Cottage door beside himself with excitement and said: 'If two cows are crossing the road, there must be a point where there is only one and that's what we must find.' Unlike poor Denniston, we were well trained in Carrollian logic and could get the point. Apparently Dilly told Hut 6: 'Give me a Lever and a Rock and I can move the universe.' Perhaps that was our contribution to Archimedes. Dilly's bright ideas sparked off like Catherine wheels and Margaret Rock might be trying to pin down the latest one while Mavis Lever was still struggling with yesterday's, which might well be a winner and might have been forgotten in the excitement of today's. It was not like that in the days when he had Gordon Welchman and Alan Turing as assistants, as they had too many bright ideas of their own to assist with Dilly's.

Denniston did his best to come to grips with Dilly's requirement of the type of staff he said in his report would be needed for the lobster production line. Up until this point, the staff consisted of Dilly and seventeen girls, of whom only Dilly himself and two of us girls, Margaret and myself, were German linguists and therefore capable of taking part in his lobster hunts. Dilly told Denniston he needed at least two more linguists, who must have time to learn, for serendipity's sake, what we knew we wanted and what might be useful.

'All hunters must know the tricks of the machine,' Dilly said. 'We must proceed as with the Italian Enigma by the careful study and correction of messages before they leave us. Any other system of arbitrary correction by those who do not understand the machine plans and cannot avail themselves of Morse corrections is repugnant and unthinkable.'

We did indeed have to make intercept corrections from time to time, when a Morse error could contradict an otherwise good lobster or throw-on. Of course, Dilly was already into this in Room 40 days, when interception was not of the high standard that now came to Bletchley Park from the 'Y' stations such as Beaumanor. He had invented a table of syllabic metre words to come to terms with Morse. I can only remember the beginning, 'Gallantly and Furiously, he fought at Waterloo, against the Barbarian.' We preferred just to run an eye down the Morse code chart on the wall.

Denniston clearly had personal talks with Dilly as to how his section should now develop and a letter on Christmas Day to Valentine Vivian, who was in overall charge of counter-espionage within SIS, takes the matter forward:

> With regard to Knox's success and the resultant labours, I would suggest that the series be issued as ISK [Illicit Services Knox]. Secondly, it will be necessary for the emending party to be reinforced to deal with some 50–100 extra telegrams per day and I suggest this is an opportunity to develop the ISOS hut on lines parallel to Hut 3.

Hut 3 was the intelligence-reporting section for the Hut 6 codebreakers working on the German army and air force messages and Denniston suggested that an SIS counter-espionage expert be put on each Hut 3 reporting shift to cover the material produced by Dilly's section. It was not just the Abwehr Enigma messages that were to be designated ISK; Dilly's section was in future to bear his name. Officially, it was referred to as Illicit Services Knox, matching up with Illicit Services Oliver Strachey, but it soon became generally known as Intelligence Services Knox, which greatly pleased him.

Panic set in at MI5 and Bletchley Park when in November 1941, just as Dilly's Spy Enigma was being broken, Agatha Christie published a counter-espionage detective novel called *N or M?*, in which her protagonists Tommy and Tuppence attempted to track down two German secret agents believed to be in Britain. There was horror when it was discovered that the novel included a character called Major Bletchley. As Dilly was known to be a friend of Christie's and had been party to her detection club rules, he was asked to find out what she knew, in order to prevent any further breaches of security. He invited her to tea at Courns Wood and over Olive's scones it appeared that she had never heard of Bletchley Park and she clearly didn't know Dilly worked there. It then emerged that once she had been stuck on the horrible station when changing trains and took revenge by giving the name of Bletchley to one of her least lovable characters. It was with great relief that another cup of tea was poured out for her. Intelligence Services Knox had not been compromised before it even started after all.

ELEVEN

Dilly's 'personal scouts'

By the time Dilly's Cottage Enigma research section became the ISK section on Christmas Day 1941, he had worked himself to the limits of endurance and his failing health was obvious for all to see. In future, he would have to work at home for much of the time and only be able to make occasional visits to Bletchley Park. To make matters worse for the administration of the new section, whose small staff was now receiving 100 or more messages a day, Margaret Rock became seriously ill in January and was away for several months. Dilly was devastated by the news early in February that Edward Travis was to replace Alastair Denniston, who was now put in charge of the diplomatic section in London. A major reorganisation of GC&CS had taken place with new orders and schedules of the kind that Dilly detested. On 13 February 1942, news came from Travis's office that Peter Twinn was 'to regard himself as in charge until Knox's return. He will continue to visit from time to time.'

Dilly made an appointment to see Stewart Menzies at Broadway Buildings to protest about Denniston's removal and wrote in a memorandum to Twinn that

> despite not infrequent differences of opinion, I realized that A.G.D., unlike the present chiefs, who had no pretensions, or at any rate, no claims to any knowledge of cryptography, had almost always been an able and understanding critic of failures or successes. Further, his constitutional attitude had always been correct, whereas Travis's methods were often, to put it mildly, lamentably direct.

Robin Denniston said that Dilly had always been a good family friend. Olive and Denniston's wife had known each other since Room 40 days, when they had worked together. From their official letters, it can be seen that Denniston and Dilly were always 'frank and open' with each other and that Denniston did his best to make allowances for Dilly's eccentricities, fully appreciating his contribution to GC&CS. It was Denniston who had had the good sense to seek out 'professor types' when recruiting Second World War codebreakers, as was done in Room 40 days. Although he was never entirely at ease with scholars, he established a *modus vivendi*. However, Dilly frequently reminded him that by their training scholars had the capacity to see things through intellectually, whatever the challenge, and should not be impeded by counter-productive 'need to know' regulations.

Concerning his interview with 'C', Dilly also noted in his memorandum that he had

> *pointed out very forcibly that I had the most capable section anyone could want, that their work had been wonderful and that I could not tolerate any interference with the personnel or their methods. The Brigadier was on the whole very cordial and I was glad that he realized what exceptional work had been done by some of the girls. He insisted that in case of difficulties arising I should not hesitate to refer to him.*

So long as he remained nominal head of ISK and could keep in close touch, Dilly was quite at ease with the arrangement that Twinn, who had worked for him in the early days, should take over the day-to-day running of ISK. Keith Batey, one of Gordon Welchman's 'wranglercoves', who had previously been seconded from Hut 6 to assist with breaking the Abwehr machine, had also found favour and became a high-powered member of the team. By the end of the war, we ended up 100-strong, including two bank managers to act as registrars, by which time we had moved from the Cottage to Elmer's School and the former Hut 6 and finally to Block G, which also housed ISOS.

Before the end of the war, we had solved 140,000 messages from almost every country of strategic importance from South America to the Far East and from Scandinavia to Africa. From the earliest days after Dilly's original break, we dealt with an extensive network of the main Balkan cities, covering the whole of eastern occupied Europe as far afield as Salonika and Warsaw. Of particular significance were those dealing with Tito and Yugoslavia. It was of great importance to Winston Churchill to make the right decision whether to support the royalist Chetniks under Mihailović or the communist Partisans under Tito, both of them fiercely resisting the invasion while at the same time fighting each other. On 28 February 1942 the Prime Minister received the Abwehr report that the Chetniks were being forced out of eastern Bosnia by the Partisans and that 'in future the communists are the only ones to be reckoned with'. With reluctance, Churchill knew we would have to back Tito with his links to the Comintern. SIS was of course unaware that a Russian agent, John Cairncross, the so-called Fifth Man, had been infiltrated into Hut 3 and was already supplying Moscow with Abwehr decrypts, sometimes identical with those distributed from Bletchley Park, which were passed on to Tito.

We had to work hard to keep track of the German operators, who as well as those working for Abwehr included those members of Himmler's Sicherheitsdienst (SD) working in occupied countries. Dilly was at ISK at the beginning of February 1942 to witness the birth of a new Abwehr machine network, which I was able to break on his methods. This was known as GGG after the call-sign of the Abwehr office in Algeciras, one of its chief users, and was of great interest to Dilly as it involved German spying on the Strait of Gibraltar, our key to the Mediterranean. Abwehr offices in Tetuan, Ceuta and Algeciras sent daily reports to the Abwehr station in Madrid concerning shipping movement and the arrival and departure of aircraft, which were then sent on to Berlin on the main Abwehr Enigma. We had always kept our eyes open for a day when the time and length of the intercepted messages pinpointed the actual repeat message with a minimum of textual additions and had in fact found one. As we suspected, for security reasons, the Abwehr would not have allowed the outstations to have their main multi-turnover Enigma machine used for communication with Berlin, so that we were looking for a 'K' machine with rewired wheels; its four-letter indicators showed that it had a settable *Umkehrwalze*. Having successfully fitted the cipher and text crib, Dilly's 'buttoning-up' method produced the wiring of the right-hand wheel. Rodding and charting could then take place for routine message-breaking with the additional information provided by the indicators.

Operation Goldeneye, the scheme to keep an eye on Spain through our Spanish embassy, was put in place after Hitler's 'Felix' directive, which followed the fall of France in May 1940 and aimed at invading Spain and seizing Gibraltar so as to control the whole of the Mediterranean. It was directed by Captain Alan Hillgarth, the British naval attaché in Madrid. The invasion of Spain did not take place, but at the end of 1941 the Germans decided that the Mediterranean was to be their navy's main theatre of operations. Dilly began to realise what vast ramifications the Madrid-based Abwehr provided, not only for Mediterranean intelligence but for cryptographical successes, because of the leads from one machine to another in the network of information. On 19 March, he put the case to Stewart Menzies, having discussed the matter with his friend Admiral Godfrey.

> *I sketched my idea of an investigation of Enemy Intelligence and pointed out how necessary it was for me to have some say in the matter of distribution. The ISOS people and I now listened in to the Enemy Intelligence at four points and even if one failed the fixture was complete. But did it all go to the same place? There was danger of one Admiralty branch panicking because of cessation on another line to another branch. We must be certain that Cowgill and Birch were in touch and then we could use our resources to get the maximum general yield ... I wanted an active effort to detect all other lines on which these enemy reports travelled and break the outstanding Kriegsmarine Enigma. I wished my personal scouts to have a large and unhampered range.*

This recorded interview with Menzies makes it quite clear how active Dilly still was behind the scenes, particularly in the 'matter of distribution' of the intelligence his ISK section was now providing under the cover of the ISOS section, which, as well as dealing with Abwehr hand ciphers, also undertook the analysis of the ISK Enigma messages. For security's sake, to conceal the breaking of the Abwehr machine, the difference between ISK and ISOS was only known to a few. Dilly was not satisfied that Felix Cowgill, the head of Section V, the SIS counter-espionage section, was passing all the information back to Frank Birch, head of the Bletchley Park naval section. ISOS under its new head, Denys Page, would pass the Abwehr intelligence on to Cowgill at Section V's headquarters at Glenalmond, St Albans. Birch in Hut 4 dealt with ULTRA Hut 8 intelligence but was missing out on the naval information that was increasingly coming from the analysed ISK messages. Cowgill was notorious for trying to keep ULTRA secrets under his own control, fearing they would be compromised, and he tried to restrict combined intelligence consultations.

Admiral Godfrey, as director of naval intelligence, on the other hand, was doing all he could to promote the Naval Intelligence Division's Room 39 as the 'co-ordinating section'. He was getting increasingly alarmed about the Abwehr spying activities in the Mediterranean, revealed by GGG. Lieutenant-Commander Ewen Montagu, who represented Godfrey on the XX Committee, later confirmed how much had to be done 'off the record' and 'under the table' behind Cowgill's back to get access to the deciphered messages. Montagu's Room 39 colleague Ian Fleming was Godfrey's personal assistant and liaison officer with Bletchley Park, which he visited about once a fortnight, co-ordinating with Birch. Dilly had worked with Fleming from the early days, when Godfrey was looking for 'cunning schemes' for pinching naval keys. He would have appreciated Fleming's ingenuity and ability to get things moving, but we have no means of knowing what he would have thought of his post-war creation of James Bond and his fantasy world.

Co-ordination over intelligence on the Abwehr was not only a question of gaining from joined-up intelligence, it was vital from the point of view of breaking new ciphers when messages were passed on from one network to another on different machines or ciphers. A 'pass-on', a message passed in one network in a decipherable cipher and then on the Abwehr Enigma, or vice versa, would provide a crib, which is why Dilly wanted an 'active effort to detect all other lines on which these enemy lines travel and break the outstanding *Kriegsmarine*'. This was another name for the Enigma machine codenamed Seahorse at Bletchley, which was used for messages between Berlin and the German naval attaché in Tokyo. Dilly urged Peter Twinn to see that an extra watch was put on the ISK traffic to look for a pass-on. It was Nigel de Grey as Edward Travis's deputy who was responsible for allocating new traffic and organising exchanges, which annoyed Dilly. 'Exchanges were all very well', he said, 'but my attitude was, and had been for the past fifteen years, that I could not tell whether I wanted anything until I had seen it.' Dilly also made it known that he 'wished my personal scouts to have a large and unhampered range'. There is no doubt that Dilly was manipulating his own spy network from Courns Wood.

Dilly was in constant touch with Twinn and was concerned that the ISK section was not getting sufficient feedback from St Albans about the new GGG traffic, but the time had come for Twinn to make his own stand. He therefore wrote to Travis on 4 May requesting improved liaison with SIS:

During the four months I have been in this section I have had no communication with anyone outside Bletchley Park and left in the dark. We have now provided decodes of the whole of GGG traffic from 14 February until today and during the last fortnight we have broken five days of a completely new network but I have had no comment on the importance or non-importance of these two groups or indeed anything to show that they have been recognized as something new.

A laconic reply was soon received from Travis to the effect that he had dealt with the situation with Section V: 'I think things will improve.'

Improvements there certainly were and Dilly might even have come round to conceding that Travis was an effective operator. Admiral Godfrey, who was still able to consult his greatly admired go-ahead predecessor 'Blinker' Hall, had undoubtedly been the one responsible for the change of heart about GGG at Section V. When there was any important movement of ships through the Strait, such as a Malta convoy, Godfrey arranged for a 'rush service' to be put into operation at Hanslope, which intercepted our

Abwehr traffic, and also for disseminating the information derived from ISK's GGG messages. We called our middle decoding stage in the process 'jumbo rush'; this might have been because it was 'rushed' to us by Travis, whose nickname was Jumbo. We knew that action stations meant men's lives at risk and working round the clock, but were seldom aware of the reason for any particular jumbo rush.

The SIS officer Kim Philby, who had been a reporter in the Spanish Civil War, was now put in charge of the Iberian desk in Section V, with the task of watching and frustrating the activities of the Abwehr in Spain and Portugal. Many of us remember Philby's liaison visits to ISOS at Bletchley Park from St Albans. Although he was already spying for the Russians they were then our ally and he was as keen as everybody else to defeat the Nazis. He wrote about his work in Section V in a book published in 1968, *My Silent War*, which refers to ISK's activities and even mentions Dilly Knox by name as having broken the Abwehr machine; this was six years before Frederick Winterbotham first revealed that the breaking of German Enigma machines had greatly contributed to the outcome of the war.

On the very day that Dilly Knox broke the Abwehr machine, 8 December 1941, the whole course of the war changed, as that was also the day that America joined the war. Churchill later wrote of his relief, after hearing the news of the Japanese attack on Pearl Harbor, that 'once again in our long island history we should emerge, however mauled or mutilated, safe and victorious. We should not be wiped out. Our history would not come to an end ... I went to bed and slept the sleep of the saved and thankful.' Hitherto, it had largely been a case of keeping the enemy off our shores, but the Americans now urged positive action to liberate Europe. Churchill was not ready to embark on the main invasion across the Channel and instead proposed to President Franklin D. Roosevelt that the Allies destroy Field Marshal Erwin Rommel's Armeegruppe Afrika prior to an attack from the Mediterranean on 'the soft underbelly of Europe'. The Admiralty would be much concerned with the safety of the armada of Allied troopships that would have to pass through the Strait of Gibraltar for amphibious landings. Dilly's ISK section and its penetration of the German secret service messages gave Churchill the trump card he needed.

Godfrey was determined to bring operations and intelligence together, which was the reason that Twinn's protest about lack of interest in the GGG Mediterranean traffic received an immediate response. As soon as GGG was broken in February 1942, Dilly and Godfrey knew that it was directly involved in the enemy surveillance of the Strait. Spying on our shipping was at first a haphazard affair, mostly by telescopes on Spanish fishing boats or lighthouses; one message we received of a Royal Navy battleship making its way to the Atlantic reported its name as 'Beware of the Propellers'! However, in March the messages began to refer to a state-of-the-art surveillance apparatus between Algeciras and Spanish Morocco, which would come into operation in April. Godfrey knew how vital it was to find out what it was, as the Allies were planning north African landings for the autumn in an operation to be called 'Torch'. Ian Fleming was already acting as his representative on Operation Goldeneye and was now put in charge of this new focus on Franco and the Mediterranean. Fleming was determined to frustrate, by one means or another, what he called the enemy's 'detailed and deadly watch' on the Strait of Gibraltar.

The ISK decodes had revealed that the Germans had codenamed their surveillance operation 'Bodden'. Philby realised that this was the name of the stretch of water between islands in the Baltic Sea and the mainland; one of these islands was home to Peenemünde, the site of the German missile scientific research establishment where the apparatus would have been tested. Combining the information from the GGG decodes with photographic intelligence of the sites, Dr R. V. Jones, head of the scientific section of SIS, soon diagnosed Bodden as a great heat-seeking infra-red searchlight across the strait. It was not long before Godfrey and the First Sea Lord, Admiral Sir Dudley Pound, received a detailed report with proposals for counter-measures, including lagging of funnels. Unfortunately, in his excitement Pound revealed the top secret source of the information to people who were not cleared to know. Jones, who had a wicked sense of humour, saved the day by turning the tables and saying that the information had not come from codebreaking, since we hadn't broken any German codes. It was a cover for a very secret source who had access to the Madrid Abwehr and went by the name of 'el Hatto'. Arthur Hatto was in fact the Bletchley Park ISOS specialist who processed the intelligence from the ISK decodes and he was not amused when the story got around, insisting that everybody should have known that Hatto was 'a good Anglo-Saxon name'.

The next step was to decide what action should be taken on the Bodden enterprise before Operation Torch was activated. Fleming, who was always ready for action of any sort, wanted the SOE to blow the Bodden sites up, but Philby, when he came to write *My Silent War*, commented wryly that he 'doubted whether anyone on our side would really welcome a James Bond-like free-for-all in Spain'. Captain Hillgarth, who throughout Goldeneye had worked so hard on keeping Spain out of the war, persuaded Godfrey against such an action and the Foreign Office, which was anxious not to let offensive action increase the influence of pro-Nazi ministers around General Franco, certainly preferred to play the diplomatic card. Having discussed it with Churchill, our ambassador, Sir Samuel Hoare, told Franco that we had become aware that he had allowed the Germans to set up surveillance sites wearing Spanish uniforms, thereby infringing Spanish neutrality. On 29 May 1942, the ISK section decoded a message on the main Abwehr machine from Madrid to Berlin reporting that 'the Golfers had become aware of Bodden South and have lodged a note of complaint with the Spanish government'. Much to our amusement, the Germans always referred to the UK as 'Golf Course'. However, pressure was put on Franco, who had no wish to be drawn into the war, and there was no further serious breach of neutrality on Spain's part. The fear of Franco providing air-bases from which the Luftwaffe could attack Gibraltar's airfield and dockyard or bomb the allies taking part in the planned Torch landings had now receded. Even though the Foreign Office had watered down Fleming's gung-ho Goldeneye proposals, he always remembered with satisfaction his Goldeneye mission and named his postwar home in his Jamaican paradise, where James Bond was born, after the operation.

A complete picture of the Abwehr in Spain had been built up thanks to Goldeneye spying and the ISK decodes. We knew the names, pseudonyms, cover and real functions of the staff at Madrid HQ and the many outstations. As Cowgill said, 'we even knew what they had for breakfast'. One of our decodes from Algeciras to Madrid had revealed that 'Axel' had bitten 'Caesar', who was now in hospital. Philby rightly guessed that Axel was not a fellow agent but the guard dog procured for the Bodden South apparatus. A Goldeneye officer investigated and reported that a certain Albrecht Carbe had been admitted to hospital with a dog bite at the right time. Caesar's cover was now blown and another piece of the German secret service jigsaw had been put together. The head of the Abwehr, Admiral Wilhelm Canaris, had a major interest in maintaining an effective Spanish organisation. He had been closely involved with General Franco in the Civil War and, as Hitler's spymaster, had been entrusted with key elements of Operation Felix; it was Canaris's ambition to see the Germans seize Gibraltar.

During 1942, the ISK Abwehr decodes became even more important and took on an operational dimension. Up to now, the information that the double agents had been sending out to their controllers was largely confined to false reports of dockyard activity, mine-laying, bomb damage, information generally designed to give a false picture of German successes in their bombing campaign and British preparations for the defence of the UK. Now that Allied invasions were being planned and protection needed for the convoys, the double agents could send out misleading information about their destinations to controllers in Madrid or Lisbon, which would be reported to Berlin. Our ISK section would then read the exchange of messages and the comments and questions of the Abwehr bosses allowed the XX Committee to tell whether the bait had been swallowed or not and to what extent the agent's credibility was trusted.

It was Dilly's great achievement in breaking the Abwehr Enigma used on the higher-level Abwehr communications links that allowed the XX Committee to be absolutely certain their deception operations were working. By the spring of 1942, the information collected from the ISK decrypts had built up such a good picture of Abwehr operations that MI5 was able to state categorically that it now controlled all the German agents operating in Britain and that it knew precisely what value the Germans put on their reports.

The whole Double Cross operation was shrouded in complete secrecy. Only a very few people at NID12, the naval intelligence department that handled the reports from Bletchley, were allowed to see the XX messages, which carried a docket marked 00, indicating that their security was even higher than mere Top Secret. This may be the reason Fleming gave James Bond the designation 007. Churchill insisted on seeing every message and not just a synopsis, as he relished the cloak-and-dagger nature of it all.

The XX Committee's first success in creating what Churchill would later describe as the 'bodyguard of lies' came during Operation Torch, the amphibious landings in north Africa in November 1942. For months, the double agents had been sending reports designed to make the Germans believe that troop build-ups and Allied convoys were related to attacks on France and Norway, and the relief of Malta.

The key double agents used in Operation Overthrow, a Torch deception plan, included the Dane Wulf Schmidt, codenamed Tate, who was ostensibly living in a house in north London and reported extensive troop movements across south-east England; Friedl Gärtner, codenamed Gelatine, an Austrian secretary in MI5, who played the part of a female agent who reported gossip among senior officers and civil servants suggesting preparations for invasions of northern Europe; and two Norwegians, Helge Moe and Tor Glad, who had been sent to Scotland by the Germans on a sabotage mission. They immediately gave themselves up and were codenamed Mutt and Jeff, after two hapless characters in a US newspaper cartoon. They reported on troops preparing for mountain and arctic warfare in Scotland apparently in preparation for an invasion of Norway. But the star turn was undoubtedly Garbo, the most accomplished of fraudsters.

Garbo was a Spaniard, Juan Pujol Garcia, who entirely of his own volition, partly for cash and partly because he hated the Germans, was sending them false reports from Lisbon based on nothing more than a Blue Guide to Britain, a Portuguese book on the Royal Navy and an Anglo-French vocabulary of military terms. He claimed to have a wide network of sub-agents in Britain feeding him information and eventually he was taken over by the British and brought to London where his attempts to sabotage the German intelligence service could be controlled by the XX Committee. Garbo's fictitious sub-agents reported widespread troop movements in southern England that might be expected before an invasion of France. He also warned the Abwehr that suggestions that the

Allies did not have enough ships ready for an invasion of France were deliberate rumours 'to confuse you'. His Abwehr controller told him it was 'of the greatest importance' that he get as much information as possible on any movements and preparations for an invasion, 'especially the Isle of Wight and regions of Wales'. As the official historian noted, 'Garbo did his best to oblige'.

With both Hitler and Field Marshal Gerd von Rundstedt, the German commander in western Europe, convinced the Allies intended to invade France and Norway that summer, it was clear from the Abwehr communications deciphered by the ISK section that the double agents' warnings were reinforcing that view. Back-up was always given for the misinformation. An American intelligence officer, Lewis Powell, a future justice of the Supreme Court, was amazed when his troopship arrived at Bristol and was very publicly issued with skis before heading off in a northerly direction; only after a circuitous journey did they find themselves passing through the Strait of Gibraltar to join the rest of the armada. Once it was obvious that the Allied fleets were heading for the Mediterranean, the double agents had to tell their controllers that they were after all destined for Malta, Crete or Sicily.

Remarkably the combined Allied fleet passed safely through the Strait of Gibraltar at the dead of night and proceeded full steam ahead along the Mediterranean. But suddenly it made a sharp turn south to land on beaches at Oran and Algiers in preparation for driving Rommel out of north Africa. If ever an operation was unlikely to succeed it was this one. To land first 90,000 men and later another 200,000 with all their supplies, across 1,500 miles of sea from Britain and 3,000 miles from America, would only be possible with complete signals security and keeping the enemy guessing as to their destination until the last moment. Mercifully, the Italian fleet was out of action after the Battle of Matapan.

The XX Committee cleverly modified Garbo's reports as the Torch landings approached. On 29 October, he told his Abwehr controller: 'I do not wish to make further predictions about the future objective, only I can assure you that an operation of great importance is imminent and I think I fulfil my duty by advising you of this danger.' He did eventually report that the Allies intended to invade French North Africa but too late for the Germans to do anything.

The Abwehr was completely taken in. 'Your last reports were magnificent,' his controller told him, 'we are sorry they arrived late.'

Back at Bletchley Park, we were flat out on a jumbo rush throughout this period; for these occasions, Dilly's girls had acquired a toy elephant, which was brought out of the cupboard for the duration. When we put on the early morning radio news after nights of slogging and heard that our troops had safely landed in north Africa, we knew what jumbo rush was all about. So successful was Operation Torch and its 'bodyguard of lies' that Rommel only heard about it on his radio at the same time as we did. Jumbo was patted on his back and returned to the cupboard for the next rush.

As a result of the invasion of north Africa, we acquired another Abwehr machine. Godfrey had authorised Ian Fleming to set up a joint service combat unit for amphibious landings which would make their way to the enemy HQ in order to seize codes and other secret material before they could be destroyed. This followed an example set by the Germans in Crete. Fleming's 'Red Indians', as he referred to them, were originally called the Special Engineering Unit and subsequently the 30 Assault Unit, their motto being 'Attain by Surprise'. They were given commando training with additional training in safe-breaking, interrogation and what they should look for. On this particular occasion, in conjunction with the Americans, they captured a 'KK' rewired multi-turnover Abwehr machine used for a link that had not been broken before; it was a Vichy French network run by the German Armistice Commission, in whose offices the machine was discovered, and six-weeks' back-traffic was soon broken. But it was not quite as easy as it sounds, as the Abwehr were notorious for thinking up ingenious methods of indicating and we had to keep our wits about us to solve the system. The type of indicator on the KK machine was the same as that used by the German armed forces, making it look as though the window positions were for a machine with three wheels. An indicator was chosen by the operator at random and set up and any three letters enciphered. The final window position was noted and the first three letters of it used as the message setting. The original indicator was then set up again and the message setting enciphered, giving the second three-letter group. Thus, after the recipient had deciphered the indicator, the first three letters were already set up on the machine and all that remained to do was to turn the right-hand wheel to read the same as the *Umkehrwalze*.

Plans for the invasion of southern Europe, once the African shores of the Mediterranean were cleared of Axis forces, were already in place. This time the landing point really would be Sicily, to attack Churchill's 'soft underbelly' of Europe. The invasion was to be called Operation Husky and would have as its bodyguard not a double agent but a dead body. The body, supposedly that of a British officer who had been in a crashed aircraft, was dropped off the southern coast of Spain, close enough to ensure it washed ashore. He was carrying a number of documents, including a photograph of a fictional fiancée and two love letters but more importantly a letter from Lord Mountbatten, the Chief of Joint Operations, which referred jocularly to sardines. The Spanish were known to collaborate with the Abwehr and it was rightly assumed that the documents would be shown to the Germans who would draw the natural conclusion from Mountbatten's joke that the Allies' first target would be Sardinia. The operation was dubbed Mincemeat and Duff Cooper, chairman of the Cabinet Security Committee at the time, wrote a novel based on it, called *Operation Heartbreak*, and Ewen Montagu, who had taken part in the deception, wrote an officially sanctioned account in *The Man Who Never Was* in 1953, which sold nearly two million copies; but the real truth could not be told.

It was crucial that the Allies know the German high command's reaction to the deception operation and only ISK could reveal that. Jumbo was taken out of his cupboard again. Churchill was at the Trident conference in Washington in May 1943 when he received with great glee a message saying: 'Mincemeat swallowed whole.' Hitler himself had said: 'The planned attack will be directed mainly against Sardinia and the Peloponnese.' We even knew the Abwehr were delighted that they had worked out what was meant by 'sardines'. The XX Committee particularly enjoyed that. The Germans moved troops to Sardinia, reducing their defences on Sicily, which was the real target. Husky's success, with its 'bodyguard of lies', would provide an excellent precedent for the deception plans for the D-Day landings, the first stage of Operation Overlord, the invasion of Europe.

The ISK and ISOS decrypts allowed SIS, MI5 and the XX Committee to build up a very detailed picture of the Abwehr and the Sicherheitsdienst, including their operating methods, cover addresses and the names of their officers and agent handlers. It also ensured that German agents coming to Britain were identified and arrested, and could therefore be bought into the Double Cross system, but that was not its only contribution. It allowed the British to foil attempts at sabotage, especially of shipping from Gibraltar; it gave a detailed picture of extensive Spanish government help to the Abwehr, enabling the Foreign Office to protest to the Spanish and restrain their collaboration; and it provided material which could be used to obtain further information from German agents under interrogation.

By far the greatest contribution made by the ISK decrypts, however, was to building up the Double Cross system to the point that it could be used as an extensive 'bodyguard of lies' to protect the forces taking part in the D-Day landings. Churchill had told Josef Stalin, during the Tehran conference in late November 1943, that 'in wartime, truth is so precious that she should always be attended by a bodyguard of lies'. The XX Committee set about using the Double Cross agents to create those lies.

Allied commanders had selected Normandy as the best landing place for the massed invasion force, but they knew that any amphibious force would automatically find itself at a disadvantage and that with sufficient forces the Germans could well throw them back into the sea. So for months beforehand the Double Cross agents were used to provide overwhelming evidence of an entirely fictitious plan under which the Normandy landings were a feint designed to draw German forces away from the real point of attack on the Pas de Calais. A fictitious 1st United States Army Group (FUSAG), led by the US war hero General George Patton, was notionally created to lead the assault on the Pas de Calais. By the beginning of 1944, the XX Committee was controlling fifteen double agents, four of whom were the key players in Churchill's 'bodyguard of lies'. As with Torch, Garbo was to be the most important of those agents. The other three were the Pole Roman Garby-Czerniawski, codenamed Brutus; the Yugoslav Duško Popov, codenamed Tricycle; and a Frenchwoman, Natalie 'Lily' Sergueiev, codenamed Treasure.

Between them Tricycle and Brutus passed the Abwehr reports on the mythical FUSAG and its troops preparing for the invasion in south-east England that were so detailed that the Germans were able to compile its complete order of battle even down to the insignia painted on the side of the vehicles of its different units. Treasure meanwhile reported on a supposed lack of troops in south-west England that would persuade the Germans there were no plans for a major assault on Normandy. Dummy tanks and invasion landing craft were left in the open in the Kent ports and mobile wireless vehicles travelled around sending out hundreds of radio messages to simulate the communications of an army based in the south-east while complete wireless silence was imposed on the real troops in the south-west.

Yet again, however, it was Garbo who played the key role. In the early hours of 6 June 1944, D-Day, Garbo made repeated attempts to warn his Abwehr controller that the Allied forces were on their way, knowing it would be too late for the Germans to do anything about it, but building up their trust in him. Then shortly after midnight on 9 June, as the Allied advance faltered and with two Panzer divisions on their way to reinforce the German defences in Normandy, Garbo sent his most important message. The Normandy landings were only a feint, he said. Three of his agents were reporting troops massed across East Anglia and Kent and large numbers of troop and tank transporters waiting in the eastern ports ready for the main assault:

> *After personal consultation on 8 June in London with my agents Donny, Dick and Derrick, whose reports I sent today, I am of the opinion, in view of the strong troop concentrations in south-east and east England, that these operations are a diversionary manoeuvre designed to draw off enemy reserves in order to make an attack at another place. In view of the continued air attacks on the concentration area mentioned, which is a strategically favourable position for this, it may very probably take place in the Pas de Calais area.*

Garbo's warning went straight to Hitler, who ordered the two Panzer divisions to the Pas de Calais, to defend against what he expected to be the main thrust of the invasion, and awarded Garbo the Iron Cross. Had the two divisions continued to Normandy, it is arguable that the Allies may well have been thrown back into the sea. On 11 June, we deciphered a message from Berlin to Garbo's controller in Madrid saying that Garbo's reports 'have been confirmed almost without exception and are to be described as especially valuable. The main line of investigation in future is to be the enemy group of forces in south-eastern and eastern England.'

These intercepts of Abwehr Enigma messages were vital to Allied commanders' confidence in the plans, confirming that the Germans believed that the main thrust of the allied attack would be on the Pas de Calais. Admiral Sir Bertram Ramsay, in charge of the amphibious landings at Eisenhower's Supreme Headquarters for the Allied Expeditionary Forces, wrote in his diary on the eve of D-Day: 'We must trust in our invisible assets to tip the balance in our favour.' That trust was well justified. Even at the end of the war, the German generals believed that the Allies had intended to make their main attack on the Pas de Calais and only changed their minds because of the strength of the German forces based there. Reminded of the deception twenty-two years later, Eisenhower laughed and said: 'By God, we fooled them, didn't we?'

Sadly, Dilly did not live to see what was – in all probability – the most important contribution to the war made by his great triumph in breaking the Abwehr Enigma.

TWELVE

Farewell

My most enduring memory of Dilly is of staying at Courns Wood in his last spring. He had invited me over to see the 'loveliest of trees, the cherry now' in full bloom under the guest bedroom. He was still passionate about his trees and I learned a lot about the Chiltern woodlands that weekend; but it could no longer be the strenuous planting or sawing and splitting of wood he so loved to do. I just helped him shake pine cone seeds into tobacco tins for scattering. I hope my efforts for posterity have come to maturity in the Naphill woods. Flourishing outside the village hall was the Atlantic cedar he had planted for the celebration of King George VI's coronation in 1937. Today it is lit up every Christmas.

While Olive was getting the supper Dilly got out the photographs of the *Mimiambi* fragments from the Greek papyri and showed me how he had put them together. At least we had a table to spread them out on and one can only wonder how he managed to do it on his knees on the train from High Wycombe to London and the reaction of his fellow commuters reading their newspapers.

Olive had greeted me with an apology that the laundry hadn't come and would I mind sleeping in Ronnie's sheets as he had just left. Dilly added that it was all right to do so because he was very clean. Ronnie had not come to see the cherries 'hung with snow' as he could have his fill of them in Housman's own Shropshire, where he was living in a convent engaged in translating the Bible into English for Roman Catholics. It was this on which he had been consulting Dilly, as he had just got to the Epistles and for St Paul's visit to the Corinthians, and he too was battling with Greek papyri. Dilly said he had translated more of it than Ronnie as his brother's Greek was not up to standard. He felt that Ronnie ought to know more about the Corinthians and their way of life in the same way in which he had sought out the world behind Herodas when editing his mimiambics. He had also tried to steep himself in the German mindset when coming to terms with the Abwehr.

Churchill had perceptively assessed, when referring in 1919 to Room 40's successful codebreaking, that it had needed 'a study of the psychology of the persons sending out the messages and a sort of instinctive "flair" for the kind of things they are saying', which was different from 'intelligence analysis'. Dilly had been able to take his time reading the stacks of ISOS hand cipher messages shown to him by Oliver Strachey before he broke the Abwehr Enigma and had got a good idea of the psychology of the spy people he was dealing with. Psychology had taken on a new dimension since Freud. The sixpenny Pelican series had produced his *Psychopathology of Everyday Life* just before the war and we were all into the subconscious and Freudian slips. I enrolled for the Cambridge extra-mural psychology course being given in the town as soon as I arrived at Bletchley and felt one up on everybody else as when I was at Zurich University I had heard Freud's disciple, Carl Jung, lecture.

We pursued our operator's subconscious when setting up his supposedly random indicators. Settings which could be guessed from idiosyncrasies of the operator became known as 'psillis' as an extension of Dilly's cillis, which were more attributable to the conscious slackness of the operator than determined by his subconscious. As the Abwehr had four-letter indicators there was much more Freudian scope for codebreakers. Girlfriends of course were an obvious giveaway and ROSA with her in-built lobster was a friend indeed. I became an expert in four-letter dirty German words and was dismayed when one day there was a reprimand from Berlin to operators for using obscenities when young girls were having to decode them. They meant the German girls of course, not us. Needless to say, we were furious when they were abandoned. We were prepared for anything with the Abwehr indicating systems.

Sometimes it was a new cipher boss who made life difficult for us. One, von Bentheim, decreed that in future indicators should be encoded half at a *Grundstellung* and half at a setting of a German folk song, for which my German romantics had fortunately prepared me. Sometimes the indicators had to be scrambled so that ROSAZ ROSAZ on a given key 5332142514 would be encoded at the *Grundstellung* as ZSSORAOZRA, which played havoc with boxing. It made us quite dizzy and we called it 'jitterboxing' after the new jitterbugging dance that the Americans had just taught us. I think we could rightly say in ISK that, to our knowledge, in machine cryptography our problems for variety and novelty were unequalled. We were prepared for anything, however bizarre.

There was worse to come in the summer when the Abwehr suddenly got round to realising the folly of using double indicators on a fixed *Grundstellung*, which the services had abandoned as long ago as 1938. Gone was boxing altogether, and our lovely chain-lobstering, when faced with single indicators; new methods for textual breaks for multi-turnover machines had to be made, involving making new catalogues and even our own *bombe*. Peter Twinn had worked with Alan Turing on the Letchworth *bombes* for Hut 6 and Hut 8, but if we were to have one made for our Abwehr machine it would need to have an additional electro-mechanical counter to account for the Abwehr machine having a moveable *Umkehrwalze*. Peter went to show the proposed diagram to Dilly and came back with a special name for it – Fünf, after Tommy Handley's German spy in the hilariously popular radio comedy *ITMA*, then all the rage. Fünf was in action by November and Jean Hazlerigg took charge of our Spy Enigma menus for the Wrens in the Bombe Hut to set up when all other methods failed.

There was still much hand-work to be done before resorting to programming Fünf and Twinn produced a blackboard and asked me to explain the new method to the girls. We had had to take on more staff who had never heard of Enigma before and even someone who had worked on the old system said that she had never understood what it was all about as she just got on with following Dilly's simple instructions of how to do it, so why bother about explaining new theories when she didn't need to know the old? I must have told Dilly, who was still deep in Ronnie's epistles, about my frustrations, as I have a letter back from him saying:

There is a lesson from Corinthians for you beginning: 'If after the manner of men, I have fought with beasts at Ephesus' that would appear apt enough for your efforts to teach the newcomers. A little further on we have the famous proof of the resurrection, 'if the dead rise not, then is our teaching in vain', which is a form of argument which can be paraphrased to meet all hecklings as you will see.

The hecklers were right, of course; in ISK you could drive the car perfectly well without knowing what went on under the bonnet. Later, when Keith Batey joined us permanently, he tried to give a newcomer a tutorial on how the machine worked technically and afterwards she fled, never to be seen again; it was rumoured she had had a nervous breakdown.

Dilly was very anxious that I should meet his niece, Penelope Knox, to try and persuade her to leave working for her father at *Punch* and join us in ISK. However, I did not actually meet her until 1975, when she had begun to write her biography of the Knox brothers. Naturally she would have liked to have known about Dilly's wartime work and thought that all could now be revealed after Frederick Winterbotham's book on Bletchley Park had been published in 1974. We had been told that it was now permissible to be anecdotal but on no account to give technical details of codebreaking in interviews, so we could not be much help; nor could Margaret Rock or Peter Twinn. It was only in 1982 that Gordon Welchman wrote his book on Hut 6 giving technical details of the breaking of Enigma. However, Penelope's husband paid a visit to Gustave Bertrand, whose book *Enigma* had been published in 1973, and he was able to furnish her with details about Dilly's visit to Warsaw and other contacts he had had with him. Unfortunately, Bertrand, who was no cryptographer, also offered to explain 'the early stages in the solving of Enigma', which he had never understood, and Dilly must have turned in his grave to see the resulting description of his work as recorded by Penelope.

It was decided that we must recruit some newly graduated mathematicians to join the team, at least one of whom would become a professor in later life. Dilly insisted that I should be present at the interviews, not to check their capabilities, as that would be taken care of, but to see if these males were the sort of people the girls could get along with. By then I had confessed that I had become engaged to the 'wranglercove' Keith Batey and although Dilly congratulated me heartily, he asked me if I knew that mathematicians as a breed were not usually very imaginative. I reassured him that this one was all right. When I showed Olive my engagement ring and it transpired that I had chosen it myself, she told me that Dilly had bought hers himself and given it to her in Room 40 as he thought that was what the bridegroom was meant to do. By the tone of her voice I rather detected that she too would have preferred to have been in on the choice.

Dilly wanted to hear about the visit of the Americans to see how our Abwehr machine worked. I told him that two service types came, one large and bullying with two ribbons and the other lean and acquiescent with one. After five minutes, the leader said: 'We've sure got your machine taped now,' which of course he hadn't. The other one made what we thought was quite an intelligent observation to be crushed by 'Don't be ridiculous' and he said meekly: 'Sorry, it was only an idea.' He awoke our maternal instincts and as we had managed to get the ingredients for a chocolate cake together, which we baked in the kitchen for their visit, we made sure he was given a much larger piece. When they left they said that they had never had such hospitality, nor met such charming people. My note ended: 'I hope we are not going to have a whole string of Doughboys to drive dizzy.' I think it was the lack of hierarchy that amazed all the Americans. Anybody, however junior, with a bright idea was listened to in ISK and often it worked. William Friedman, America's top codebreaker, on a visit to Bletchley Park in 1943 was astounded at what he regarded as a bunch of amateurs could produce. 'In a technical sense, we are ahead,' he said. 'But in a practical sense, judged by accomplishments, these amateurs have very largely surpassed us in detail, attention to minutiae, digging up every bit of intelligence possible and applying high-class thinking, originality and brains to the task.'

Admiral Godfrey made a point of visiting Courns Wood as often as he could to tell Dilly how strategic deception was being planned as a result of his Abwehr break, now that Torch, the first Allied operation, was scheduled for the autumn; this was something which was not known to the staff in ISK itself of course, where to us it would just be action stations jumbo rush when it happened. On one occasion, Dilly told Godfrey that he was sure he would get better if he had a cruise and asked him to try and get him on an Arctic convoy; the astounded admiral could only say that these were not vessels to recuperate on. We knew Dilly had said he wanted some sea air and thought he just meant a yachting trip on the Fal with Frank Birch as in the old days, but alas not even this could take place. Peter Twinn and I continued to visit Courns Wood regularly to keep Dilly informed of ISK progress and were taken by official car. There was one driver who seemed to think we were out for a joy ride and was determined that we should see all the sights of Buckinghamshire – Chequers, Ishbel Macdonald's pub and some speed trials, but we told him not to waste time and petrol and take the shortest route.

At this time, Margaret Rock had for several months been working with Dilly at Courns Wood on an 'isolated problem' which was not connected with Abwehr. She was able to drive Dilly over, sometimes bearing lovely fruit, which we ate in the garden at Elmer's School. She was very secretive about the work but as it had no bearing on ours we knew better than to ask her. It has been suggested that Dilly was working on Soviet ciphers before he died and this may well be true. Russia was our ally and officially we had ceased to read their traffic, but in March 1942 'C' and the director general of the security services decided that some Russian systems should be worked. Dilly had of course worked on Comintern and with the great Russian codebreaker, Ernst Fetterlein, and it might have been the answer to let him work on it away from mainstream codebreaking. Margaret and I went on to work on Russian at Eastcote after the war. But 'need to know' was just as strict then and I did not ask her if that was what she and Dilly were doing in 1942. Margaret Rock did come back to hold the fort for the jumbo rush before Operation Torch when Keith and I were married in London with Peter Twinn as best man. Dilly sent us a lovely wedding present and said that if the Muse hadn't left him he would have composed my wedding hymn.

Soon afterwards Dilly was admitted to University College Hospital and when I visited him his brother Evoe was by his bedside and they were roaring with laughter composing Dilly's last words. They were reading from a book of collected famous last words called *The Art of Dying*, which Dilly handed to me when I left. I still have it. Dilly's last words were in fact: 'Is that Ronnie outside in the corridor bothering God about me?' He wrote a pentelope for his epitaph:

A wanderer on the path [A]
That leads through life to death, [E]
I was acquainted with [I]
The tales they tell of both [O]
But found in them no truth [U].

Dilly died at home on 27 February 1943, aged fifty-eight, and was buried in his woodlands, where Olive's ashes would later be scattered. John Maynard Keynes, who was present, described his old friend as 'sceptical of most things except those that really matter, that is affection and reason'.

Just before he died, Dilly was appointed as a Companion of the Order of St Michael and St George 'for services to his country'. It was explained to Olive that security conditions precluded a more illustrious honour. Dilly insisted on getting dressed to receive the emissary from Buckingham Palace and, typically, he sent the decoration to ISK with a touching note saying it was really meant for them. It was heartening to know that he regarded ISK and what he called the 'Cottage tradition' as the fulfilment of his career. The official farewell letter shows that, until the very last moment, he was insisting that codebreaking and intelligence work were inseparable and that the secrecy of 'need to know' and 'working in blinkers' was counter-productive. His letter ended: 'In bidding farewell and closing down the continuity but not, I hope, the traditions of the Cottage, I thank once more the section for their unswerving loyalty. Theirs I remain

Affectionately

A. D. Knox.'

Dear Margaret [Rock]

Mavis [Batey]

Peter [Twinn]

Rachel etc.

[Denys] Page

Peggy [Taylor]

Very many thanks for your, and the whole section's, very kind messages of congratulations. It is of course, a fact that the congratulations are due the other way and that awards of this sort depend entirely on the support from colleagues and associates to the Head of the Section. May I, before proceeding, refer them back.

It is, I fear, incumbent upon me at the same time to bid farewell. For more than ten years, I have taken up with A.G.D. the position that (a) there is no proper distinction between research cryptography and cipher and intelligence work, (b) that it is as improper to ask a person of any degree of education to run a key-setting bureau, as to ask him or her to run a typewriting section, (c) that it is impossible to edit or translate satisfactorily without a precise knowledge of the cipher in question, (d) latterly we have recruited during and shortly before the war from the Universities; and Academic tradition does not understand the idea that a half-fledged result should be removed from the scholar who obtains it and handed over to another. The discoverer loses all interest in further discovery and the recipient has no interest in the offspring of another's brain. Still more doubtful is the case of 'Research'. Until we know who will handle and circulate any result we get, the irrepertum aurum *of our search will very probably be* sic melius situm.*

I have recently arranged with the authorities to attempt a line which should give wider scope though it will be of far less importance. In bidding farewell and in closing down the continuity but not, I hope, the traditions of the Cottage, I thank once more the section for their unswerving loyalty. Theirs I remain

Affectionately

A. D. Knox

The original letter, written in green ink on blue paper, an old naval tradition, can be found in The National Archives (Public Record Office) HW 25/12

* The Latin is a quote from Horace, *Odes III*, 3, 49, *irrepertum aurum et sic melius situm* – 'the gold unfound and so the better placed'.

Introduction to the appendices

Dilly began to investigate the characteristics of the Enigma machine as soon as he had access to one, probably as early as 1925. With an actual machine in front of him, he could tell how the keyboard letters were connected to the entry plate, and by battery testing could determine the internal wiring of the wheels. By tapping messages out to himself he could then begin to experiment on ways in which the wiring could be ascertained, using his own 'crib' for the cipher text. A method for breaking the wheel wiring was essential as the manufacturers had indicated that to increase security the wiring of the original wheels could be changed.

The instructions given to ordinary German soldiers, the *Schlüsselanleitung für die Chiffriermaschine Enigma*, included an example using a real machine which would have given Dilly some of the answers if only SIS had agreed to pay for it when it was first offered to them by the French in 1931. Appendix 1 is a translation of those instructions, which explain how the machine was set up to encipher a message. The technique Dilly invented to break the machine was by 'rodding' and 'buttoning-up', which he first put into practice with operational messages in the Spanish Civil War in 1937, when Mussolini and Franco obtained from Hitler improved 'K' models of the commercial Enigma machine with rewired wheels.

Throughout the chapters in this book, there is frequent mention of Dilly's system of rodding for breaking messages. Appendix 2, written by Frank Carter for the Bletchley Park Trust, explains how the rods were made specifically to match each machine. Although it refers to the rods' original use for the un-*Stecker*ed Enigma machine, there were occasions when rodding could be applied to the *Stecker*ed German service machine, such as the 'routine operation' put in place in confirming the authenticity of the 'crib message' provided in the 1930 operator's manual when Dilly stripped off the *Stecker* as a reciprocal substitution super-encipherment. His fundamental methods for breaking Scherbius's original machine had been a vital step in cryptanalysis, allowing later complications, such as the multi-turnover nature of the Abwehr machine, to be dealt with as they arose. As stated in the appendix, the rods used are those made for the German Railways 'K' model machine, broken on Dilly's methods in 1940. The term 'rotor', as is now normal in modern cryptographic texts, has replaced the word 'wheel', which was always used at Bletchley Park, being a near translation of *Walze*, the word used in the German description of the Enigma machine.

Appendix 3, also written by Frank Carter for the Bletchley Park Trust, explains 'buttoning-up'. The author is very grateful to Frank for providing these detailed explanations of Dilly's techniques. Frank in turn would like to thank Keith Batey, the author's husband, for his assistance in their compilation. Appendix 4 is Dilly's wonderfully idiosyncratic description for Alastair Denniston of the 'lobster hunt' that preceded the breaking of the Abwehr Enigma, and Appendix 5, compiled by Ralph Erskine, gives a complete list of the machines broken by Dilly's ISK section.

SECRET

Directions for Use of Keys for the Enigma I Cipher Machine

I. Distribution of Keys

1. Within a given district (e.g. a Division, or on manoeuvres one side, etc.) one 'district key' is in force.
2. For communication beyond the limit of this district 'transverse key' is employed.

II. Keys

3. Each 'key' contains all necessary directions for setting the cipher machine for the period of one month, as follows:
   (a) Directions for the position of the wheels, changed every three months.
   (b) Directions for the setting of the tyres (changed daily).
   (c) Directions for the basic setting (changed daily).
   (d) Directions for plug connections (changed daily).
4. While the above directions are similar and hold good for all users of the cipher machine, the choice of the message key is left (with one or two restrictions) to the encipherer. Hence the 'key' contains no directions for setting the 'message key'.

III. Setting the Key

5. The directions for the position of the wheels give the order, from left to right, in which the individual wheels are to be inserted, e.g.: II I III.

6. The directions for setting the tyres give the setting of the tyres of each individual wheel, e.g.: II:24 I:13 III:22.

7. The directions for the basic setting give the figures which must be set in the three windows from left to right, e.g.: 06 15 12.

8. Directions for plug connections indicate which twin sockets are to be connected to each other by means of the twin plug leads, e.g.: 1/13 6/9 14/22 16/19 20/21 23/26. (Each of these figures denotes a particular twin socket and the stroke separates the numbers of the twin sockets that are to be connected together, thus socket 1 has to be connected to socket 13, 6 to 9, 14 to 22, etc.)

9. Every message is enciphered using a particular message key. This is chosen at will from the range of figures 01 01 01 to 26 26 26. For every message on the same day a new message key must be used for the starting point. It is forbidden to encipher two or more messages on the same day using the same message key.

10. The recipient of the message is informed secretly of the chosen message key. The figures of the message key are replaced by the corresponding letters on the plugboard (e.g.: 1 is replaced by A, 13 by M, etc.), and using the basic setting the keys are pressed twice in succession. The resulting six letters are prefixed to the message which is being enciphered with this message key.

IV. Example

A. Enciphering

11. Key in force for the day:
    Position of the wheels: II I III; Setting of the tyres: II:24 I:13 III:22; Basic setting: 06 15 12; Plug connections: 1/13 6/9 14/22 16/19 20/21 23/26

12. A message to be enciphered at 1035 reads: 'Feindliche Infanteriekolonne beobachtet. Anfang Südausgang Bärwalde. Ende 3 Kilometer ostwärts Neustadt.' [Hostile column of infantry observed. Extends from the south exit of Bear Woods to position 3 kilometres east of Neustadt.] As 'ch' is replaced by 'q', 'ä' by 'ae', and 'ü' by 'ue', and punctuations are replaced by Xs, the message is enciphered in the following form: FEINDLIQE INFANTERIEKOLONNE BEOBAQTET X ANFANG SUEDAUSGANG BAERWALDE X ENDE DREI KM OSTWAERTS NEUSTADT.

171

13. The sender selects the [arbitrary] message key 01 02 12 and converts it into letters on the plugboard, this reads A B L. In accordance with Para III, 10, the key is pressed twice in succession (with a basic setting 06 15 12), and the letters PKPJXI will result. As the message in five-figure groups follows immediately after these letters, they are written down in the following form: PKPJX I.

14. Then, after setting the message key 01 02 12, the clear text is enciphered by pressing the keys. The resulting letters are written down after the above six letters. Thus the first four letters of the message are added to the I in Para IV, 13 above and the remainder are likewise divided into five-letter groups: PKPJX IGCDS EAHUG WTQGR KVLFG XUCAL XVYMI GMMNM FDXTG NVHVR MMEVO UYFZS LRHDR RXFJW CFHUH MUNZE FRDIS IKBGP MYVXU Z

15. The following precede the enciphered text:
    (a) Time group (four figures)
    (b) Number of letters (two or three figures)
    (c) To be able to see at once that the message was enciphered using the machine, an arbitrary three-figure number. The enciphered message therefore reads as follows: 1035-96-341 PKPJX IGCDS EAHUG etc., etc.

    Should a message be longer than 180 letters, then it is to be divided. The second and third portions are always to be enciphered with a different message key, which is to be disguised in the prescribed way.

16. On conclusion of enciphering, the final figures appearing in the windows are to be altered by casual rotation of the wheels.

B. Deciphering

17. The enciphered message reads: 1035-96-341 PKPJX IGCDS EAHUG WTQGR KVLFG XUCAL XVYMI GMMNM FDXTG NVHVR MMEVO UYFZS LRHDR RXFJW CFHUH MUNZE FRDIS IKBGP MYVXU Z.

18. The directions preceding the message which give the key for the day also show the position of the wheels, tyre settings and plug connections for that day. The machine is set according to these. Using the basic setting, the first six letters PKPJXI are typed. The resultant letters are ABLABL.

19. The letters ABL are looked for on the plugboard and the corresponding figures 1 2 12 are substituted. These show the message key chosen by the sender (01 02 12).

20. These figures are now set in the windows and the enciphered message is typed, omitting the first six letters (PKPJXI). The result is the deciphered message as shown in Para IV, 12.

These instructions for use of the Enigma machine appear in the National Archives, Public Record Office file HW 25/9.

Author's note

The effect of the *Stecker*- or plugboard on an Enigma cipher was first to encipher the plain text with the reciprocal substitution given by the plugboard connections then, once the wheels had enciphered the result, to encipher the cipher text still further with the same substitution. This effect could be stripped off to reveal the text the machine would have produced without the plugboard. In the example given in this manual, the *Stecker* were plugged across 1/13, 6/9, 14/22, 16/19, 20/21 and 23/26 (see paragraph 11 on page 171). The figures represent the position of the letter in the German alphabet, thereby producing the following reciprocal pairs: A/M, F/I, N/V, P/S, T/U, W/Z. So A became M and M became A and so on.

This table illustrates how the effect of the *Stecker* was stripped off both the cipher text and the plain text.

Cipher	G	C	D	S	E	A	H	U	G	W	T	Q	G	R	K	V	L	F	G	X
*Stecker*ed	G	C	D	P	E	M	H	T	G	Z	U	Q	G	R	K	N	L	I	G	X
(The wheel system enciphers G to I etc.)																				
*Stecker*ed	I	E	F	V	D	L	F	Q	E	F	V	I	M	V	U	E	R	F	E	K
Plain	F	E	I	N	D	L	I	Q	E	I	N	F	A	N	T	E	R	I	E	K

This process produced the modified crib required for the buttoning-up procedure, where G equals I, C equals E etc.

G	C	D	P	E	M	H	T	G	Z	U	Q	G	R	K	N	L	I	G	X
I	E	F	V	D	L	F	Q	E	F	V	I	M	V	U	E	R	F	E	K

The message was ninety letters long. So once the effect of the *Stecker* was stripped off the enciphered text, Dilly had a ninety-letter crib with which to determine the wheel wiring of an un-*Stecker*ed machine through his routine 'buttoning-up' method (see Appendices 2 and 3).

APPENDIX 2

'Rodding'

This technique (invented by Dilly Knox in 1937) was used to break messages that had been enciphered on Enigma machines that did not have a plugboard. The first commercial version of Enigma was of this type and a few countries adopted it for use by their armed services, after equipping it with different sets of rotors. The Italian navy used the machine during the Spanish Civil War, and continued to do so in a limited way after their entry into the Second World War in June 1940. In March 1941 rodding was used to break some important Italian messages, which lead to the dramatic and successful action in the Mediterranean, known as the Battle of Matapan. A new exhibition at Bletchley Park gives an account of these events and includes some detailed information showing how the first success was achieved. The following notes explain the basic principles of the technique by means of an illustrative example.

Like most of the methods used at BP, rodding required a crib with which to begin; however, this technique did not provide a complete sequence of characters from the plain text, but only a very fragmented one, and considerable linguistic skill was required to fill in the gaps, not unlike that required for solving crossword puzzles. Every correct inference made about the content of a message obtained in this way could then be used as an extension of the crib, and this would enable the process to be continued.

The versions of the Enigma machine without a plugboard had entry discs on which the letter terminals followed the sequence QWERTZUIOASDFGHJKPYXCVBNML in a clockwise sense when viewed from the right-hand side, in contrast to the standard service Enigma machines, for which the sequence was ABCD ... XYZ.

The basic idea used in 'rodding' can be explained by means of a diagram, in which an imaginary fixed disc with twenty-six electrical contacts is shown between the right-hand rotor of the Enigma machine and the remaining components of the rotor/reflector system on the left.

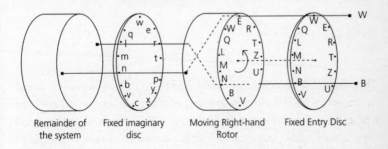

| Remainder of the system | Fixed imaginary disc | Moving Right-hand Rotor | Fixed Entry Disc |

Consider the contacts on the input disc, and suppose that the effect of the RH rotor is to connect contact 'W' to the contact 'n' on the imaginary disc. Likewise suppose that the effect of the RH rotor is to connect contact 'B' to the contact 'r' on the imaginary disc. If the letter W happens to be enciphered as B on the Enigma, then the pair of contacts 'n' and 'r' on the imaginary disc must be electrically connected through the remaining part of the Enigma system. For each position of the RH rotor there will be thirteen of these pairs of contacts on the imaginary disc, all of them being 'mutually disjoint', i.e. no two pairs have a common contact. For any given position of the RH rotor, the twenty-six letters on the entry disc will be directly connected to an individual contact on the fixed imaginary disc, and if the internal wiring of the RH rotor is known, then these can be determined. Since the rotor can be set to twenty-six different positions, the complete set of results can be presented in the form of a 26x26 tabulation, known as the 'rod square' table for the rotor.

The rod square table for 'Rotor I' used with the three-rotor, 'QWERTZU' version of the machine (without a plugboard), known as the 'Railway' Enigma, is shown below. The lower case letters in the column at the left represent the contacts on the imaginary disc, and the numbers in the top row represent the twenty-six possible positions of the rotor. The table gives the connections between the imaginary disc contacts and the entry disc contacts for all positions of the rotor. (For this table the rotor ring-setting used was 'Z'. Then the 1st column in the table corresponds to the rotor position 'A', the 2nd to position 'B' etc.) For example, the table shows that contact 't' on the imaginary disc is connected to contact 'C' on the entry disc when the rotor is at its tenth position.

Rod square for Rotor I

Contact points on the imaginary disc

	1	2	3	4	5	6	7	8	9	10	11	12	13	14	15	16	17	18	19	20	21	22	23	24	25	26
q	C	U	L	H	I	V	Y	R	P	S	D	M	T	K	W	G	B	J	B	F	X	N	O	Q	M	A
w	I	Q	J	O	B	X	T	Y	D	F	L	Z	P	E	H	N	K	N	G	C	M	A	W	L	S	V
e	W	K	A	N	C	Z	X	F	G	Q	U	Y	R	J	M	P	M	H	V	L	S	E	Q	D	B	O
r	P	S	M	V	U	C	G	H	W	I	X	T	K	L	Y	L	J	B	Q	D	R	W	F	N	A	E
t	D	L	B	I	V	H	J	E	O	C	Z	P	Q	X	Q	K	N	W	F	T	E	G	M	S	R	Y
z	Q	N	O	B	J	K	R	A	V	U	Y	W	C	W	P	M	E	G	Z	R	H	L	D	T	X	F
u	M	A	N	K	P	T	S	B	I	X	E	V	E	Y	L	R	H	U	T	J	Q	F	Z	C	G	W
i	S	M	P	Y	Z	D	N	O	C	R	B	R	X	Q	T	J	I	Z	K	W	G	U	V	H	E	L
o	L	Y	X	U	F	M	A	V	T	N	T	C	W	Z	K	O	U	P	E	H	I	B	J	R	Q	D
a	X	C	I	G	L	S	B	Z	M	Z	V	E	U	P	A	I	Y	R	J	O	N	K	T	W	F	Q
s	V	O	H	Q	D	N	U	L	U	B	R	I	Y	S	O	X	T	K	A	M	P	Z	E	G	W	C
d	A	J	W	F	M	I	Q	I	N	T	O	X	D	A	C	Z	P	S	L	Y	U	R	H	E	V	B
f	K	E	G	L	O	W	O	M	Z	A	C	F	S	V	U	Y	D	Q	X	I	T	J	R	B	N	S
g	R	H	Q	A	E	A	L	U	S	V	G	D	B	I	X	F	W	C	O	Z	K	T	N	M	D	P
h	J	W	S	R	S	Q	I	D	B	H	F	N	O	C	G	E	V	A	U	P	Z	M	L	F	Y	T
j	E	D	T	D	W	O	F	N	J	G	M	A	V	H	R	B	S	I	Y	U	L	Q	G	X	Z	K
k	F	Z	F	E	A	G	M	K	H	L	S	B	J	T	N	D	O	X	I	Q	W	H	C	U	P	R
p	U	G	R	S	H	L	P	J	Q	D	N	K	Z	M	F	A	C	O	W	E	J	V	I	Y	T	G
y	H	T	D	J	Q	Y	K	W	F	M	P	U	L	G	S	V	A	E	R	K	B	O	X	Z	H	I
x	Z	F	K	W	X	P	E	G	L	Y	I	Q	H	D	B	S	R	T	P	N	A	C	U	J	O	J
c	G	P	E	C	Y	R	H	Q	X	O	W	J	F	N	D	T	Z	Y	M	S	V	I	K	A	K	U
v	Y	R	V	X	T	J	W	C	A	E	K	G	M	F	Z	U	X	L	D	B	O	P	S	P	I	H
b	T	B	C	Z	K	E	V	S	R	P	H	L	G	U	I	C	Q	F	N	A	Y	D	Y	O	J	X
n	N	V	U	P	R	B	D	T	Y	J	Q	H	I	O	V	W	G	M	S	X	F	X	A	K	C	Z
m	B	I	Y	T	N	F	Z	X	K	W	J	O	A	B	E	H	L	D	C	G	C	S	P	V	U	M
l	O	X	Z	M	G	U	C	P	E	K	A	S	N	R	J	Q	F	V	H	V	D	Y	B	I	L	N

Rotor positions

It will be observed that the letters in all the diagonals running from top right to bottom left in the table follow the order of the cyclic sequence of the letters on the entry disc, i.e. Q, W, E, R, T, Z, U … B, N, M, L. This phenomenon can be explained by considering a particular case. The table shows that at the 15th position of the rotor, contact 'Z' on the entry disc is directly connected to the contact 'v' on the imaginary disc. Suppose that the RH rotor rotates forwards (i.e. anti-clockwise when viewed from the right-hand side) by one position at a time to give the sequence of positions 15, 16, 17, 18, 19, 20, 21 etc., while the contact selected on the fixed entry disc is changed 'backwards' (i.e. also anti-clockwise) by one position at a time, giving the corresponding sequence of contacts: Z, T, R, E, W, Q, L, M, N… The combination of these two actions will, on each occasion, cause the electrical signal to be conveyed to the same contact on the right-hand face of the RH rotor, and hence to a particular contact on its left-hand face.

As this rotor is advancing by one position each time, this particular left-hand contact will move backwards (anti-clockwise) relative to the fixed contact points on the imaginary disc, giving the sequence of contact points v, c, x, y, p, k, j… on it. This behaviour is illustrated in the following diagram, and confirms that the patterns in the diagonals in the rod square table consist of letter sequences running top right to bottom left, in the same order as those for the contacts on the RH side of the entry disc, i.e. Q, W, E, R, T, Z, U…

	15	16	17	18	19	20	21
j							L
k						Q	
p					W		
y				E			
x			R				
c		T					
v	Z						

Contact points on the imaginary disc

Rotor positions

The rods

A set of twenty-six rods is made up from the individual rows of a rod-square table. Originally three sets would have been needed, one for each of the three rotors used in the machine. These sets were colour coded to avoid confusion.

	1	2	3	4	5	6	7	8	9	10	11	12	13	14	15	16	17	18	19	20	21	22	23	24	25	26
q	C	U	L	H	I	V	Y	R	P	S	D	M	T	K	W	G	B	J	B	F	X	N	O	Q	M	A
u	M	A	N	K	P	T	S	B	I	X	E	V	E	Y	L	R	H	U	T	J	Q	F	Z	C	G	W

Two examples are shown with a pair of rods (for 'rotor I') aligned side by side. The 1st rod shows that for the succession of RH rotor positions 1, 2, 3, 4, 5, 6 ... 26, the corresponding sequence of contacts on the entry disc, C, U, L, H, I, V, Y, R, ... M, A, are all connected to contact 'q' on the imaginary disc. Likewise the 2nd rod shows that for the same succession of rotor positions the corresponding sequence of contacts on the entry disc, M, A, N, K, P, T, S, B, ... G, W, are all connected to contact 'u'.

Suppose that the letter V from a cipher message is known to represent the plain-text letter T, and that this occurs when the RH rotor is at its 6th position. Then it follows as a consequence of the reciprocal relationship between the two letters V and T, (each being the encipherment of the other), that the two terminals 'q' and 'u' on the imaginary disc must be electrically connected together through the remaining components of the Enigma machine. The letters q and u are known as the 'rod coupling' letters, and the diagram shows the pair of rods 'q' and 'u' coupled together side by side with the pair of letters (V, T) at position 6. Now suppose that the third letter of the cipher message happens to be B (appearing at the 8th position on the second rod), then as a result of the same rod coupling it should be evident that the corresponding plain-text letter must be R. Thus by means of the rods one known letter of the plain text crib has enabled an additional letter to be deduced. The validity of this deduction is, however, dependent on two conditions:

1. That the pair of rods is taken from the correct set for the RH rotor originally used.
2. That a middle rotor 'turnover' (TO) has not occurred between the 6th and 8th positions in the cipher.

The application of this useful property of the rods can be extended. A general description of the procedure is hard to formulate, but an understanding can be obtained by means of an illustrative practical example. A message was enciphered on the 'Railway' Enigma machine (which has an adjustable reflector) configured in the following way: rotor order 3, 2, 1; ring settings 'ZZZZ'; reflector setting 'F'; rotor settings 'LCZ'. The cipher message obtained was as follows:

MLXVK SCLDU HOHSV FKXKU SDVRP NGCYA T
(31 characters)

A description follows showing how the process of 'rodding' can be used to recover the plain text, given the accurate starting crib 'CODEX' (X was commonly used as a 'space' mark).

The procedure would originally have begun with the lengthy task of trying in turn each of the three possible rotors that might have occupied the RH location in the machine together with its possible initial position (there are up to $3 \times 26 = 78$ possible configurations to try). Each could be tested by finding the corresponding set of pairs of rod couplings and checking them for inconsistencies (i.e. no two to contain a common letter). If, for a particular combination of rotor and initial position, no inconsistencies occurred in the set of rod couplings derived from the crib, then there was a good chance that it was the correct combination. (Much time and effort would have been required to find the correct combination by this process of elimination.)

In the demonstration example this protracted task (and another described later on) has been avoided (dishonestly!) by the prior knowledge of the Enigma configuration used. (In reality 'rodding' must have been an extremely tedious process, requiring great patience as well as skill.) The crib and cipher provide the following pairs of reciprocal characters (bigrams):

$$(M\ C)\ (L\ O)\ (X\ D)\ (V\ E)\ (K\ X)$$

The five corresponding pairs of rod couplings (shown in the following table) for rotor I, starting in its 1st position, are (u q) (t s) (o y) (r k) (b x), and there are no inconsistencies between them.

Using the rods for Rotor I starting at its 1st position, the five pairs of coupled rods arising from the crib are shown. These rod pairs contain the bigrams obtained from the crib and cipher characters, but in addition, outside the range of the crib, there are some places where a letter on one of the rods matches a letter in the cipher, and at these places the letter on the other rod provides an additional character of the plain text (assuming that no prior middle rotor TO has taken place) These pairs of letters are shown in the diagrams in bold type.

	1	2	3	4	5	6	7	8	9	10	11	12	13	14	15	16	17	18	19	20	21	22	23	24	25	26	27	28	29	30	31
	M	L	X	V	K	S	C	L	D	U	H	O	H	S	V	F	K	X	K	U	S	D	V	R	P	N	G	C	Y	A	T
	C	O	D	E	X																										
u	M	A	N	K	P	T	S	B	I	X	E	V	E	Y	L	R	H	U	T	J	Q	F	Z	C	G	W					
q	C	U	L	H	I	V	Y	R	P	S	D	M	T	K	W	G	B	J	B	F	X	N	O	Q	M	A					
t	D	L	B	I	V	H	J	*E*	O	C	Z	P	Q	*X*	Q	K	N	W	F	T	E	G	M	S	R	Y					
s	V	O	H	Q	D	N	U	*L*	U	B	R	I	Y	*S*	O	X	T	K	A	M	P	Z	E	G	W	C					
o	L	Y	X	U	F	M	A	V	T	N	T	C	W	Z	K	O	U	P	E	H	I	B	J	*R*	Q	D					
y	H	T	D	J	Q	Y	K	W	F	M	P	U	L	G	S	V	A	E	R	K	B	O	X	*Z*	H	I					
r	P	S	M	V	U	C	G	H	W	I	X	T	K	L	Y	L	J	*B*	Q	D	R	W	F	N	*A*	E					
k	F	Z	F	E	A	G	M	K	H	L	S	B	J	T	N	D	O	*X*	I	Q	W	H	C	U	*P*	R					
b	T	B	C	Z	K	E	V	S	R	P	*H*	L	*G*	U	I	C	Q	F	N	A	Y	*D*	Y	O	J	X					
x	Z	F	K	W	X	P	E	G	L	Y	*I*	Q	*H*	D	B	S	R	T	P	N	A	*C*	U	J	O	J					
	C	O	D	E	X		E			I	G	X			B			C	Z	A											

The eight-letter word '??E??I?G' in the partially recovered plain text between the two 'space' characters (X) very probably ends with 'ING', and taking into account the crib 'CODE', it is realistic to assume that this word is probably 'BREAKING'. (This is an example of the type of linguistic assumption that had to be made.)

The probable extension of the plain text arising from this assumption leads to the following new bigrams and rod couplings shown below:

- At the 6th place, (S B) gives rod couplings (a n), providing the bigram (A V) at the 15th place.
- At the 7th place, (C R) gives rod couplings (l z), confirming the bigram (U K) at the 10th place.
- At the 9th place, (D A) gives rod couplings (w v), providing the bigram (K X) at the 17th place.
- At the 12th place, (O N) gives rod couplings (m h), which provides no useful results.

The new pairs of rods giving additional information are shown below.

	1	2	3	4	5	6	7	8	9	10	11	12	13	14	15	16	17	18	19	20	21	22	23	24	25	26	27	28	29	30	31
	M	L	X	V	K	S	C	L	D	U	H	O	H	S	V	F	K	X	K	U	S	D	V	R	P	N	G	C	Y	A	T
	C	O	D	E	X	B	R	E	A	K	I	N	G	X			B					C		Z	A						
a	X	C	I	G	L	S	B	Z	M	Z	V	E	U	P	*A*	I	Y	R	J	O	N	K	T	W	F	Q					
n	N	V	U	P	R	B	D	T	Y	J	Q	H	I	O	*V*	W	G	M	S	X	F	X	A	K	C	Z					
l	O	X	Z	M	G	U	C	P	E	*K*	A	S	N	R	J	Q	F	V	H	V	D	Y	B	I	L	N					
z	Q	N	O	B	J	K	R	A	V	*U*	Y	W	C	W	P	M	E	G	Z	R	H	L	D	T	X	F					
w	I	Q	J	O	B	X	T	Y	D	F	L	Z	P	E	H	N	*K*	N	G	C	M	A	W	L	S	V					
v	Y	R	V	X	T	J	W	C	A	E	K	G	M	F	Z	U	*X*	L	D	B	O	P	S	P	I	H					
	C	O	D	E	X	B	R	E	A	K	I	N	G	X	A		X	B				C		Z	A						
	C	O	D	E	X	B	R	E	A	K	I	N	G	X	A		X	B				C		Z	A						

The message has now become 'C O D E X B R E A K I N G X A ? X B ? ? ? C ? Z A'. The conjecture 'C O D E X B R E A K I N G X A T X B L E T C H L E Y' might seem to be a possibility but there is a clash at the 24th and 25th places in the cipher with the pair of letters Z and A given earlier by the rods. However, their advanced locations in the cipher make it probable that a TO of the RH rotor will have occurred before the 24th place, and that consequently these letters are incorrect. Taking into account that the letter C at the 22nd place appears to be correct, it seems likely that a middle rotor TO has occurred either between the 22nd and 23rd or between the 23rd and 24th places in the cipher. Assuming the conjecture 'ATXBLETCHLEY' to be correct then up to the 23rd place in the cipher the following new bigrams appear: (F T), (K L), (U E), (S T) and (V H). However only (K L) at the 19th position, with the rod coupling (i d), gives a useful result by providing the valuable confirmation of the letter pair (V H) at the 23rd position, thus indicating that the TO almost certainly must occur between the 23rd and 24th positions. This rod coupling is shown below.

	1	2	3	4	5	6	7	8	9	10	11	12	13	14	15	16	17	18	19	20	21	22	23	24	25	26	27	28	29	30	31
	M	L	X	V	K	S	C	L	D	U	H	O	H	S	V	F	K	X	K	U	S	D	V	R	P	N	G	**C**	**Y**	**A**	**T**
	C	O	D	E	X																										
	C	O	D	E	X	B	R	E	A	K	I	N	G	X	A		X	B				C		Z	A						
	C	O	D	E	X	B	R	E	A	K	I	N	G	X	A	T	X	B	L	E	T	C	H	L	E	Y					
i	S	M	P	Y	Z	D	N		C	R	B	R	X	Q	T	J	I	Z	K	W	G	U	*V*	H	E	L					
d	A	J	W	F	M	I	Q	I	N	T	O	X	D	A	C	Z	P	S	L	Y	U	R	*H*	E	V	B					
	C	O	D	E	X	B	R	E	A	K	I	N	G	X	A	T	X	B	L	E	T	C	H	L	E	Y					

The message now appears to be 'C O D E X B R E A K I N G X A T X B L E T C H L E Y ? ? ? ? ?' (with a middle rotor TO taking place between the letters H and L).

Dealing with a turnover of the middle rotor

The next stage of the work requires an understanding of the effect of a middle rotor TO, which will change the rod coupling letter pairs in the way shown in the following diagrams.

The first diagram (Fig. 1) shows the pair of contacts (α and β) on the imaginary disc connected to the pair of contacts 'P' and 'Q' on the entry disc through the RH rotor, before the middle rotor TO has taken place. The second diagram (Fig. 2) shows how two contacts (δ and γ) on the LH rotor are connected to the pair of contacts (α β) on the imaginary disc through the middle rotor, before the TO. The third diagram (Fig. 3) shows how the same two contacts (δ and γ) are connected to the pair of contacts ($\alpha 1$ $\beta 1$) on the imaginary disc through the middle rotor after the TO.

The diagrams show that both of the pairs of contacts (α β) and ($\alpha 1$ $\beta 1$) on the imaginary disc are connected to the contacts (δ γ) through the middle rotor, in just the same way as the contacts (P and Q) on the entry disc are connected to the contacts (α β) through the RH rotor. This means that the correct relationships between the contacts (α β), ($\alpha 1$ $\beta 1$) and (δ γ) will appear in the rod square table for the middle rotor, as shown in the following diagram.

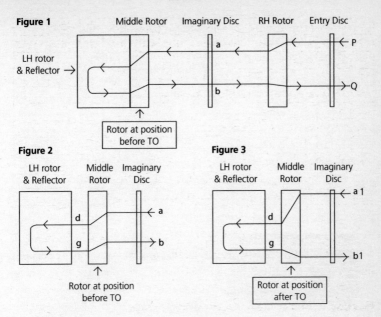

Figure 1

Middle Rotor   Imaginary Disc   RH Rotor   Entry Disc

LH rotor & Reflector →

Rotor at position before TO

Figure 2

LH rotor & Reflector   Middle Rotor   Imaginary Disc

Rotor at position before TO

Figure 3

LH rotor & Reflector   Middle Rotor   Imaginary Disc

Rotor at position after TO

It follows that the correct rod square table for the middle rotor will contain a pair of adjacent columns (i.e. those corresponding to the 'pre' and 'post' middle rotor TO positions) that will satisfy the following conditions:

1. One pair of corresponding cells in these two columns will contain the two elements α and α1.
2. A second pair of corresponding positions in the same columns will contain the two elements β and β1.
3. The positions of these two adjacent columns in the table will give the 'pre' and 'post' TO positions of the middle rotor.

(As the upper case letters in the rod square tables are now being used to represent contacts on the imaginary disc, these entries in the table must be changed (mentally) to their lower case forms.)

The diagram shows that once the rod square has been correctly identified, and its original setting (s1) has been found, then any rod coupling (α β) found before the TO can be used to find the corresponding rod couplings (α1 β1) after the TO and vice-versa.

Part of the rod square for the middle rotor

	1	2	3		s1 (pre-TO)	s2 (post-TO)		
q								
w								
δ					α	α1		
γ					β	β1		

A procedure for identifying the middle rotor (from the two remaining ones), together with its position before the TO, is as follows. First consider the following bigrams that must occur after the TO:

- At the 24th position, bigram (R L) gives the rod coupling (o w).
- At the 25th position, bigram (P E) gives the rod coupling (k i).
- At the 26th position, bigram (N Y) gives the rod coupling (l t).

(None of these couplings happen to provide any additional letters of the plain text.)

An important point is that these couplings must correspond to others that were valid before the TO had occurred, and which could be found from the appropriate column of the rod square table for the correct middle rotor, provided that the TO position of this rotor were known.

If assumptions are made for both the identity of the middle rotor and its starting position, then the appropriate two columns of the rod square table for this rotor can be used to find a set of corresponding 'pre-TO' rod couplings from the known 'post-TO' couplings given above. If, however, either of these assumptions are wrong, then it is very likely that logical inconsistencies will occur between these and the original 'pre-TO' couplings previously found, and when this happens two or more of the couplings will have a letter in common. Otherwise the couplings need to be checked to see if they give 'promising' letters of plain text when set up against the cipher. Originally a tedious process of elimination (involving up to 2 × 26 = 52 trials) would have been necessary to find the correct combination of assumptions. To see how this works in practice remember that the pre-TO rod couplings enumerated earlier were (u q), (t s), (o y),(r k), (b x), (a n), (l z), (w v), (m h) and (i d).

Rod square for rotor II

	1	2	3	4	5	6	7	8	9	10	11	12	13	14	15	16	17	18	19	20	21	22	23	24	25	26
q	Z	S	**D**	**J**	Q	Y	K	I	T	M	U	N	G	X	H	A	C	F	O	W	V	H	L	B	R	Y
w	D	F	**K**	**W**	X	P	O	Z	L	I	M	H	C	J	S	V	G	A	E	B	J	Q	N	T	X	U
e	G	P	**E**	**C**	Y	A	U	Q	O	L	J	V	K	D	B	H	S	R	N	K	W	M	Z	C	I	F
r	Y	R	**V**	**X**	S	I	W	A	Q	K	B	P	F	N	J	D	T	M	P	E	L	U	V	O	G	H
t	T	B	**C**	**D**	O	E	S	W	P	N	Y	G	M	K	F	Z	L	Y	R	Q	I	B	A	H	J	X
z	N	V	**F**	**A**	R	D	E	Y	M	X	H	L	P	G	U	Q	X	T	W	O	N	S	J	K	C	Z
u	B	G	**S**	**T**	F	R	X	L	C	J	Q	Y	H	I	W	C	Z	E	A	M	D	K	P	V	U	M
i	H	D	**Z**	**G**	T	C	Q	V	K	W	X	J	O	E	V	U	R	S	L	F	P	Y	B	I	L	N
o	F	U	**H**	**Z**	V	W	B	P	E	C	K	A	R	B	I	T	D	Q	G	Y	X	N	O	Q	M	J
a	I	J	**U**	**B**	E	N	Y	R	V	P	S	T	N	O	Z	F	W	H	X	C	M	A	W	L	K	G
s	K	I	**N**	**R**	M	X	T	B	Y	D	Z	M	A	U	G	E	J	C	V	L	S	E	Q	P	H	O
d	O	M	**T**	**L**	C	Z	N	X	F	U	L	S	I	H	R	K	V	B	Q	D	R	W	Y	J	A	P
f	L	Z	**Q**	**V**	U	M	C	G	I	Q	D	O	J	T	P	B	N	W	F	T	E	X	K	S	Y	A
g	U	W	**B**	**I**	L	V	H	O	W	F	A	K	Z	Y	N	M	E	G	Z	R	C	P	D	X	S	Q
h	E	N	**O**	**Q**	B	J	A	E	G	S	P	U	X	M	L	R	H	U	T	V	Y	F	C	D	W	I
j	M	A	**W**	**N**	K	S	R	H	D	Y	I	C	L	Q	T	J	I	Z	B	X	G	V	F	E	O	R
k	S	E	**M**	**P**	D	T	J	F	X	O	V	Q	W	Z	K	O	U	N	C	H	B	G	R	A	T	L
p	R	L	**Y**	**F**	Z	K	G	C	A	B	W	E	U	P	A	I	M	V	J	N	H	T	S	Z	Q	D
y	Q	X	**G**	**U**	P	H	V	S	N	E	R	I	Y	S	O	L	B	K	M	J	Z	D	U	W	F	T
x	C	H	**I**	**Y**	J	B	D	M	R	T	O	X	D	A	Q	N	P	L	K	U	F	I	E	G	Z	W
c	J	O	**X**	**K**	N	F	L	T	Z	A	C	F	S	W	M	Y	Q	P	I	G	O	R	H	U	E	V
v	A	C	**P**	**M**	G	Q	Z	U	S	V	G	D	E	L	X	W	Y	O	H	A	T	J	I	R	B	K
b	V	Y	**L**	**H**	W	U	I	D	B	H	F	R	Q	C	E	X	A	J	S	Z	K	O	T	N	P	S
n	X	Q	**J**	**E**	I	O	F	N	J	G	T	W	V	R	C	S	K	D	U	P	A	Z	M	Y	D	B
m	W	K	**R**	**O**	A	G	M	K	H	Z	E	B	T	V	D	P	F	I	Y	S	U	L	X	F	N	C
l	P	T	**A**	**S**	H	L	P	J	U	R	N	Z	B	F	Y	G	O	X	D	I	Q	C	G	M	V	E

If the middle rotor is assumed to be rotor II, initially set to its 1st position, then from the 1st and 2nd columns of this rod square, the three post-TO rod couplings (o w), (k i) and (l t) are found to have the corresponding pre-TO couplings (j u), (w k), and (r p). Comparing these with the list of couplings given above, it can be seen that all three are inconsistent, (for example the couplings (u q) and (j u) are contradictory); this implies that at least one of the initial assumptions must be wrong.

If the setting of the assumed middle rotor (still rotor II) is changed to position 3, then the 3rd and 4th columns of the rod square table give the corresponding pre-TO couplings (r k), (b x) and (t s). As each of these appears on the original list of couplings, there are no inconsistencies, and consequently the two assumptions (i.e. that the middle rotor is rotor II and that it was set to the 3rd position) are probably correct. The rod pairs for these couplings also confirm some of the bigrams found previously, thus providing further evidence that these assumptions are the correct ones. By using the 3rd and 4th columns in the rod square in the reverse order, the remaining original rod couplings can be used to find their corresponding post-TO couplings, and two of them providing additional information are (u q) → (b v) and (l z) → (h g).

The new rod coupling (b v) gives at the 31st place the bigram (K T), and the new coupling (h g) gives at the 30th place the bigram (R A).

1	2	3	4	5	6	7	8	9	10	11	12	13	14	15	16	17	18	19	20	21	22	23	24	25	26	27	28	29	30	31	
M	L	X	V	K	S	C	L	D	U	H	O	H	S	V	F	K	X	K	U	S	D	V	R	P	N	G	C	Y	A	T	
C	O	D	E	X	B	R	E	A	K	I	N	G	X	A		X	B			C		Z	A								
C	O	D	E	X	B	R	E	A	K	I	N	G	X	A	T	X	B	L	E	T	C	H	L	E	Y						
																									b	T	B	C	Z	*K*	E
																									v	Y	R	V	X	*T*	J
																									h	J	W	S	*R*	S	Q
																									g	R	H	Q	*A*	E	A
C	O	D	E	X	B	R	E	A	K	I	N	G	X	A	T	X	B	L	E	T	C	H	L	E	Y				R	K	
C	O	D	E	X	B	R	E	A	K	I	N	G	X	A	T	X	B	L	E	T	C	H	L	E	Y	X	P	A	R	K	

The two additional bigrams give the plain text letters R and K, so that the plain text becomes 'C O D E X B R E A K I N G X A T X B L E T C H L E Y ? ? ? R K', credibly leading to the message:

C O D E X B R E A K I N G X A T X B L E T C H L E Y X P A R K

Concluding remarks

In addition to the meticulous care that would have been necessary during the elimination procedures described above, the wartime successes required considerable linguistic ability and creative imagination. It was often necessary to make correct inferences about the context of messages expressed in German or Italian, based only on the fragmentary evidence of some of the letters contained in them.

If the reader does not consider the deductions made in this example to be plausible, it is suggested that a visit to the exhibition at BP might be of interest, as some of the deductions actually made during the breaking of a genuine cipher message on display are quite surprising and show that much higher levels of skill and imagination were required for success than are suggested by the somewhat contrived example given above.

A brief historical post-script

The following short summary on how the first break was made in 1940 may give the reader some insight into the difficulties encountered at the time.

When the Italians entered the war in June 1940, it was thought likely that their navy might still be operating the same type of Enigma machine as they had used at the time of the Spanish Civil War, and the attempts to break their ciphers were based on this assumption. For the technique of 'rodding' to succeed it was essential to have accurate cribs, and initially a serious difficulty was the lack of knowledge about the stereotyped forms of text that were likely to occur in the Italian messages.

In the absence of anything more specific, Dilly Knox instructed his assistants (a group of young women known as 'Dilly's girls') to use 'PERX' as a crib for the first four characters of each intercepted signal (= 'FOR' followed by a 'space') and, for those cases when this did not lead to any inconsistencies between the crib and the first four letters of a cipher message, to record any other letters that could be found by the rods in the hope that these might provide some clues about the plain text.

These assistants worked continuously for three months at this task without having any success until September 1940, when one of them, Mavis Lever, a nineteen-year-old student whose university course had been interrupted by the war, achieved a remarkable break. With the message on which she was then working, for a particular starting position for the 'green' rotor (i.e. rotor I), the rods had given the letter S in the 4th place, which clashed with the letter X in the crib (i.e. resulting in the letter sequence 'PERS' instead of 'PERX', as was anticipated).

If Miss Lever had obeyed her instructions, she would have rejected this rotor starting position and gone on to try the next one. However in a moment of inspiration she decided to assume that the crib 'PERX' was in fact wrong and guessed that it was 'PERSONALE'. After making this assumption and continuing with the 'rodding' process, she was gratified to find that the additional letters of plain text then given by the rods made good sense, so that the first part of the message turned out to be 'P E R S O N A L E X P E R X S I G N O R X...' (X = 'space'). (More information on how this was done is to be found in the exhibition.)

This was a most remarkable and valuable achievement, as it proved (after three months' effort!) that the Italians were indeed still using the same early version of the Enigma machine. From this message and others, which were subsequently broken, a vocabulary of useful cribs was built up which greatly increased the effectiveness (and speed) of the 'rodding' technique.

Frank Carter

Appendix 3

'Buttoning-up'

(A method for recovering the wiring of the rotors used in an un-Steckered Enigma)

The description in Appendix 2 of the codebreaking technique known as 'rodding' shows how the rod square tables for the Enigma rotors were used to make the required sets of rods. However, before a particular table could be constructed it was first necessary to determine the complete sequence of letters in the left-hand column of the table, known as the 1st upright. From this upright it was then possible to construct the entire table, and also find the internal wiring of the corresponding rotor.

Clearly the establishment of a procedure for finding the 1st upright was of fundamental importance, and in the following notes an account is given of the one originally devised by the veteran codebreaker 'Dilly' Knox. These include an illustrative example to demonstrate the effectiveness of the procedure, which involved a process referred to by Knox as 'buttoning-up'.

In order to understand what is to follow, it is essential to have read the notes on 'rodding' in Appendix 2.

During the Spanish Civil War the Italian navy made some use of the commercial Enigma machine but with differently wired rotors, and it was in 1937 that Knox recovered the internal wiring of these. The so-called 'Railway' Enigma has the same basic structure as the machine used by the Italians, and as a computer emulation of it happens to be available, it has been used instead of the Italian machine, to generate the cipher messages used in these notes.

Rod square for Rotor I

	1	2	3	4	5	6	7	8	9	10	11	12	13	14	15	16	17	18	19	20	21	22	23	24	25	26
q	C	U	L	H	I	V	Y	R	P	S	D	M	T	K	W	G	B	J	B	F	X	N	O	Q	M	A
w	I	Q	J	O	B	X	T	Y	D	F	L	Z	P	E	H	N	K	N	G	C	M	A	W	L	S	V
e	W	K	A	N	C	Z	X	F	G	Q	U	Y	R	J	M	P	M	H	V	L	S	E	Q	D	B	O
r	P	S	M	V	U	C	G	H	W	I	X	T	K	L	Y	L	J	B	Q	D	R	W	F	N	A	E
t	D	L	B	I	V	H	J	E	O	C	Z	P	Q	X	Q	K	N	W	F	T	E	G	M	S	R	Y
z	Q	N	O	B	J	K	R	A	V	U	Y	W	C	W	P	M	E	G	Z	R	H	L	D	T	X	F
u	M	A	N	K	P	T	S	B	I	X	E	V	E	Y	L	R	H	U	T	J	Q	F	Z	C	G	W
i	S	M	P	Y	Z	D	N	O	C	R	B	R	X	Q	T	J	I	Z	K	W	G	U	V	H	E	L
o	L	Y	X	U	F	M	A	V	T	N	T	C	W	Z	K	O	U	P	E	H	I	B	J	R	Q	D
a	X	C	I	G	L	S	B	Z	M	Z	V	E	U	P	A	I	Y	R	J	O	N	K	T	W	F	Q
s	V	O	H	Q	D	N	U	L	U	B	R	I	Y	S	O	X	T	K	A	M	P	Z	E	G	W	C
d	A	J	W	F	M	I	Q	I	N	T	O	X	D	A	C	Z	P	S	L	Y	U	R	H	E	V	B
f	K	E	G	L	O	W	O	M	Z	A	C	F	S	V	U	Y	D	Q	X	I	T	J	R	B	N	S
g	R	H	Q	A	E	A	L	U	S	V	G	D	B	I	X	F	W	C	O	Z	K	T	N	M	D	P
h	J	W	S	R	S	Q	I	D	B	H	F	N	O	C	G	E	V	A	U	P	Z	M	L	F	Y	T
j	E	D	T	D	W	O	F	N	J	G	M	A	V	H	R	B	S	I	Y	U	L	Q	G	X	Z	K
k	F	Z	F	E	A	G	M	K	H	L	S	B	J	T	N	D	O	X	I	Q	W	H	C	U	P	R
p	U	G	R	S	H	L	P	J	Q	D	N	K	Z	M	F	A	C	O	W	E	J	V	I	Y	T	G
y	H	T	D	J	Q	Y	K	W	F	M	P	U	L	G	S	V	A	E	R	K	B	O	X	Z	H	I
x	Z	F	K	W	X	P	E	G	L	Y	I	Q	H	D	B	S	R	T	P	N	A	C	U	J	O	J
c	G	P	E	C	Y	R	H	Q	X	O	W	J	F	N	D	T	Z	Y	M	S	V	I	K	A	K	U
v	Y	R	V	X	T	J	W	C	A	E	K	G	M	F	Z	U	X	L	D	B	O	P	S	P	I	H
b	T	B	C	Z	K	E	V	S	R	P	H	L	G	U	I	C	Q	F	N	A	Y	D	Y	O	J	X
n	N	V	U	P	R	B	D	T	Y	J	Q	H	I	O	V	W	G	M	S	X	F	X	A	K	C	Z
m	B	I	Y	T	N	F	Z	X	K	W	J	O	A	B	E	H	L	D	C	G	C	S	P	V	U	M
l	O	X	Z	M	G	U	C	P	E	K	A	S	N	R	J	Q	F	V	H	V	D	Y	B	I	L	N

Both of these versions of the Enigma machine (which did not have plugboards) had an entry disc on which the electrical contacts were connected to the keyboard in the sequence QWERTZUIOASDFGHJKPYXCVBNML (in a clockwise sense when viewed from the right-hand side of the machine). As a logical consequence of this, the letters in all the diagonals (from top right to bottom left) of the rod squares form cyclic sequences of letters in the order shown above. As described elsewhere, a set of rods was based on the strips formed by dividing the corresponding rod square into its 26 individual horizontal rows.

The basis of the method that Knox employed to find the 1st upright from a rod square depended upon the property of the diagonals in the rod squares described above, and on the way in which the rods were to be used to decipher messages. Initially of course the details of both the rod squares and the individual rods would not have been known.

The 'rod square' table for Rotor I from the 'Railway' Enigma is shown opposite, and it will be observed that the letter sequences in the diagonals in the table (top right–bottom left) do conform to the cyclic QWERTZU... sequences previously described.

Two of the rods formed by individual rows from this table are shown below side by side, and above them a short sequence of letters from a message in cipher (it is supposed that the rods are correctly aligned with the cipher and are paired through the machine as described in the notes on 'rodding' in Appendix 2).

```
  Q G A N P Y C F Y M H
```

e	W	K	A	N	C	Z	X	F	G	Q	U	Y	R	J	M	P	M	H	V	L	S	E	Q	D	B	O
z	Q	N	O	B	J	K	R	A	V	U	Y	W	C	W	P	M	E	G	Z	R	H	L	D	T	X	F

```
  W ? O B ? ? ? ? A ? ? ?
```

The four letters from the message that have been deciphered by the rods are W, O, B and A. Note that two adjacent letters in the cipher message (A and N) happen to be the same as a pair of adjacent letters on the upper rod, and this leads to the corresponding pair of adjacent letters O and B on the lower one. A pair of adjacent letters on the same rod was referred to by Knox as a 'beetle', so that the letter pair AN is one example of a beetle and the letter pair OB is another.

If in a cipher message two successive letters form a beetle in the correct rod position, the corresponding deciphered letters will form a beetle on another rod.

In their original fixed locations in the rod square it is unlikely that the two rods will be in adjacent rows, and usually they will be separated from each other by an unknown number of other rows, as is the case for the pair of rods in the example. These are shown in their true locations in the following diagram, which only illustrates the relevant part of the rod square.

The two corresponding rows from the rod square (beetles outlined)

	1	2	3	4	5	6	7	8	9	10	11	12	13	14	15	16	17	18	19	20	21	22	23	24	25	26
q																										
w																										
e	W	K	A	N	C	Z	X	F	G	Q	U	Y	R	J	M	P	M	H	V	L	S	E	Q	D	B	O
r																										
t																										
z	Q	N	O	B	J	K	R	A	V	U	Y	W	C	W	P	M	E	G	Z	R	H	L	D	T	X	F
u																										
i																										

The diagonals in this rod square will have the invariant property previously described, namely that the letters in each diagonal always conform to the cyclic sequence based on the letter order of the terminals on the entry disc. For the version of Enigma machine being used here, as already noted the letters in each diagonal reading from top right to bottom left are in the cyclic sequence QWERTZUIOASDFGHJKPYXCVBNML. Using this information it is possible to insert additional letters into the cells of the diagonals, to the left and below each of the beetles shown in the following diagram, which conform to this cyclic sequence. (Some additional empty rows have been introduced into the diagram in order to avoid overlaps between these additional letters.) This provides a useful starting point for an explanation of the procedure used to recover the letter sequence forming the 1st upright in a rod square.

W	K	A	N	C	Z	X	F	G	Q	U	Y	R	J	M	P	M	H	V	L	S	E	Q	D	B	O
	S	M																							
D	L																								
Q																									
Q	N	O	B	J	K	R	A	V	U	Y	W	C	W	P	M	E	G	Z	R	H	L	D	T	X	F
	A	N																							
S	M																								
L																									

Consider the above diagram from a point of view in which there is no prior knowledge about the structure of the upright, but it is known that the two 'Enigma alphabet' letter pairs (AO) and (NB) occur at the 3rd and 4th positions in the message (i.e. A would encipher as O at the 3rd position, and N would encipher as B at the 4th position). The sequences of letters in the two 'descending' diagonals from the two letters A and N are respectively ASD and NMLQ, and likewise the two 'descending' diagonals from the pair of letters O and B are respectively OAS and BNML. It will be observed that as a consequence of these sequences, the 1st upright contains the two pairs of adjacent letters DQ and SL.

Alternatively from another point of view if it is assumed that the 1st upright contains the letter pair DQ, then the existence of the two alphabet letter pairs AO and NB jointly leads to the conclusion that the 1st upright will also contain the letter pair SL.

This conclusion can also be established by the use of the following procedure:

- The two letters A and O at the 3rd position are replaced by the corresponding two letters D and S at the 1st position in their 'descending' diagonals.

- Likewise the two letters N and B at the 4th position are replaced by the corresponding letters Q and L at the 1st position in their descending diagonals.

In this way the two Enigma letter pairs AO and NB are replaced by two new letter pairs, DS and QL. (This is the process that was originally referred to by Dilly Knox as 'buttoning-up'.) The new letter pairs DS and QL lead directly to the two deductions D→S and Q→L, which when considered jointly give the same result as before (i.e. that if the 1st upright contains the letter pair DQ, it must also contain the letter pair SL). This procedure is illustrated in the diagram and tables below.

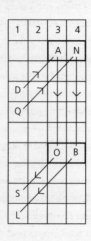

Enigma letter pairs occurring at the designated positions

-1	2	3	4
		A O	
			N B

corresponding pairs of 'buttoned up' letters in the 1st column

1	2	3	4
		D S	
			Q L

The final conclusion can be obtained directly from the table containing the pairs of 'buttoned-up' letters, without any reference to the diagram. In general, once such a table has been constructed from a number of Enigma letter pairs, it can be used to derive the deductions for adjacent letter pairs in the 1st upright without any further reference to the sequences of letters in the diagonals.

The process of buttoning-up is carried out by using the diagonal sequence QWERTZUIOASDFGHJKPYXCVBNML. For example suppose that letter X from an Enigma pair occurs at the 6th position. Then, beginning at X in the above sequence, a displacement of five positions down the diagonal (from right to left) will lead to M, the corresponding 'buttoned-up' letter at the 1st position. If instead the given letter from an Enigma pair happened to be N then a displacement of five positions down the diagonal will lead to the 'buttoned-up' letter E (a consequence of the cyclic nature of the diagonal sequence).

In order to apply this process usefully, it is first necessary to discover a number of Enigma alphabet letter pairs for about six consecutive positions of the Enigma rotors. (An analysis by Alan Turing showed that roughly around 100 Enigma alphabet letter pairs are required.) All of the letters in the alphabet pairs are then 'buttoned up' and by means of them, an initial assumption about the identity of one pair of adjacent letters on the 1st upright can be used to make logical conclusions about other adjacent letter pairs, which in turn can then be used as the basis for further similar conclusions. If the initial assumption happens to be false, then this will soon become evident, as logical contradictions will arise between some of the outcomes.

These ideas lead to a procedure in which a sequence of possible initial assumptions are tested one by one, until a correct assumption is found that does not lead to any inconsistent conclusions and indeed is very likely to generate some confirmatory (repeated) ones.

Success in the task of identifying Enigma alphabet letter pairs depends upon finding cribs for the intercepted cipher messages. The precise pre-war circumstances that enabled Knox and his colleagues to obtain a sufficient number of these letter pairs are not known, but it is believed that during the Spanish Civil War the Italian navy sometimes transmitted signals that had been enciphered with the same Enigma configuration. Provided that a sufficient number of these had been intercepted and identified, they would have provided a set of messages 'in depth', enabling the task in hand to be successfully completed.

Given such a set of messages in depth, and starting with one or two cribs based on likely words, it is possible to find cribs for the others by using the reciprocal rule imposed on Enigma encipherments, and also applying some of the skills of a solver of crosswords. Once this task has been completed, then from the resulting Enigma alphabet letter pairs, the 1st upright in the rod square table can be found, this in turn leading to the wiring of the corresponding rotor.

The following contrived list of clear texts and enciphered texts will be used as a basis for a practical illustrative example of the task of finding the 1st upright in a rod square. (A number of these were composed by someone with real wartime experience of this type of work, and are reminders of episodes from the past that were in some way related to cryptology.)

1	**E**	N	**E**	**M**	Y	X	S	I	**G**	**H**	T	E	**D**
	U	X	Q	B	E	J	Y	O	Z	W	P	H	X
2	**P**	**E**	**R**	S	**O**	N	**A**	L	**X**	**F**	O	R	
	F	K	T	D	C	H	K	E	S	E	B	X	
3	I	N	**F**	**O**	**R**	**M**	**A**	**T**	**I**	**O**	**N**	X	
	Y	X	M	X	L	Y	K	Z	P	V	M	R	
4	R	E	C	E	**I**	**V**	E	**D**	**X**	**Y**	**O**	**U**	R
	G	K	K	V	P	T	V	X	S	P	B	C	S
5	I	M	M	E	D	I	A	**T**	E	**X**	**F**	**O**	R
	Y	J	F	V	V	D	K	Z	V	S	J	N	S
6	A	C	T	I	O	N	X	**T**	**H**	I	**S**	**X**	D
	S	V	R	Q	C	H	O	Z	W	L	X	R	X
7	P	L	E	A	S	E	X	S	E	N	**D**		
	F	O	Q	C	N	P	O	G	V	M	E		
8	**R**	E	**P**	O	R	T	X	N	O	**W**			
	G	K	W	X	L	V	O	J	U	H			
9	A	C	K	N	O	**W**	L	E	D	G	E	**X**	
	S	V	C	L	C	Z	H	L	A	D	D	R	
10	T	O	D	**A**	Y	X	I	S					
	Z	L	X	C	E	J	Z	G					
11	F	R	**O**	M	**X**	A	**D**	M	I	R	**A**	**L**	T	Y
	P	Q	Z	B	K	R	B	F	P	T	Y	Q	E	K
12	F	R	**O**	M	**X**	**W**	A	R	X	**O**	**F**	**F**	I	**C**	E
	P	Q	Z	B	K	Z	K	B	S	V	J	Y	U	B	M

13	**S**	E	N	D	X	**A**	D	D	R	E	S	S	**X**	
	A	K	L	S	K	R	B	X	L	F	X	W	D	
14	**N**	**O**	**T**	**H**	I	N	G	X	T	O	X	**R**	E	**P**
	X	L	R	K	P	H	M	D	F	V	S	X	T	O
15	**M**	**E**	**R**	**R**	**Y**	**X**	**C**	**H**	**R**	I	S	T	**M**	**A**	S
	C	K	T	T	E	J	R	K	L	L	X	B	P	Q	R
16	**F**	**O**	**R**	**X**	**C**	**A**	**P**	**T**	**A**	**I**	**N**	**X**	
	P	L	T	O	O	R	F	Z	D	L	M	R	
17	**B**	**L**	**E**	**T**	**C**	**H**	**L**	**E**	**Y**	**X**	**P**	**A**	**R**	**K**
	J	O	Q	R	O	N	H	L	M	S	T	K	S	Y
18	**H**	**E**	**A**	**V**	**Y**	**X**	**A**	**T**	**T**	**A**	**C**	**K**	
	L	K	G	E	E	J	K	Z	F	Q	U	A	
19	**D**	I	S	**P**	**A**	**T**	**C**	**H**	**X**	**N**	**O**	**W**	
	V	W	Y	G	U	V	R	K	S	M	B	S	
20	**O**	**P**	**E**	**R**	**A**	**T**	**I**	**O**	**N**	**X**	
	Q	H	Q	T	U	V	Z	I	C	S	
21	**W**	**A**	**R**	**X**	**O**	**F**	**F**	**I**	**C**	**E**	
	K	U	T	O	C	Q	P	O	N	F	
22	**A**	**D**	**V**	**A**	**N**	**C**	**E**	**X**	
	S	G	J	C	S	G	V	D	

In order to obtain a set of cipher messages in depth, all the clear text sequences shown in the above list were enciphered on the Railway Enigma emulation, using the same key: rotor order 3,2,1; ring settings ZZZZ; message settings FLCZ.

From the above tabulation a number of Enigma alphabet letter pairs were obtained, and Table I (below) gives these letter pairs, all from the first six positions in the messages. (For example at the 2nd position, AU indicates that A is enciphered as U and U is enciphered as A). Table II shows the corresponding letter pairs at the 1st position obtained by means of the 'buttoning-up' process. (Note that the first column is the same in both tables.)

Table I

1	2	3	4	5	6
AS	AU	AG	AC	AU	AR
BJ	CV	CK	BM	CO	CG
CM	DG	EQ	DS	DV	DI
DV	EK	FM	EV	EY	EP
EU	IW	JV	HK	IP	FQ
FP	LO	LN	IQ	KX	HN
GR	MJ	OZ	LN	LR	JX
HL	NX	PW	OX	NS	MY
IY	PH	RT	PG		VT
NX	QR	SY	RT		WZ
OQ	XN	XD			
TZ					
WK					

Table II

AS	SI	DJ	FN	GS	HO
BJ	VB	BY	LW	MF	LY
CM	FH	GV	HG	JL	KF
DV	RP	TE	ZM	UB	IB
EU	OE	HQ	PX	DV	PZ
FP	QA	PN	SR	CN	XE
GR	LK	WL	EQ	RI	CM
HL	MC	SI	DB	WH	RN
IY	YJ	XR	CK		QA
NX	WT	ZU	UI		US
OQ		FC			
TZ					
WK					

Table II will be used extensively in the following work and it is important to understand how the entries in it were derived from those in Table I. As an example consider the letter pair DV in the 5th column of Table I. By means of the diagonal sequence QWERTZUIOASDFGHJKPYXCVBNML, the letter D is replaced by the letter J (four places forward in the sequence). Likewise the letter V is replaced by the letter L (again four places forward). Note that the resulting letter pair (JL) appears in the 5th row of Table II.

By means of the information in this table, the somewhat lengthy process of constructing the 1st upright in the rod square for the right-hand rotor can begin. Without any prior knowledge about this upright, the strategy used will be to carry out a search for a correct letter pair contained in it. The choice will be made systematically from the list of possibilities A/B, A/C, A/D etc., so that if the hypothesis 'A/B' (i.e. A is above and adjacent to B) is found to lead to inconsistencies then a fresh start will be made using the next hypothesis, 'A/C', and so on. The correct hypothesis related to letter A will be readily identified as it will be the only one not leading to any inconsistent conclusions.

From the initial hypothesis A/B and the information contained in Table II, the following conclusions can be made:

- Letter pair AS in the 1st column indicates that A→S and the letter pair VB in the 2nd column indicates that B→V. Jointly these show that A/B→S/V. As the letter pair AS occurred in the 1st column of the table, this result can be expressed more precisely as AB–1–SV.
- Likewise in the 2nd column letter pair QA indicates that A→Q and in the 3rd column letter pair BY indicates that B→Y. Jointly these show that A/B→Q/Y. As the letter pair QA occurred in the 2nd column of the table this result is expressed more precisely as AB–2–QY.

The result S/V obtained above also leads to further conclusions:

- Letter pair SI (2nd column) indicates that S→I and letter pair GV (3rd column) indicates that V→G. Jointly these show that S/V→I/G or SV–2–IG.
- Letter pair SR (4th column) indicates that S→R and letter pair DV (5th column) indicates that V→D. Jointly these show that S/V→R/D or SV–4–RD.

Starting with the result Q/Y obtained above, letter pair OQ (1st column) indicates that Q→O, and letter pair YJ (2nd column) indicates that Y→J. Jointly these show that Q/Y→O/J or QY–1–OJ. Starting with the result R/D obtained above, letter pair GR (1st column) indicates that R→G. However, letter D does not appear in the letter pairs from the 2nd column of the table and consequently no conclusion for this letter can be made, and the process cannot be completed. However, the occurrence of the letter pair RP (2nd column) and the letter pair DJ (3rd column) jointly show that R/D→P/J or RD–2–PJ. In addition the letter pair XR (3rd column) and the letter pair DB (4th column) jointly show that R/D→X/B or RD–3–XB. These results are shown in the diagram below.

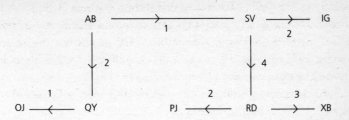

The two conclusions O/J and P/J are inconsistent and the conclusion X/B is inconsistent with the initial assumption A/B, which consequently must be false. The procedure must now be repeated with the next initial assumption, 'A/C', and the details of this are shown (in a somewhat more abbreviated form) below:

- AS (1st column) and MC (2nd column): A/C→S/M or AC–1–SM.
- QA (2nd column) and FC (3rd column): A/C→Q/F or AC–2–QF.

Starting again with S/M:
- SI (3rd column) and ZM (4 column): S/M→I/Z or SM–3–IZ.
- SR (4th column) and MF (5th column): S/M→R/F or SM–4–RF.
- GS (5th column) and CM (6th column): S/M→G/C or SM–5–GC.

These results are shown in the diagram below.

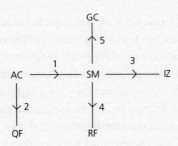

One of the conclusions reached is G/C, which conflicts with the initial assumption A/C, so that the assumption A/C is false.

Starting with the initial assumption 'A/D':

- QA (2nd column) and DJ (3rd column): A/D→Q/J or AD–2–QJ.

Starting again with Q/J:

- OQ (1st column) and YJ (2nd column): Q/J→O/Y or QJ–1–OY.
- EQ (4th column) and JL (5th column): Q/J→E/L or QJ–4–EL.

Starting again with O/Y:

- OE (2nd column) and BY (3rd column): O/Y→E/B or OY–2–EB.

These results are shown in the diagram below.

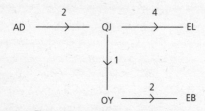

The conclusions E/L and E/B are clearly inconsistent and hence the assumption A/D is false. This procedure must be repeated to systematically test in turn the initial assumptions A/E, A/F etc.

When the assumption A/K is tested, the results are strikingly different. A large number of conclusions are obtained which do not logically conflict with one another, and some do indeed provide confirmation of others that have already been found. Some of these conclusions are shown below and are followed by a diagram showing the rather complex way in which they are related to each other. (In order to reduce as far as possible the length of the work, all of the confirmations have been omitted except for one that has been shown as an illustrative example.)

Starting with the assumption A/K:

- AS (1st column) and EK (2nd column): A/K→S/L or AK–1–SL.

Starting with S/L:
- SI (2nd column) and WL (3rd column): S/L→I/W or SL–2–IW.
- GS (5th column) and LY (6th column): S/L→G/Y or SL–5–GY.

Starting with I/W:
- IY (1st column) and WT (2nd column): I/W→Y/T or IW–1–YT.
- UI (4th column) and WH (5th column): I/W→U/H or IW–4–UH.

Starting with Y/T:
- YJ (2nd column) and TE (3rd column): Y/T→J/E or YT–2–JE.

Starting with U/H:
- EU (1st column) and FH (2nd column): U/H→E/F or UH–1–EF.
- ZU (3rd column) and HG (4th column): U/H→Z/G or UH–3–ZG.

Starting with J/E:
- BJ (1st column) and OE (2nd column): J/E→B/O or JE–1–BO.
- DJ (3rd column) and EQ (4th column): J/E→ D/Q or JE–3–DQ.
- JL (5th column) and XE (6th column): J/E→L/X or JE–5–LX.

Starting with E/F:
- OE (2nd column) and FC (3rd column): E/F→O/C or EF–2–OC.
- EQ (4th column) and MF (5th column): E/F→Q/M or EF–4–QM.

Starting with Z/G:
- ZM (4th column) and GS (5th column): Z/G→M/S or ZG–4–MS.

Starting with B/O:
- UB (5th column) and HO (6th column): B/O→U/H or BO–5–UH.

Starting with D/Q:
- DV (1st column) and QA (2nd column): D/Q→V/A or DQ–1–VA.

Starting with M/S:
- CM (1st column) and SI (2nd column): M/S→C/I or MS–1–CI.
- MF (5th column) and US (6th column): M/S→F/U or MS–5–FU.

Starting with C/I:
- FC (3rd column) and UI (4th column): C/I→F/U or CI–3–FU. (Note: this is a confirmatory conclusion.)
- ~~CK (4th column) and RI (5th column): C/I→K/R or CI–4–KR.~~
- CN (5th column) and IB (6th column): C/I→N/B or CI–5–NB.

Starting with F/U:
- FH (2nd column) and ZU (3rd column): F/U→H/Z or FU–2–HZ.

Starting with H/Z:
- WH (5th column) and PZ (6th column): H/Z→W/P or HZ–5–WP.

Starting with N/B:
- NX (1st column) and VB (2nd column): N/B→X/V or NB–1–XV.
- PN (3rd column) and DB (4th column): N/B→P/D or NB–3–PD.

Starting with G/Y:
- GR (1st column) and YJ (2nd column): G/Y→ R/J or GY–1–RJ.

Starting with W/P:
- WK (1st column) and RP (2nd column): W/P→K/R or WP–1–KR.
- WT (2nd column) and PN (3rd column): W/P→T/N or WP–2–TN.
- WL (3rd column) and PX (4th column): W/P→L/X or WP–3–LX.

This rather protracted procedure has now been carried far enough for it now to be possible to deduce the complete letter sequence in the 1st upright. The following diagram will be very helpful in this final stage of the work.

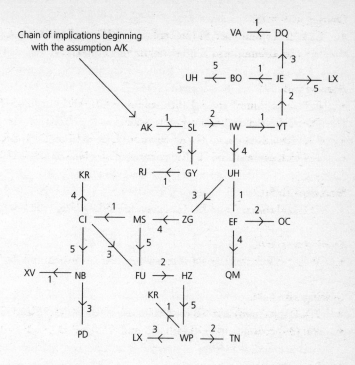

Chain of implications beginning with the assumption A/K

Combining the results

The initial assumption that the letter pair AK forms a fragment of the upright leads to a long chain of conclusions for other letter pairs on the upright that is both consistent and confirmatory, and these are shown in the final diagram below. When they are combined the result is a complete list of 26 ordered letters that form the required 1st upright.

Beginning with the letter pair AK, the above diagram can be used to list all the conclusions about the adjacent letter pairs existing in the 1st upright into an appropriate order: AK, KR, RJ, JE, EF, FU, UH, HZ, ZG, GY, YT, TN, NB, BO, OC, CI, IW, WP, PD, DQ, QM, MS, SL, LX, XV, VA. Combining these then leads to the upright sequence:

A K R J E F U H Z G Y T N B O C I W P D Q M S L X V (A)

This is a cyclic sequence that is closely related to the electrical connections between the contact 'pins' on the right-hand side of the rotor and the 'plate' contacts (denoted by the sequence of letters q, w, e, r, t, z, u etc.) on an imaginary fixed reference disc on the left hand side of the rotor. The fact that the letter A appears at the beginning of the sequence is of no significance and this has only happened because the initial assumption A/K was used to obtain all of the subsequent conclusions.

If it is assumed that, for the 1st position in each message, pin 'C' on the rotor was connected to plate 'q' on the fixed reference disc (through the internal wiring of the right-hand rotor), then the connections between these two sets of contacts will be as shown in the following table:

q	w	e	r	t	z	u	i	o	a	s	d	f	g	h	j	k	p	y	x	c	v	b	n	m	l
C	I	W	P	D	Q	M	S	L	Z	V	A	K	R	J	E	F	U	H	Z	G	Y	T	N	B	O

Reference to the rod square given earlier confirms that this corresponds to the 1st upright correct for Rotor I when set to ring setting 'Z' and rotor position 'A'.

A more practical version of this table can be constructed in the following way. Assign the numbers 1, 2, 3, 4 … 26 to the corresponding letters in the list q, w, e, r, t … l appearing in the 1st row and also to the corresponding capital letters in the 2nd row (e.g. both letters 'q' and 'Q' will be replaced by '1'; both letters 'w' and 'W' will be replaced by '2'). The table will then be transformed to:

1	2	3	4	5	6	7	8	9	10	11	12	13	14	15	16	17	18	19	20	21	22	23	24	25	26
21	8	2	18	12	1	25	11	26	20	22	10	17	4	16	3	13	7	15	6	14	19	5	24	23	9

This table shows the internal core wiring connections from the 26 contacts on the left-hand face of the rotor to the corresponding contacts on the right-hand face.

A final version gives the same connections but now considered in the opposite direction, from the right-hand face of the rotor to the left-hand one:

1	2	3	4	5	6	7	8	9	10	11	12	13	14	15	16	17	18	19	20	21	22	23	24	25	26
6	3	16	14	23	20	18	2	26	12	8	5	17	21	19	15	13	4	22	10	1	11	25	24	7	9

Concluding remarks

It is believed that 'Dilly' Knox developed the technique of 'rodding' in 1936. In the following year he was first able to apply this method to 'live' messages, after he had determined the rod squares for the Enigma rotors then in use by the Italian navy. This early work paid dividends later on, when in 1940/41 by means of 'rodding', some important Italian naval signals yielded the intelligence that resulted in the dramatic British success at Matapan. In 1941 Knox achieved perhaps his greatest success by breaking the Abwehr Enigma, in which the 'buttoning-up' procedure had again been usefully applied.

Frank Carter

Appendix 4

Report on the 'Lobster Enigma'

I. Solution

This was based on a theory, an observation and a procedure devised by the head of the section. These were:

(a) The key-blocks were too scanty to be evaluated. Evaluation could only occur if we availed ourselves of two staggered settings of the key-blocks, e.g.

ABCD	or	ABCD
BCDE		KLMN

A sufficient hunt was made for these with the aid of Mr. Freeborn but no instances occurred. This was in itself suspicious.

(b) It was no great surprise to the aforesaid Officer when he found what was wanted standing, like the abomination of desolation, precisely where it should not – on a single setting, e.g. (1) ABCD (2) BCDE (3) ???? (4) ???? (5) BCDH (6)CDEI (7) ???? (8) ????

(c) It became clear with these data
   (1) that the diagonal was QWERTZU. No other fact emerged.
   (2) that we had to deal with frequent carries affecting all four wheels.
   (3) that we still had only partial evaluation of two of the four columns and could not guess the rest.

(d) He then decided that, as everything that has a middle has also a beginning and an end that sometimes we should have, e.g. (1) ???? (2) ???? (3) ???? (4) ???? (5) ABCD (6) BCDE (7) ????(8) ????

(e) The first phenomenon he named 'a crab' and condemned as useless; the second he named 'a lobster' and ordered an intensive hunt on 'saga' methods (the box).

(f) The hunt was up and scent was good. One very fine 'lobster' (among others) was caught, and after two days Miss Lever, by very good and careful work, succeeded in an evaluation which contained sufficient non-carry units to ascertain the green wheel.

(g) The blue wheel was sometimes harder and on semi-saga methods several evaluations were made, two of which coincided.

(h) The red wheel proved very difficult. We diagnosed an apparent red wheel as a 'double' wheel (red and green) and Mr. Rees definitely proved this by obtaining the *Umkehrwalze* couplings.

(i) The compound wheel was later dissected by him and the red wheel which usually carries obtained.

(j) An element of surprise was the discovery that the carry is cyclometric, a fact which suggests that we may be ready to decode before the machine. To decode such carries except on the machine would need an enormous staff.

(k) There are snags ahead. To get the first key onto the messages we still need much fortune and a complete study of all parallel material. All subsequent keys up to the fourth and fifth will be very hard; after that they will more probably prove laborious.

(l) Since the old rod system cannot be used an alternative method is being provided. It cannot be ready for three weeks.

(m) Meantime staff must be collected or adjusted and it is necessary to consider this carefully.

II. Staff

It is obvious that a most careful and immediate study of our output will sooner or later be necessary. This cannot be done except on the system of supervising the outgoing traffic as is done in Hut 8, and on the Italian Enigma. It is more necessary for us than for Hut 8 since we must always solve by trial and error at least one position of message for every key.

The linguistic (German) staff at present consists of three, Miss Lever, Miss Rock and myself. As we shall also have to direct all the solutions and may have to work shifts, at least two more linguists must be chosen and have time to learn (a) what we know we want, (b) what might be useful. All hunters must know all the tricks of the machine.

The existing system of crib-hunting by proxy has yielded the Italian Enigma in two years the total of 0 (nought) cribs. I should add that I am using 'cribs' in the widest sense of the term. A long 'crib' in the ordinary sense is no longer necessary. We must proceed as with the Italian Enigma by the careful study and correction of messages before they leave us. Any other system of arbitrary correction by those who do not understand machine plans and cannot avail themselves of Morse corrections is repugnant and unthinkable.

We need, therefore:
(a) Two more scholars for watch, the watch probably proceed to message solution.
(b) A certain increase of general staff at the earlier possible moment.
(c) Three or four machines and relays of decoders, cannot watch results off machines in another Hut.

With regard to (b) I suggest the gradual return from the Naval Hut of the Cottage staff. They were first loaned intermittently and are now really on a continuous loan. They are not doing work up to their capacity and should, in my opinion, be replaced by a Wren section. Return could be gradual. Some could be spared for (c), the machines. There would then remain (a) which is a matter of urgent moment. I would welcome a private discussion.

A. D. Knox
(I shall be away tomorrow, ADK)
28 October 1941

APPENDIX 5

Abwehr and SD cipher machines attacked by the ISK section

1. Group II Enigma Called the *Zählwerk* (counter) Enigma by the Germans; also called the Lobster Enigma by ISK

Solved by Dilly Knox in October 1941. The principal Abwehr Enigma, with multi-notched rotors (11, 15 and 17 notches), used until the end of 1944 for European communications.

Called 'Group II' after the Radio Security Service name for the radio circuits carrying its traffic.

The Abwehr became aware that the *Zählwerk* Enigma could be broken by a 10-letter crib. Users were then instructed to encipher messages twice, but appear not to have done so.

The machine was withdrawn from German military attachés in 1943. It ceased to be supplied to the Abwehr after 23 November 1943, and was largely replaced by the KD Enigma and Cipher Machine 41 (see below) towards the end of 1944.

2.	GGG Enigma	Solved by Mavis Batey (née Lever) in February 1942. An Enigma used by the Abwehr solely for communications between Madrid and several outstations situated round the Strait of Gibraltar.

There were about 500 signals a month from February 1942 onwards, of which 90 per cent were readable.

3.	KK Enigma	Captured in November 1942 at Blida in Algeria. An Enigma with multi-notched rotors (11, 15 and 17 notches) used by the German Armistice Commission in Vichy France and north Africa.
4.	'Green' South American Enigma	Solved in December 1942. An Enigma with multi-notched rotors (11, 15 and 17 notches) used by the Abwehr for communications between Germany and South America.
5.	Canary Islands Enigma	Solved by Margaret Rock in May 1943. Used for maintaining a weather ship reporting service between Berlin and the Canaries.
6.	SD Enigma	Solved by Keith Batey in August 1943. Used by the Sicherheitsdienst for European communications, including Berlin–Turkey.
7.	'Red' South American Enigma	Solved in January 1944. An Enigma with multi-notched rotors (11, 15 and 17 notches) used from November 1943 by the Abwehr and Sicherheitsdienst for communicating with South America.

The first two groups and last two groups in its traffic were identical to make it look like Naval Enigma, although signals were also sometimes sent in 5-letter groups.

8.	KD Enigma	Solved in January 1945. Used between Berlin and Madrid and Lisbon. A machine with multi-notched rotors (nine on each rotor) and a rewirable reflector. The 'D' reference suggests that the rewirable reflector was the same as the 'D' reflector introduced by the German air force in January 1944.
		Replaced the Group II Enigma for security reasons (see above).
9.	Cipher Machine 41 (Schlüsselgerät 41 (SG 41))	Introduced on 12 October 1944.
		A Hagelin-type machine, with six pin wheels whose motion was very irregular – the wheels sometimes moved backwards. Even when pure key was available, the wheel settings and pin patterns could not be reconstructed.
		A few messages in depth were read by GC&CS, but the machine could not be solved during the war, and remained a mystery. A post-war US Signal Security Agency report described it as 'a remarkable machine'.
		The SG 41 was intended to supersede Enigma for the Abwehr's European communications but was only in use on certain internal networks when the war ended.
		It was designed by *Regierungsoberinspektor* Fritz Menzer, who had become a massive bane for the ISOS and ISK sections by introducing numerous reforms to the Abwehr's ciphers. About 11,000 machines were ordered by the German army and Luftwaffe, but only about 1,000 were produced.

10.	The Service Enigma (Wehrmacht (plugboard) Enigma)	Keys were solved at various times. This machine was used by the SD and the Brandenburg division, an Abwehr commando unit.
11.	Kryha	First used on 6 May 1943, and solved in May 1943. Used for communicating with South America.

The first two groups and last two groups in its traffic were identical to make it look like Naval Enigma.

Kryha was a relatively simple mechanical machine with two concentric cipher discs, each with a changeable alphabet. The inner disc rotated as each letter was enciphered. An adjustable gearwheel gave a variable 'kick' to the inner disc's movement.

Curiously, the SD continued to use Kryha even after its use was 'excluded since cipher text can be read like plain language' – an overstatement, but one erring on the side of caution.

12.	Hagelin	Probably the Hagelin C 48. Messages were partially solved at various times. Used occasionally for the ship-reporting service from Madrid.

13.	First Italian 'K' Enigma	A rewired commercial 'K' machine. Solved in April 1937 by Dilly Knox. Used by the Italians and Spaniards in the Spanish Civil War. Used during that war and the Second World War (with a minor modification) until late 1940 for some Italian naval communications.
		New rotors were introduced about the end of 1940.
		The 'Matapan' signals were enciphered on this machine.
		The Italian Navy held very few such machines.
14.	Second Italian Enigma	Solved in July 1943. A rewired version of the previous machine. Used for some naval communications.
15.	Spanish military attaché (SMA) Enigma	Solved by Keith Batey in November 1943. Used for military attaché communications between Madrid, Berlin, Rome, Vichy and Berne.
		For some of the SMA decrypts, see TNA PRO HW 18/168 (messages sent between the Spanish government and its naval, military and air attachés in Berlin and Rome).

GC&CS also read about 5,200 Abwehr messages enciphered on 'Tunny' (the Lorenz SZ 40/42 teleprinter cipher attachment). The resulting decrypts were known as ISTUN. The Abwehr also used the Siemens and Halske T52 teleprinter cipher machine. It is unlikely that GC&CS broke much, if any, Abwehr T52 traffic.

Glossary

Abwehr The German armed forces intelligence service.

Additive Figures added to a cipher message using non-carrying arithmetic during the super-encipherment process.

Alphabet Paired reciprocal letters in same position on the Enigma machine.

ARCOS All-Russian Co-operative Society, trade organisation which provided cover for Soviet intelligence activities in the UK in the 1920s.

B1A MI5 section that controlled the double agents ostensibly operating in the UK.

Beetle Term invented by Dilly Knox to define two clicks on the same rod, also known as a direct click.

Blue The various Enigma ciphers were originally identified by colours. Blue was the Luftwaffe practice Enigma cipher machine.

Boil A technique invented by Dilly Knox which exploited the fact that no letter could be enciphered as itself. Cipher texts were catalogued on a chart to identify letters that never appeared at certain points in the message and were therefore likely plain text.

Bomba **(pl.** *bomby***)** Polish electro-mechanical device designed to assist in breaking Enigma keys.

Bombe Ultra-fast electro-mechanical machine for recovering Enigma daily keys by testing a crib and its implications at all possible wheel or rotor orders and initial settings, inspired by but not based on the Polish *bomby*.

Boxing The process of cataloguing box-shapes, i.e. forming chains of letters from indicators doubly enciphered on a *Grundstellung*, so that the enciphered indicators

TQZ   PYC
POW   RTI

will box as TPR.

Box-shapes The patterns formed by enciphered indicators during the pre-war period when the *Grundstellung* did not change.

BP Bletchley Park.

Buttoning-up A method for recovering the wiring of the rotors used in an Enigma cipher machine that did not have the *Stecker* or plugboard (See Appendix 3).

'C' Title of the head of SIS, known as Chief. 'C' was originally derived from the first letter of the surname of the first chief of SIS, Mansfield Cumming. For security reasons, Cumming was only referred to as 'C'. The title was inherited by his successor, Admiral Hugh Sinclair, by which time it had become an abbreviation for 'Chief'. It remains in use to this day.

Call-sign The designation given to a wireless station on a communications circuit or network to allow ease of identification, often used in a preamble to identify the originator and intended recipients of the message.

Cilli A German procedural error, first spotted by Dilly Knox, in which the operator uses the rotor finishing positions in one part of a multi-part Enigma message as the *Grundstellung* for the next part. Derived from CIL, the basic position of the message in which the mistake was first discovered.

Cipher A cryptographic system in which letters or numbers represent plain-text units (generally single letters) in accordance with pre-arranged rules.

Click Confirmations of probable cribs of individual letters. There are two kinds of clicks: direct clicks are those in which both letters of the crib occur side by side on the same rod; Dilly called this a beetle. The other is a cross-click where one of the crib letters is on one rod and the second on the other; Dilly called this a starfish.

Click chart A chart compiled at Dilly's instigation to show all occurrences of clicks.

Code A cryptographic system, generally set out in a codebook, in which groups of letters or numbers represent plain-text words or phrases.

Comintern Communist International, organisation set up by Moscow with the intention of spreading communism worldwide.

Crab Term invented by Dilly Knox to define two lobsters four places apart on the key-block.

Crib Probable plain text guessed at from previous usage and tested out against the cipher text to break a message.

Cyclometer A machine devised by Polish codebreaker Marian Rejewski comprising two sets of rotors connected by electric wires which he used to produce a catalogue of early Enigma rotor cycles.

Depth The correct alignment of ciphered text that has been enciphered by the same length of key.

Diagonal The order in which keys on the Enigma machine were wired to the entry plate, QWERTZU in the un-*Stecker*ed machines, ABCDE in the Wehrmacht machines.

DID Director Intelligence Division. British head of naval intelligence in the First World War.

Direction-finding Locating the sender of a message by plotting bearings to the origin of the radio signals received at two or more locations.

Discriminant (German *Kenngruppe*) A group in the preamble showing the cipher system in use.

DNI Director Naval Intelligence. British head of naval intelligence in the Second World War.

Female A letter in the second group of a doubly enciphered Enigma message key which repeats a letter in the corresponding position in the first group, e.g. AFO, CFK.

FUSAG Notional First US Army Group alleged to be under General Patton that was central to the Allied D-Day deception plans suggesting the main attack would be on the Pas de Calais.

GC&CS Government Code and Cypher School, the British codebreaking and cipher security organisation between 1919 and 1945.

GGG Abwehr Enigma used between Berlin and stations in Spain.

Grundstellung The basic original position of the rotors at which the message key is enciphered or deciphered.

Herivel tip A method used to deduce the daily *Ringstellungen* from a series of *Grundstellungen* at the start of the cipher period. Named after John

Herivel, who first realised that some operators would use the ring settings as *Grundstellungen* in this way.

Hollerith Punched-card equipment used for rapid searches of data at Bletchley Park.

Hut 3 The section at Bletchley Park which issued intelligence reports based on the German army and Luftwaffe Enigma messages deciphered in Hut 6.

~~**Hut 4**~~ The naval section at Bletchley Park, led by Frank Birch, which issued intelligence reports based on the German naval Enigma messages deciphered in Hut 8.

Hut 6 The section at Bletchley Park which deciphered German army and Luftwaffe Enigma messages.

Hut 8 The section at Bletchley Park which deciphered German naval Enigma messages.

Indicators A group of letters or symbols showing the cipher system being used.

ISK Illicit Services Knox, also Intelligence Services Knox, the designation given to both the section that deciphered German intelligence service Enigma machines and the resulting decodes throughout the war.

ISOS Illicit Services Oliver Strachey, also Intelligence Services Oliver Strachey, the designation given to both the section that deciphered German intelligence service hand ciphers and the resulting decodes throughout the war.

Jeffreys sheets A catalogue of the effect of any two wheels or rotors and the reflector in the Enigma machine. Not to be confused with Zygalski sheets.

K model Improved early commercial Enigma machine with turnover on the wheel instead of the tyre.

Key A series of numbers or symbols used to encipher text. In terms of Enigma, this meant the initial settings of the various parts of the machine for a given period of time, usually a day.

Key-block A group of indicators enciphered using the same *Grundstellung*.

Kriegsmarine The name used by the German navy from 1935 to 1945.

Lobster Term invented by Dilly Knox to define a message enciphered using an Abwehr Enigma machine, in which all four wheels turn over at the same time. Also known as a four-wheel turnover.

Luftwaffe German air force.

Mask Codename of the 1930s operation, in which Dilly Knox played a leading role, to intercept and decipher messages between Moscow and Comintern representatives worldwide.

Menu A series of linked plain and cipher pairs based on cribs or predictions of original plain text used as instructions for setting up a *bombe*.

MEW Ministry of Economic Warfare.

MI1b The First World War military intelligence department that dealt with signals intelligence, both collection and decryption.

MI5 British domestic counter-espionage and security service, more properly known as the Security Service.

Netz See Zygalski sheets.

NID Naval Intelligence Division, the Admiralty's intelligence organisation.

NID25 Naval Intelligence Division 25, the Royal Navy's signals intelligence branch during the First World War, better known as Room 40. This is where Dilly Knox worked and was the inspiration for *Alice in NID25*.

OIC Operational Intelligence Centre, the Second World War naval intelligence organisation which used co-ordinated intelligence to plot enemy shipping worldwide.

Pinch A piece of cryptographic material, which could be anything from a list of keys to a cipher machine, stolen or captured from the enemy and used to assist in codebreaking.

Preamble The information given at the start of a message, normally in a standard format, which gives such details as the message serial number;

the originator; the intended recipients; the time and date the message was initiated; the priority; security classification; and the discriminants and keys in use.

Psilli A psychological cilli. An Enigma message setting which so closely related to the message *Grundstellung* that it could be guessed at, e.g. a *Grundstellung* of HIT might be followed by a message setting of LER.

QWERTZU The name given by Dilly Knox to the 'diagonal', the order in which the keys on the Enigma machine were wired to the entry plate. It derives from the order of the top line of the keys on a German typewriter, which was the layout used for the Enigma keys.

Radio Security Service Intercept and analysis organisation originally part of MI5, later part of SIS Section V, which dealt with illicit radio stations operating in the UK.

Red The colour coding given to the main Luftwaffe Enigma cipher.

Reichsmarine Original post-First World War name for the German navy, which was changed to Kriegsmarine in 1935.

Reichswehr The original name for the German armed forces following the First World War, changed to Wehrmacht in 1935.

Ringstellung Ring setting. The setting of the ring or tyre on an Enigma rotor or wheel.

Rodding Technique devised by Dilly Knox in 1937 to break an Enigma cipher machine that did not have the *Stecker* or plugboard (See Appendix 2).

Rotor Rotating disc on an Enigma cipher machine with wired electrical contacts which, with a number of other rotors, contributes to the encipherment process. Also known as a wheel, from the original German *Walze*.

Saga Method of 'boxing' throw-on indicators.

SD Sicherheitsdienst, the Nazi Party's internal intelligence service, effectively Nazi Germany's civilian intelligence service during the Second World War. It also took over all functions of the Abwehr in 1944.

Section V The SIS counter-espionage section during the Second World War.

Section VIII The SIS communications section during the Second World War.

Sigint Signals intelligence – the general term for the processes of interception of electronic signals, codebreaking, analysis and intelligence processing.

SIS Secret Intelligence Service, British foreign intelligence service, more commonly known as MI6.

Slides An insecure method of producing the indicators in which the operator slides his fingers over several adjacent keys in order to produce the indicator, e.g. WER.

SLU Special Liaison Unit, an intelligence unit attached to Allied commanders which passed them ULTRA intelligence.

Starfish Term invented by Dilly Knox to define two clicks in which one is on one rod and the second is on another rod, also known as a cross-click.

Stecker Shortened form of *Steckerverbindung*, the connections used on the plugboard added to the German armed forces Enigma machines to provide greater security.

Substitution cipher A cipher in which one letter is substituted by another but retains its position in the message.

Super-encipherment A system in which an already encrypted message is enciphered to give it an increased level of security.

Supermarina The Italian Admiralty.

Throw-on indicators A pair of letters representing two encipherments of the same letter at two different positions in indicators that have been enciphered twice on a *Grundstellung*.

Traffic The messages passing on a communications network or circuit.

Traffic analysis The study of wireless communication networks and the exploitation of operators' signals procedure and plain language conversations.

Transposition cipher A cipher in which the positions of individual letters or figures change their positions within a message.

Turnover Movement of a wheel produced by the movement of the next wheel to its right.

Typex The British cipher machine, based on Enigma but crucially never broken by the Germans.

Tyres Alternative name for the rings on the rotors or wheels.

ULTRA The top secret codeword attached to the security classification applied to intelligence derived from the breaking of high-grade ciphers. The security classification at the top and bottom of such intelligence was rendered as Top Secret Ultra.

Umkehrwalze The reflector which sent the electrical signal back through the wheels or rotors to complete the letter's encryption.

Wehrmacht All three branches of the German armed forces.

Wheel Rotating disc on an Enigma cipher machine with wired electrical contacts which, with a number of other wheels, contributes to the encipherment process. Use of the word 'wheel' derives from the original German *Walze*. Also known as a rotor.

Wheel track Sequence of turnovers on the Abwehr machine wheels.

Y Service The intercept and direction-finding service, which until October 1943 also carried out traffic analysis and broke low-grade codes and ciphers.

Zygalski sheets Lettered sheets with holes punched in them showing which combination of wheel or rotor starting positions and orders produced females. By suitably aligning the relevant sheets on top of each other, the *Ringstellungen* and the wheel or rotor order were revealed by the coincidence of holes in some sheets. Also known as *Netz*.

Notes

Foreword

Page ix   'The only codebreaker': William Friedman, the founder of modern American codebreaking, also solved cipher machines, but not during the Second World War. Although he is sometimes described as 'the man who broke Purple', the Japanese Foreign Ministry's cipher machine, its solution was a team effort, with the real team leader being Frank Rowlett. See 'Preliminary Historical Report on the Solution of the B Machine', National Archives and Records Administration, College Park (NACP), MD, RG 457, Entry 9032, Historic Cryptographic Collection, Pre-World War I Through World War II (HCC), Nr. 2344.

Page ix   '10,500 people': note 2 to the Table 'Expansion of the "Services" Branch of GC&CS March 1942–August 1945' in 'British Sigint, 1914–1945', vol. 3: TNA PRO HW 43/3.

Page ix   'Very little was known': see, for example, David Kahn, *Codebreakers: the Story of Secret Writing*, p.275, Scribner, New York, 1996, referring briefly to his work in the First World War; Kim Philby, *My Silent War*, MacGibbon & Kee, London, 1968, p. 61, with a few lines on his solution of Abwehr Enigma.

Page x   'A technical history': J. K. Batey, M. L. Batey, M. Rock and P. F. G. Twinn, 'A History of the Solution of Unsteckered Enigmas and Abwehr Machine Cyphers 1941–1945' (catalogued as 'GC&CS Secret Service Sigint Volume II: Cryptographic Systems and their Solution. I Machine Cyphers': TNA PRO HW 43/7).

Page x   'Amateur cryptanalysts can now solve ': Geoff Sullivan and Frode Weierud have solved more than seventy authentic German army Enigma daily keys, without the benefit of cribs (probable plain text used as the basis for 'menus' for the bombes – fast key-finding aids): see Geoff Sullivan and Frode Weierud, 'Breaking German Army Ciphers', *Cryptologia* (2005), vol. 29, pp. 193–232; also at http://www.tandf.co.uk/journals/pdf/papers/ucry_06.pdf (accessed 1 July 2009). GC&CS seldom, if ever, achieved that, and found German army Enigma signals even more difficult to solve than Kriegsmarine Enigma messages.

    The M4 Message Breaking Project has broken two genuine Kriegsmarine messages enciphered on four-rotor Enigma (out of three intercepts available), again without cribs: http://www.bytereef.org/m4_project.html (accessed 1 July 2009).

Page x   'Not an isolated example': There are many examples, especially in the TNA PRO HW 43 series. Thus GCHQ continues to withhold files HW 43/33 and 34 on 'The Japanese Fleet General Purpose System' (JN 25) although the US Navy, which broke far more JN 25 systems than GC&CS, has released a full account of its codebreaking methods in 'Techniques and Procedures used in the Cryptanalysis of JN-25 by Station Negat': NACP, RG 38, Radio Intelligence Publications, RIP 171. The decision to withhold HW 43/33 and 34 is redolent of GCHQ's earlier decision to withhold all the Room 40 files.

    GCHQ even continues to classify some German secrets from the Second World War, such as Ticom I-38 (report on interrogation of Lt. Frowein of OKM/4 SKL/III, on his work on the security of the German naval four-wheel Enigma) – see the withholding card in TNA PRO HW 40/176. Frowein merely recounts how he solved messages enciphered on the four-rotor Kriegsmarine Enigma, using punched cards. To claim that information on such methods endangers British security almost sixty-five years later beggars belief. The report is available elsewhere, yet there is not the slightest indication that national security has suffered as a result.

Such ridiculous classification decisions virtually destroy any confidence one might otherwise have in GCHQ's judgment about the classification of wartime documents.

Page x   'Paradoxically, the American': http://www.gpo.gov/congress/commissions/secrecy/pdf/03sum.pdf, p.xxi (accessed 1 July 2009).

Page x   'The US Homeland Security': Homeland Security Advisory Council, 'Top Ten Challenges Facing the Next Secretary of Homeland Security', http://www.fas.org/irp/agency/dhs/topten.pdf (accessed 1 July 2009).

A deputy under-secretary of defence, counter-intelligence and security told a Congressional sub-committee in 2004 that 50 per cent of the United States government's defence secrets might be overclassified: see *Too Many Secrets: Overclassification as a Barrier to Critical Information Sharing*, US Government Printing Office, 2005, testimony of Carol A. Haave, p. 82, (http://bulk.resource.org/gpo.gov/hearings/108h/98291.pdf, accessed 1 July 2009); William Leonard, the director of the Information Security Oversight Office, put the figure as 'over 50 percent': ibid., p. 83.

Page xi   'Dilly specialised': On the A to C machines, see Dr Siegfried Türkel, *Chiffrieren mit Geraten und Maschinen,* Verlag Ulr. Mosers Buchhandlung (J. Meyerhoff), Graz, 1927, pp. 71–94; Cipher A. Deavours and Louis Kruh, *Machine Cryptography and Modern Cryptanalysis*, Artech House, Dedham, MA, 1986, pp. 94–6.

Page xi   'The main Abwehr Enigma': The Germans called it the 'counter' (*Zählwerk*) Enigma because it had a counter for the number of letters enciphered; it was sometimes described by the Allies as a 'Group II' machine.

Page xi   'Most regrettably': F. H. Hinsley and C. A. G. Simkins, *British Intelligence in the Second World War, vol. IV: Security and Counter-intelligence,* HMSO, London, 1990, p. 108. On Sicherheitsdienst (SD, the intelligence service of the Nazi Party) Enigma, see ibid., p.182, fn. In 1943, the main Abwehr ('counter') Enigma was employed between Berlin, Madrid, Lisbon, Paris, Bordeaux and the Italian and Balkan cities: GISK 1 in 'Descriptions of German Cipher Types GISOS, GIMP, GISK and GISKXY' (NARA HCC, Box 606, Nr. 1587). For details of the Abwehr Enigma machines and their characteristics, see 'Descriptions of German Cipher Types GISOS, GIMP, GISK and GISKXY'; 'Tentative List of Enigma and other Machine Usages' (HCC, Box 580, Nr. 1417).

Page xii   '25 December 1941': TNA PRO HW 19/85.

Page xii   'Rejewski mathematical methods': Marian Rejewski, 'How the Polish Mathematicians Broke Enigma', in Władysław Kozaczuk, *Enigma: How the German Machine Cipher Was Broken, and How It Was Read by the Allies in World War Two,* tr. Christopher Kasparek, University Publications of America, MD, 1984, p. 246.

Page xii   'Inspired guess': Ralph Erskine, 'The Poles Reveal their Secrets: Alastair Denniston's Account of the July 1939 Meeting at Pyry', *Cryptologia* (2006), vol. 30, p.300.

Page xii   'Cape Verde Operation': See Ralph Erskine and Frode Weierud, 'Naval Enigma: M4 and its Rotors', *Cryptologia* (1987), vol. 11, p. 235.

Page xii   'Dilly showed remarkable': If Dilly's recommendation had been implemented earlier, Hut 8 (naval Enigma) would probably not have had to confess to 'an episode in the history of the section over which even the least sensitive of us would gladly draw a veil of considerable opacity'. It had failed to recognise that Porpoise (Süd), an Enigma key used in the Mediterranean, was employing an outmoded indicating system. If it had known about the system in time, it 'could certainly have been reading it for some months, possibly since 1941'. Hut 6 did know, but no arrangements had been made to inform Hut 8: see C. H. O'D. Alexander, 'Cryptographic History of Work on the German Naval Enigma' (PRO HW 25/1), p. 38; Ralph Erskine, 'Naval Enigma: An Astonishing Blunder', *Intelligence and National Security* (1988), vol. 3, no. 1, p. 162.

Page xiii   'Burials of essential documents': Knox, undated note about a meeting on 19 March 1942 with 'the Brigadier' (Brigadier Stewart Menzies – 'C'), TNA PRO HW 25/12.

Page xiii   'Over sixty years later': *The 9/11 Commission Report, Final Report of the National Commission on Terrorist Attacks upon the United States*, p. 417: http://www.9-11commission.gov (accessed 1 July 2009).

Page xiii   'Dilly ensured': Knox to Denniston, letter, 7 January 1940: TNA PRO HW 14/3.

Page xiii   'Learned crucial information': The History of Hut 6, vol. I', p.53: PRO HW 43/70; F. H. Hinsley and others, *British Intelligence in the Second World War, vol. III, part 2*, HMSO, London, 1984, p. 952.

Page xiii   'After he returned': 'The History of Hut 6, vol. I', p.55.

Page xiii   'A method, "cillies"': On cillies, see Ralph Erskine, 'Cillies', in Ralph Erskine and Michael Smith (eds), *Action This Day: Bletchley Park from the Breaking of the Enigma Code to the Birth of the Modern Computer*, Bantam, London, 2001, p. 453.

Page xiii   'Provided excellent "cribs"': 'Notes on the History of ISOS': TNA PRO HW 19/316. The ISOS section was 'entirely dependent upon busts and cribs from ISK' for solving traffic on some of the main Abwehr networks for several months in 1944: ibid., para. 21.

Page xiv   Magisterial official history': F. H. Hinsley and others, *British Intelligence in the Second World War: Its Influence on Strategy and Operations*, three volumes in four parts, HMSO, London, 1979, 1981, 1984 & 1990.

Page xiv   'To be of value': On the importance of ISK and ISOS, see Hinsley and Simkins, *British Intelligence in the Second World War, vol. IV*, p. 281.

Page xiv   'Constantly had to struggle': See further, E. D. R. Harrison, 'British Radio Security and Intelligence, 1939-43': *The English Historical Review* (2009), vol. CXXIV, no. 506, pp. 53–93; Hinsley and Simkins, *British Intelligence in the Second World War, vol. IV*, p. 132.

Page xiv   'Kim Philby': See Anthony Cave Brown, *Treason in the Blood: H. St. John Philby, Kim Philby, and the Spy Case of the Century*, Robert Hale, London, 1995, p. 330; cf. Desmond Bristow, with Bill Bristow, *A Game of Moles: The Deceptions of an MI6 Officer*, Warner, London, 1993, pp. 33, 264.

Page xv   'Pas de Calais and Belgium' : See Michael Smith, 'Bletchley Park, Double Cross and D-Day', in Erskine and Smith (eds), *Action This Day*, p. 299.

Chapter 1: The making of a codebreaker

Page 1   'A profitable talk in the summerhouse': Penelope Fitzgerald, *The Knox Brothers*, Coward, McCann & Geoghegan, New York, 1977, p. 26.

Page 2   'Like Herrick': Edmund Arbuthnott Knox, *Reminiscences of an Octogenarian 1847–1934*, Hutchinson, London, 1934.

Page 3   'In August 1892 she died': see Fitzgerald, *Knox Brothers*, p. 37.

Page 4   'A death grapple': see 'Mothering famous people', *Daily Chronicle*, 12 May 1930.

Page 4   'Mrs K and the girls picking up the balls': see Evelyn Waugh, *The Life of the Right Reverend Ronald Knox*, Chapman & Hall, London, 1959, p. 67.

Page 5   'Ronnie used Baconian reasoning': see Ronald Clark, *The Man Who Broke Purple: The Life of The World's Greatest Cryptologist, Colonel William F. Friedman*, Weidenfeld & Nicolson, London, 1977, p. 219.

Page 7   'I was not unprepared for difficulties': Knox, *Reminiscences of an Octogenarian*.

Page 9   'A most loathsomely untidy, unintelligible, illegible condition': Fitzgerald, *Knox Brothers*, pp. 66–7.

Page 10   'You must forgive me': ibid., pp. 71, 91–2.

Page 10   'Loved by all': ibid., pp. 78–9; 'University Intelligence', *The Times*, 12 February 1907.

Page 10   'Too austere and uncongenial': ibid., p. 119.

Page 11   'His argument was so clever that nobody could contradict it': ibid., p. 94.

Chapter 2: Room 40

Page 14   'This sort of Nelsonian exercise had to be abandoned': see Robin Denniston, *Thirty Secret Years: A .G. Denniston's Work in Signals Intelligence 1914–1944*, Polperro Heritage Press, Clifton-upon-Teme, 2007, p. 34.

Page 14   'Arms rigid in death': Winston S. Churchill, *The World Crisis, vol. I: 1911–1914*, Thornton Butterworth, London, 1923, p. 251.

Page 14   'Communication with merchantmen': see Patrick Beesly, *Room 40: British Naval Intelligence 1914–18*, Hamish Hamilton, London, 1982, pp. 3–4.

Page 14   'Begin codebreaking in real earnest': ibid., p. 7.

Page 14   'Three additional copies': see Denniston, *Thirty Secret Years*, p. 34.

Page 15   'The wish that Ewing would "associated himself continuously" with this work': Christopher Andrew, *Secret Service: The Making of the British Intelligence Community*, Heinemann, London, 1985, p. 90.

Page 15   'Although the bombarded towns...': Churchill, *The World Crisis*, p. 264.

Page 16   'There can be few purely mental experiences...': ibid., p. 335.

Page 17   'The Log became an object of hatred...': Denniston, *Thirty Secret Years*, p. 35.

Page 18   'One of our torpedo boats will be running out': Andrew, *Secret Service*, p. 92.

Page 18   'An excellent choice': TNA PRO HW 3/3 'Narrative of Captain Hope', Appendix to *History of Room 40 OB*.

Page 18   'In preparation for the war': see Mavis Batey, *From Bletchley with Love*, Bletchley Park Trust, Milton Keynes, 2008, p. 3; Godfrey memoirs cf p44.

Page 20   'Working in the censorship department': David Kahn, *The Codebreakers: The Story of Secret Writing*, Scribner, New York, 1996, p. 285.

Page 21   'Earlier in this account...': Churchill, *The World Crisis*, p. 606.

Page 21   'These signal books...': ibid., p. 607.

Page 24   'The telegram was first sorted to Knox...': TNA PRO HW 3/177.

Page 24   'I've got a telegram': see David Ramsay, *'Blinker' Hall, Spymaster: The Man Who Brought America into World War I*, History Press, Stroud, 2008, Chapter XI for account of the Zimmermann telegram from Hall's unpublished autobiography.

Page 26   'The ensuing outrage': Joachim von zur Gathen, 'Zimmermann Telegram: The Original Draft', *Cryptologia* (2007), vol. 31, pp. 2–37; David Kahn, 'Edward Bell and His Zimmermann Telegram Memoranda', *Intelligence and National Security* (1999), vol. 14 no. 3, pp. 143–59; TNA PRO HW 3/177 De Grey personal account of the breaking of the Zimmermann telegram.

Page 27   'Dilly's future plaintive murmurs': Penelope Fitzgerald, *The Knox Brothers*, Coward, McCann & Geoghegan, New York, 1977, p. 144.

Page 28   'There was great alarm': see Beesly, *Room 40*, p. 25.

Page 28   'Dilly would marry Miss Roddam': ibid., pp. 145–6.

Page 30   'Professor Walter Bruford': CCAC Misc 20.

Page 30   'Willoughby, go and fetch the rum': see Arthur J. Marder, *From the Dreadnought to Scapa Flow: The Royal Navy in the Fisher Era 1904–1919, vol. 4: 1917: Year of Crisis*, Oxford University Press, London, 1969, p. 265.

Page 30   'Alastair Denniston went out from ID25': see Denniston, *Thirty Secret Years*, pp. 39–43.

Page 30   'My interpretation of *Alice in ID25*': copies available from the Bletchley Park Trust.

Chapter 3: Alice in ID25

Page 31   'Peace, Peace, Oh for some peace...': quoted in Patrick Beesly, *Room 40: British Naval Intelligence 1914–18*, Hamish Hamilton, London, 1982, p. 302.

Chapter 4: Between the wars

Page 41   'Its public function': Robin Denniston, *Thirty Secret Years: A.G. Denniston's Work in Signals Intelligence 1914–1944*, Polperro Heritage Press, Clifton-upon-Teme, 2007, p. 93.

Page 42   'Money was never a major consideration': see Christopher Andrew, *Secret Service: The Making of the British Intelligence Community*, Heinemann, London, 1985, p. 259.

Page 42   'Working in blinkers': TNA HW 25/12.

Page 42   'Sinclair moved the codebreakers': see Michael Smith, *The Spying Game: The Secret History of British Espionage*, Politico's, London, 2003, p. 259.

Page 43   'Our work has been done in the face of the enemy...': quoted in Denniston, *Thirty Secret Years*, p. 48.

Page 43   'The inevitable had happened...': Churchill College Archives, Cambridge, GBR/0014/CLKE, papers of William F. Clarke.

Page 44   'The task was finished in time': see Denniston, *Thirty Secret Years*, p. 100.

Page 44   'Olive did not like living in Chelsea': see Penelope Fitzgerald, *The Knox Brothers*, Coward, McCann & Geoghegan, New York, 1977, pp. 170–71.

Page 45   'Dilly caused some consternation': ibid.

Page 45   'Sir John has bought an aeroplane...': Oliver Knox, *The Oldie*, March 2002.

Page 46   'Just as Herodas...': Herodas, *The Mimes and Fragments*, ed. A. D. Knox with notes by Walter Headlam, Cambridge University Press, Cambridge, 1922.

Page 46   'A glowing achievement': W. G. Arnott, 'Walter Headlam and Herodas', *Proceedings of the African Classical Association* (1947), vol. 10.

Page 47   'Fetty, as we addressed him...': quoted in Smith, *The Spying Game*, p. 260.

Page 48   'Signals intelligence, or Sigint': see Denniston, *Thirty Secret Years*, p. 25.

Page 48   'The great Soviet plot': see Smith, *The Spying Game*, p. 78.

Page 48   'A whole network of Russian intrigue was involved': see Michael Smith and Ralph Erskine (eds), *Action This Day: Bletchley Park from the Breaking of the Enigma Code to the Birth of the Modern Computer*, Bantam, London, 2001, p. 26; Smith, *The Spying Game*, pp. 259–60.

Page 49   'The Russians lost no time in abandoning the cipher': see Andrew, *Secret Service*, p. 332.

Page 49   'Knox had a very powerful intellect...': quoted in Michael Smith, *Station X: The Codebreakers of Bletchley Park*, Channel 4 Books, London, 1998, p. 16.

Page 50   'Hungarian was successfully broken by Knox': Denniston, *Thirty Secret Years*, p. 103.

Page 50   'John Tiltman ... was recalled to England': see Ralph Erskine and Peter Freeman, 'Brigadier John Tiltman: One of Britain's Finest Cryptologists', *Cryptologia* (2003), vol. 27, p 293.

Page 50   'The arrest of a number of Soviet agents': See Smith and Erskine, *Action This Day*, pp. 28–31; Michael Smith, *Foley: The Spy Who Saved 10,000 Jews*, Politico's, London, 2004, pp. 45–50; Gill Bennett, *Churchill's Man of Mystery: Desmond Morton and the World of Intelligence*, Routledge, London, 2007, p. 191.

Page 51   'These were never publicised': Denniston, *Thirty Secret Years*, p. 35.

Page 52   'Limericks are remembered long after White Papers': quoted in Oliver Knox, obituary, *The Times*, 20 July 2002.

Page 52   'To his work he referred not at all...': quoted in Fitzgerald, *The Knox Brothers*, pp. 170, 201.

Page 53   'Dilly got to know and like Christie': see Evelyn Waugh, *The Life of the Right Reverend Ronald Knox*, Chapman & Hall, London, 1959, p. 189.

Page 53   'If Edgar Lobel was the most imposing...': quoted in Fitzgerald, *The Knox Brothers*, p. 199.

Page 54   '[Dilly] used to amuse himself...': quoted ibid., p. 198.

Page 55   'My father was talking of the frustrations of life...': ibid., pp. 195–6, 203.

Page 55   'He would earn his place as a scholar': see A. D. Knox, 'The Early Iambers', *Philologus* (1932), vol. 87. The use of syllable weight is critical to the metre of Greek classical poetry. The syllable weight depends upon the juxtaposition of the vowels and consonants within and around a syllable. A heavy syllable is known as a *longum* and a light syllable as a *brevis*. The law defined by Dilly, expanding on work carried out by Wilamowitz, is known as the 'Wilamowitz–Knox bridge'. According to that law, 'there may not be word end after the penultimate and also after the ante-penultimate *longum*'. See Seth L. Schein, *The Iambic Trimeter in Aeschylus and Sophocles: A Study in Metrical Form*, Brill, Leiden, 1979, p. 14.

Chapter 5: Enigma

Page 56   'Scherbius exhibited his machine': see David Kahn, *The Codebreakers: The Story of Secret Writing*, Scribner, New York, 1996, p. 421.

Page 57 'Decisive battles have been lost...': quoted in Ronald Lewin, *Ultra Goes to War: The Secret Story*, Hutchinson, London, 1978, p. 26.

Page 57 'In the case of war...': quoted ibid., p. 45.

Page 57 'Foss painstakingly got down to the problem': TNA PRO HW 25/10, Hugh Foss's 'Reminiscences of Enigma' (reprinted in Michael Smith and Ralph Erskine (eds), *Action This Day: Bletchley Park from the Breaking of the Enigma Code to the Birth of the Modern Computer*, Bantam, London, 2001, pp. 42–6).

Page 58 'At least 180 letters would be needed': ibid.

Page 58 'Perhaps there was an exhibition': see Smith and Erskine, *Action This Day*, p. 44.

Page 59 'The methods I used were rather clumsy...': ibid., p. 45.

Page 59 'A jointly run wireless station was set up': see Nigel West, *GCHQ: The Secret Wireless War 1900–86*, Weidenfeld & Nicolson, London, 1986, p. 102.

Page 60 'Dilly's colleague Wilfred Bodsworth was impressed': TNA PRO HW 3/1, Wilfred Bodsworth's 'Reminiscences of Naval Section 1927–1939'.

Page 60 'The Italian messages were not sent out on the commercial machine he knew': TNA PRO HW 43/7, extract from the history of ISK (Illicit Services Knox). The full report is still classified.

Page 62 '... a remarkable 1,252,962,387,456': quoted in Graham Keeley, 'Nazi Enigma machines helped Franco in Civil War', *The Times*, 24 October 2008.

Page 63 'It was important for the Admiralty': see Patrick Beesly, *Very Special Intelligence: The Story of the Admiralty's Operational Intelligence Centre 1939–1945*, Hamish Hamilton, London, 1977, p. 13.

Page 63 'Denning spent several weeks with Dilly': see Donald McLachlan, *Room 39: Naval Intelligence in Action*, Weidenfeld & Nicolson, London, 1968, p. 55.

Page 63 'A brilliant team for the Second World War': see Beesly, *Very Special Intelligence*, for a full account of OIC.

Page 64 'Asché returned the precious documents': see David Kahn, *Seizing the Enigma: The Race to Break the German U-boat Codes 1939–1943*, Houghton Mifflin, Boston, 1991, p. 59.

Page 64 'Impossible to get anything useful...': quoted ibid., p. 60.

Page 65 'An explosion of stupefaction and joy': Gilbert Bloch, 'Enigma before Ultra: Polish Work and the French Contribution', *Cryptologia* (1987), vol. 11, p. 142.

Page 66 'Dilly was already aware of the introduction of the *Stecker*': see Robin Denniston, *Thirty Secret Years: A .G. Denniston's Work in Signals Intelligence 1914–1944*, Polperro Heritage Press, Clifton-upon-Teme, 2007, p. 107.

Page 66 'The discriminants ... were isolated by Tiltman's deputy': TNA PRO HW 25/10, Cooper's 'Pre-history of Enigma'; Denniston, *Thirty Secret Years*, p. 118.

Page 68 'Their cryptographic work is less ambitious than ours...': TNA PRO HW 25/12, Denniston memo to Strachey, Knox and Tiltman dated 1 November 1938; French minutes of meetings dated 3 November 1938; Denniston to Sinclair, liaison with the French, 2 November 1938.

Page 68 'Bertrand "salvaged five Spanish Republicans"': see Denniston, *Thirty Secret Years*, pp. 116–17.

Page 69 'Dilly might well have broken Enigma': TNA PRO HW 3/83, 'Reminiscences of Joshua Cooper', 1949.

Page 69 'A random entry plate connection': TNA PRO HW 43/70-72, 'The History of Hut 6', entry by Dennis Babbage.

Page 70: 'Dilly brought no information': Denniston, *Thirty Secret Years*, pp. 117–18; Smith and Erskine, *Action This Day*, p. 45; TNA/PRO HW 25/12, assessment by Knox of relative work of the Poles, French and British, 13 January 1939.

Page 70 'The French were delighted': see Smith and Erskine, *Action This Day*, p. 45.

Page 71 'The idea was abandoned': Denniston, *Thirty Secret Years*, p. 118; Gustave Bertrand, *Enigma ou la plus grande énigme de la guerre 1939–1945*, Plon, Paris, 1973, p. 58; TNA PRO 25/12, Denniston to Sinclair, visit to Paris, 13 January 1939; F. H. Hinsley and others, *British Intelligence in the Second World War, vol. III, part 2*, HMSO, London, 1984, p. 951.

Page 71 'He dined at several high tables...': TNA PRO HW 3/83, 'Reminiscences of Joshua Cooper', 1949; Michael Smith, *Station X: The Codebreakers of Bletchley Park*, Channel 4

Books, London, 1998, p. 16. *Station X* accompanied the Channel 4 TV series of that name and includes many interviews with former Bletchley Park codebreakers.

Page 72 'He sported his oak': Andrew Hodges, *Alan Turing: The Enigma*, Simon & Schuster, London, 1983, p. 151.

Chapter 6: The Warsaw conference

Page 74 'Godfrey's mission at that time': see Donald McLachlan, *Room 39: Naval Intelligence in Action*, Weidenfeld & Nicolson, London, 1968, p. 15.

Page 74 'The 26th (Wednesday) was THE day': Penelope Fitzgerald, *The Knox Brothers*, Coward, McCann & Geoghegan, New York, 1977, p. 234; Robin Denniston, *Thirty Secret Years: A .G. Denniston's Work in Signals Intelligence 1914–1944*, Polperro Heritage Press, Clifton-upon-Teme, 2007, p. 118; Ralph Erskine, 'The Poles Reveal Their Secrets: Alastair Denniston's Account of the July 1939 Meeting at Pyry', *Cryptologia* (2006), vol. 30, pp. 294–305.

Page 75 'Knox as our expert was alongside Ciężki...': quoted in Denniston, *Thirty Secret Years*, pp. 118–20.

Page 76 'Knox was really his own bright self...': quoted ibid.

Page 76 'I am fairly clear...': TNA PRO HW 25/12, Knox to Denniston on Hotel Bristol notepaper, dated only July 1939 but almost certainly 27 July 1939.

Page 77 'Just how much Braquenié understood...': quoted in Władysław Kozaczuk, *Enigma: How the German Machine Cipher Was Broken, and How It Was Read by the Allies in World War Two*, tr. Christopher Kasparek, University Publications of America, Frederick, MD, 1984, p. 236.

Page 77 'Rejewski also recalled the jubilation': see Józef Garliński, *Intercept: The Enigma War*, J. M. Dent & Sons, London, 1979, p. 45.

Page 77 '*Nous avons le QWERTZU*': Michael Smith, *Station X: The Codebreakers of Bletchley Park*, Channel 4 Books, London, 1998, p. 19.

Page 79 'At the time of my visit...': TNA PRO HW 25/12, Knox memo headed Most Secret, Warsaw, dated 4 August 1939.

Page 80 'I hasten to say...': quoted in F. H. Hinsley and Alan Stripp (eds), *Codebreakers: The Inside Story of Bletchley Park*, Oxford University Press, Oxford, 1993, p. 127.

Page 80 '*Accueil triomphal*': see David Kahn, *Seizing the Enigma: The Race to Break the German U-boat Codes 1939–1943*, Houghton Mifflin, Boston, 1991, p. 81.

Page 80 'Rejewski himself had never denied': TNA PRO HW 25/12; Kozaczuk, *Enigma*, pp. 258, 312. Oliver Knox recalls that when Turing came to spend weekends at Courns Wood in 1939, his father would be engaged in deep discussions on mathematics with him.

Page 81 'It seems that Dilly Knox...': Gordon Welchman, *The Hut Six Story: Breaking the Enigma Codes*, Allen Lane, London, 1982, p. 15.

Page 81 'Dilly boast to Menzies': TNA PRO HW 25/12, Knox resignation letter to Brigadier (Menzies), undated.

Page 81 'The work they would be doing "did not really need mathematics"': quoted in Hinsley and Stripp, *Codebreakers*, p. 113.

Page 81 'A few old-time professionals...': quoted ibid., p. 90.

Page 82 'Rejewski had worked out the wiring': see also Kahn, *Seizing the Enigma*; Stephen Budiansky, *Battle of Wits: The Complete Story of Codebreaking in World War II*, Viking, London, 2000, pp. 98–102.

Page 82 'The Poles were then able to read messages': A. P. Mahon, 'History of Hut 8, 1939–1945', p. 16, TNA PRO HW 25/2 (reproduced in B. Jack Copeland (ed.), *The Essential Turing: Seminal Writings in Computing, Logic, Philosophy, Artificial Intelligence, and Artificial Life, plus the Secrets of Enigma*, Clarendon Press, Oxford, 2004, p. 278); C. H. O'D. Alexander, 'Cryptographic History of Work on the German Naval Enigma', TNA PRO HW 25/2; Marian Rejewski, 'How the Polish Mathematicians Broke Enigma', in Kozaczuk, *Enigma*.

Page 82 on 'boxing', in which 'chains' of related letters were derived from the indicators (the procedure was also known as 'chaining indicators'), see PRO HW 25/3, 'Mathematical Theory of ENIGMA Machine by A. M. Turing' (sometimes referred to as 'Turing's Treatise on the Enigma'), pp. 16–19.

Page 83 'It would be "possible to find the places"': TNA PRO HW 25/12, Knox memo headed Most Secret, Warsaw, dated 4 August 1939.

Page 84 'These he called "females"': see F. H. Hinsley and others, *British Intelligence in the Second World War, vol. III, part 2*, HMSO, London, 1984, p. 951.

Page 84 'He "could not possibly have finished the tasks"': TNA PRO HW 25/12, Knox memo headed Most Secret, Warsaw, dated 4 August 1939.

Chapter 7: Bletchley Park as war station

Page 85 'He paid the £7,500 asking price': see Michael Smith, *Station X: The Codebreakers of Bletchley Park*, Channel 4 Books, London, 1998, p. 20.

Page 86 'A 1920s movie palace...': Thomas Parrish, *The Ultra Americans: The U.S. Role in Breaking the Nazi Codes*, Stein & Day, New York, 1986, p. 111.

Page 86 'He recruited Richard Gambier-Parry': see Geoffrey Pidgeon, *The Secret Wireless War*, UPSO, London, 2003, pp. 50–51.

Page 86 'The aerial was slung to the top of a *Sequoiadendron giganteum*': see F. H. Hinsley and Alan Stripp (eds), *Codebreakers: The Inside Story of Bletchley Park*, Oxford University Press, Oxford, 1993, p. 307.

Page 87 '"The Park" or more simply "BP"': TNA PRO HW 14/57. The Wrens based at Woburn and Gayhurst were instructed to stop calling it Station X in November 1942.

Page 87 'The chapter on British intelligence': Richard Deacon and Nigel West, *Spy!*, BBC, London, 1980, pp. 41–65; Walter Schellenberg, *Invasion 1940* (tr. John Erickson), St Ermin's Press, London, 2000.

Page 89 'It fell to my lot': quoted in Smith, *Station X*, p. 20.

Page 90 'They reached Gustave Bertrand's wartime Cipher Bureau': see Józef Garliński, *Intercept: The Enigma War*, J. M. Dent & Sons, London, 1979, pp. 56–7.

Page 90 'The French government were paying for the Polish army': TNA PRO HW 14/7.

Page 90 'I have taken the line...': TNA PRO HW 25/12, Knox to Denniston, dated 29 September 1939; Penelope Fitzgerald, *The Knox Brothers*, Coward, McCann & Geoghegan, New York, 1977, p. 199.

Page 91 'PC Bruno was also sent copies of the "Jeffreys sheets"': TNA PRO HW 43/70-72, 'The History of Hut 6', Babbage entry, 1:122.

Page 91 'Dilly was neither an organisation man nor a technical man': Gordon Welchman, *The Hut Six Story: Breaking the Enigma Codes*, Allen Lane, London, 1982, p. 34.

Page 92 'I followed suit': ibid. p. 37.

Page 93 'Dilly was furious': ibid., pp. 54, 71.

Page 93 'Hadn't one said the right thing?': Fitzgerald, *The Knox Brothers*, p. 239.

Page 93 'Hugh Alexander, the head of Hut 8, later commented': Michael Smith and Ralph Erskine (eds), *Action This Day: Bletchley Park from the Breaking of the Enigma Code to the Birth of the Modern Computer*, Bantam, London, 2001, p. 209.

Page 94 'He was considered to be part of Dilly's team': TNA PRO HW 14/1.

Page 94 'Turing is very difficult to anchor down...': ibid.

Page 94 'The information Dilly managed to extract': TNA PRO HW 25/12. It is described in 'Turing's Treatise', an extract of which appears in B. Jack Copeland (ed.), *The Essential Turing: Seminal Writings in Computing, Logic, Philosophy, Artificial Intelligence, and Artificial Life, plus the Secrets of Enigma*, Clarendon Press, Oxford, 2004, p. 281.

Page 95 'The format FORTYQEETYY': the Poles had called this the FORTYWEEPY method.

Page 95 'He was mechanically apt': see David Kahn, *Seizing the Enigma: The Race to Break the German U-boat Codes 1939–1943*, Houghton Mifflin, Boston, 1991, p. 94.

Page 95   'This was an electro-mechanical device': see Władysław Kozaczuk, *Enigma: How the German
           Machine Cipher Was Broken, and How It Was Read by the Allies in World War Two*, tr.
           Christopher Kasparek, University Publications of America, Frederick, MD, 1984, p. 63, n. 1.

Page 95   'Which may at any time be cancelled': TNA PRO HW 25/12, letter from Knox to
           Denniston, July 1939.

Page 96   'This would greatly speed up the breaking of the Enigma messages': TNA PRO HW 14/2.

Page 96   'A meeting on 1 November 1939': TNA PRO HW 25/12.

Page 96   'What happened precisely was this...': ibid., Knox memorandum dated 3 December 1939.

Page 96   'His report to Denniston': TNA PRO HW 14/12.

Page 97   'Welchman had stipulated': Welchman, *The Hut Six Story*, p. 76.

Page 97   'As yet Turing's *bombes* were wishful thinking': TNA PRO HW 14/1.

Page 97   'They resulted from a combination of two different mistakes': see Smith and Erskine,
           Action This Day, Appendix IV, 'Cillies'.

Page 97   'Dilly in his playful way called these snakes': TNA PRO HW 43/70-72, 'The History of
           Hut 6', 1:125.

Page 98   'This became known as the "Herivel tip"': ibid., 1:213; see also John Herivel, *Herivelismus
           and the German Military Enigma*, M. & M. Baldwin, Kidderminster, 2008.

Page 98   'Testing for self-*Stecker*': Smith and Erskine, *Action This Day*, p. 54.

Page 99   'A younger colleague who had specialised in mathematical logic...': quoted in Copeland,
           The Essential Turing, p. 235.

Page 99   'The Poles had given them some wrong information': see F. H. Hinsley and others, *British
           Intelligence in the Second World War, vol. III, part 2*, HMSO, London, 1984, p. 952.

Page 100   'We eagerly awaited the opportunity...': TNA PRO HW 43/70-72, 'The History of Hut 6',
           1:126.

Page 101   'If there was a crib guess': ibid., 1:122.

Page 101   Marian Rejewski, 'Memories of My Work in the Office of Division II, Codes, Chief of Staff,
           1930–1945', *Przegląd Historyczno-Wojskowy* (2005), no. 5, pp. 132–3. 'We had the English
           to thank...': F.H.Hinsley and others, British Intelligence in the Second World War, vol 3, part
           2, p.954 (fn)

Page 101   'In the framework of the co-operation...': Rejewski, 'Memories of My Work in the Office
           of Division II, Codes, Chief of Staff, 1930–1945', p. 133.

Page 101   'Bletchley and Bruno audaciously exchanged Enigma secrets': Kozaczuk, *Enigma*, p. 87.

Page 102   'Knox had been the pioneer worker': TNA PRO HW 43/70-72, 'The History of Hut 6', 1:202.

Chapter 8: Dilly's girls

Page 106   'He was extremely allergic': TNA PRO HW 14/157, general orders on GC&CS
           organisation with charts.

Page 106   'Another resignation letter': TNA PRO HW 25/12.

Page 106   'My dear Dilly...': TNA PRO HW 14/22.

Page 106   'He had been made chief assistant': TNA PRO HW 14/1, Butler to Denniston, dated 5
           January 1940.

Page 109   'Comparable to the operations of the three Services...': Gill Bennett, *Churchill's Man of
           Mystery: Desmond Morton and the World of Intelligence*, Routledge, London, 2007, p. 177,
           quoting from TNA PRO FO 837/3, Handbook of Economic Warfare, 24 July 1939.
           Morton was largely responsible for the creation of the economic intelligence organisation.

Page 111   'Their work was devoted to "retrieving the misses"': TNA PRO HW 25/12.

Page 111   'There were catalogues called "corsets"': TNA PRO HW 25/3, 'Turing's Treatise', Section p. 141.

Page 112   'When talking to Lt-Cdr Fleming...': quoted in B. Jack Copeland (ed.), *The Essential
           Turing: Seminal Writings in Computing, Logic, Philosophy, Artificial Intelligence, and
           Artificial Life, plus the Secrets of Enigma*, Clarendon Press, Oxford, 2004, p. 289.

Page 113   'I was frequently asked if I had met the creator of James Bond': see Mavis Batey, *From
           Bletchley with Love*, Bletchley Park Trust, Milton Keynes, 2008, p. 4

Page 115   'Prof's manual was never used in the Cottage': TNA PRO HW 25/3.

Page 117   'Dilly's XALTX charts': TNA PRO HW 43/7. The rod techniques described in this chapter mostly come from a released extract from the classified history of ISK referring to the Italian machine, which we wrote in 1946.

Chapter 9: The Battle of Matapan

Page 119   'A dangerous practice': see F. W. Winterbotham, *The ULTRA Secret*, Weidenfeld & Nicolson, London, 1974, p. 18.

Page 119   'He set up Special Liaison Units': see Ronald Lewin, *Ultra Goes to War: The Secret Story*, Hutchinson, London, 1978, pp. 138–54.

Page 120   'So far as the Italian Naval Enigma is concerned...': TNA PRO HW 14/7, Knox to Denniston, 8 October 1940; Denniston to Knox, 8 October 1940.

Page 121   'There is no proper distinction': TNA PRO HW 25/12, Knox to members of ISK section, dated 3 January 1943.

Page 121   'Dilly was a genius in cryptography...': TNA PRO HW 3/16, Clarke memoir written 1954.

Page 121   'Italian Enigma intelligence would go straight from the Cottage': TNA PRO HW 3/140, Clarke's 'Early History of the Naval Section and of Italian Naval Section from 1939 to June 1941'.

Page 121   'The Italian invention of the midget submarine': see F. H. Hinsley and others, *British Intelligence in the Second World War, vol. I*, HMSO, London, 1979, p. 210.

Page 122   'Hut 3 received a decoded Afrika Korps Luftwaffe message': TNA PRO DEFE 3/686, OL9 21/3/41.

Page 123   'I was working in my tiny cabin...': personal memo to author.

Page 124   'Endeavour to make the enemy strike': TNA PRO ADM 223/88.

Page 124   'I have now decided to take 1st BS': ibid.

Page 124   'Destroyed it after perusal': see Winterbotham, *The ULTRA Secret*, p. 89.

Page 124   'A special signals link had been set up': F. H. Hinsley and others, *British Intelligence in the Second World War*, pp. 570–71. For a fuller account of the unit see TNA PRO HW3/165, 'Hut 3 History', Chapter V. I am indebted to Wilf Neal for this reference.

Page 125   'The conclusion that he decided to sail...': F. H. Hinsley and others, *British Intelligence in the Second World War*, p. 405.

Page 125   'The Italians continued to intercept': see John Winton, *Cunningham*, John Murray, London, 1998, p. 161.

Page 128   'The mastermind behind the Enigma affair': Winterbotham, *The ULTRA Secret*, p. 14.

Page 128   'Winterbotham only knew about the German air force ULTRA intelligence': ibid., p. 66.

Page 129   'Cynthia's first major assignment...': H. Montgomery Hyde, *Cynthia: The Spy Who Changed the Course of the War*, Hamish Hamilton, London, 1966.

Page 129   'Lewin ... was writing a book about ULTRA': see Lewin, *Ultra Goes to War*, Hutchinson, London, 1978, pp. 196–200.

Page 130   'Di Vita was incensed': 'Ultra and Matapan', letters, *The Times,* 18 February 1980.

Page 130   '*Affascinante signora...*': *Corriere della Sera*, 12 February 1980.

Chapter 10: Dilly and the Spy Enigma

Page 132   'Camp 020 was set up': see Oliver Hoare (ed.), *Camp 020: MI5 and the Nazi Spies*, National Archives, Richmond, 2000.

Page 132   'The double agent was to send out his false information': Michael Smith and Ralph Erskine (eds), *Action This Day: Bletchley Park from the Breaking of the Enigma Code to the Birth od the Modern Computer*, Bantam, London, 2001, Appendix 1 outlines the simple cipher given to 'Snow', the first double agent.

Page 134 'My dear Denniston...': TNA PRO HW 25/12, Knox to Denniston, undated but beginning, 'As I think you are aware...'

Page 135 'As a scholar...': TNA PRO HW14/23, Knox to Denniston, 10 November 1941.

Page 135 'At present we are encumbered...': TNA PRO HW 25/12, Knox to Menzies, undated but beginning, 'Sir, I have the honour to tender you my resignation.'

Page 135 'Dilly wanted to be in on the overall intelligence': TNA PRO HW 25/12, Knox to Denniston, undated but beginning: 'As I think you are aware...'

Page 135 'She is a very nice and remarkable woman', TNA PRO HW14/23, Knox to Denniston, 10 November 1941.

Page 135 'The report on the breaking of the Abwehr machine', TNA PRO HW 14/21, Folio 131, three-page Knox report on Lobster Enigma, dated 28 October 1941.

Page 136 'He found what was wanting standing...': ibid.

Page 137 'The hunt was up...': ibid.

Page 138 'Knox has again justified his reputation': TNA PRO 14/24, Folio 53, Denniston to Menzies, 10 December 1941.

Page 141 'An SIS counter-espionage expert': TNA PRO HW 14/25, Denniston to Vivian.

Page 142 'Intelligence Services Knox had not been compromised': see William Stevenson, *Intrepid's Last Case*, Michael Joseph, London, 1984.

Chapter 11: Dilly's 'personal scouts'

Page 143 'News came from Travis's office': PRO HW 14/21, Folio 7, De Grey to Travis, dated 13 February 1942.

Page 143 'Despite not infrequent differences of opinion...': HW 25/21, Dilly memorandum to Twinn on interview with Menzies, 19 March 1942.

Page 144 'He had "pointed out very forcefully"'...: ibid.

Page 145 'Churchill knew we would have to back Tito': Winston S. Churchill, *The Second World War, vol. V: Closing the Ring*, Cassell, London, 1952; John Cripps, 'Mihailovic or Tito? How the Codebreakers Helped Churchill Choose', in Michael Smith and Ralph Erskine (eds), *Action This Day: Bletchley Park from the Breaking of the Enigma Code to the Birth of the Modern Computer*, Bantam, London, 2001, pp. 237–63.

Page 146 'Operation Goldeneye': TNA PRO FO 371/47591.

Page 146 'I sketched my idea...': HW 25/21, Dilly memorandum to Twinn on interview with Menzies, 19 March 1942.

Page 147 'The difference between ISK and ISOS': see F. H. Hinsley and C. A. G. Simkins, *British Intelligence in the Second World War, Vol 4: Security and Counter-Intelligence*, HMSO, London, 1990, p. 108.

Page 147 'Cowgill was notorious': see Smith and Erskine, *Action This Day*, p. 288.

Page 147 'Admiral Godfrey ... was doing all he could': Patrick Beesly, *Very Special Admiral: The Life of J. H. Godfrey*, Hamish Hamilton, London, 1980, p. 228.

Page 148 'Dilly urged Peter Twinn': Smith and Erskine, *Action This Day*, p. 188; TNA PRO HW 14/35, Twinn to de Grey, 26 March 1942.

Page 148 'Dilly also made it known': HW 25/21, Dilly memorandum to Twinn on interview with Menzies, 19 March 1942.

Page 148 'During the four months I have been in this section...': HW 14/36.

Page 148 'I think things will improve': ibid.

Page 149 'Mentions Dilly Knox by name': Kim Philby, *My Silent War*, MacGibbon & Kee, London, 1968, p. 61.

Page 149 'Once again in our long island history...': Winston S. Churchill, *The Second World War, vol. III: The Grand Alliance*, Cassell, London, 1950, p. 607.

Page 150 'Fleming was determined to frustrate': see Donald McLachlan, *Room 39: Naval Intelligence in Action*, Weidenfeld & Nicolson, London, 1968, p. 205.

Page 150 'Pound revealed the top secret source': Ralph Erskine, 'Eavesdropping on Bodden: ISOS v. The Abwehr in the Straits of Gibraltar', *Intelligence and National Security* (1997), vol. 12, no. 3, p. 110; R. V. Jones, *Most Secret War*, Hamish Hamilton, London, 1978, pp. 254–9.

Page 151 '[He] doubted whether anyone on our side would really welcome': Philby, *My Silent War*, p. 40.

Page 152 'Caesar's cover was now blown': ibid., p. 38.

Page 152 'It was Canaris's ambition to see the Germans seize Gibraltar': see Heinz Höhne, *Canaris: Hitler's Masterspy*, tr. J. Maxwell Brownjohn, Secker & Warburg, London, 1979, pp. 433–4.

Page 152 'It now controlled all the German agents operating in Britain': Smith and Erskine, *Action This Day*, pp. 287–8.

Page 152 'The reason Fleming gave James Bond the designation 007': Beesly, *Very Special Admiral*, p. 321.

Page 154 'Garbo did his best to oblige': Michael Howard, *British Intelligence in the Second World War, vol. V*, HMSO, London, 1990, pp. 55–63.

Page 154 'Lewis Powell ... was amazed': see Thomas Parrish, *The Ultra Americans: The U.S. Role in Breaking the Nazi Codes*, Stein & Day, New York, 1986, p. 179.

Page 154 'Your last reports were magnificent': Howard, *British Intelligence in the Second World War*, p. 63.

Page 155 'Fleming's "Red Indians"': see David Nutting, *Attain by Surprise: The Story of 30 Assault Unit Royal Navy/Royal Marine Commando and of Intelligence by Capture*, David Colver, London, 2003.

Page 156 'The operation was dubbed Mincemeat': TNA PRO ADM 223/794. *The Man Who Never Was* and *Operation Heartbreak* were reissued in an omnibus edition by Spellmount, Stroud, 2003, with an introduction by Duff Cooper's son John Julius Norwich.

Page 156 'The planned attack will be directed mainly against Sardinia': Cooper/Montagu omnibus, p. 189.

Page 157 'It allowed the British to foil attempts at sabotage': see Smith and Erskine, *Action This Day*, pp. 292–3; Oliver Hoare (ed.), *Camp 020: MI5 and the Nazi Spies*, National Archives, Richmond, 2000.

Page 159 'We must trust in our invisible assets...': Smith and Erskine, *Action This Day*, pp. 295–300. I am indebted to David Ramsay for his father's diary entry.

Page 159 'By God, we fooled them': Institute for Studies in American Military History, 'The Crucial Deception', *Discovery: Research and Scholarship at The University of Texas at Austin*, vol. 14, no. 2.

Chapter 12: Farewell

Page 160 'Ronnie had not come to see the cherries': see Penelope Fitzgerald, *The Knox Brothers*, Coward, McCann & Geoghegan, New York, 1977, p. 246.

Page 161 'A study of the psychology of the persons sending out the messages...': Robin Denniston, *Thirty Secret Years: A .G. Denniston's Work in Signals Intelligence 1914–1944*, Polperro Heritage Press, Clifton-upon-Teme, 2007, p. 48.

Page 163 'Dilly must have turned in his grave': Fitzgerald, *The Knox Brothers*, pp. 230–34.

Page 164 'In a technical sense, we are ahead...': this remark is in William Friedman's diary for 1943, held at the National Cryptologic Museum, Maryland, USA.

Page 165 'Dilly had of course worked on Comintern': see Nigel West, *Historical Dictionary of British Intelligence*, Scarecrow Press, Lanham, MD, 2005, pp. 293–4.

Page 165 'A book of collected famous last words': Francis Birrell and F. L. Lucas, *The Art of Dying*, Hogarth Press, London, 1930.

Appendix 5

Page 210   'The principal Abwehr Enigma': Peter Twinn, 'The Abwehr Enigma', in F. H. Hinsley and
Alan Stripp (eds), *Codebreakers: The Inside Story of Bletchley Park*, Oxford University Press,
Oxford, 1993, p. 124, relied on memory in suggesting that this Enigma had 11, 15 and 19
notches.

Page 210   'A 10-letter crib': Ticom I-77 (Dr. Hüttenhain and Dr. Fricke on *Zählwerk* Enigma),
FOIA.

Page 211   '"Red" South American Enigma': for details of this machine, including photographs, see
'Description and Photos of German Cryptographic Device (Enigma)', HCC, Box 604,
Nr. 1570.

Page 211   'Signals were also sometimes sent in 5-letter groups': GISK 9 in 'Descriptions of German
Cipher Types GISOS, GIMP, GISK and GISKXY', National Archives and Records
Administration, College Park, Md., RG 457, Entry 9032, Historic Cryptographic
Collection, Pre-World War I Through World War II (HCC), Box 606, Nr. 1587.

Page 211   on Umkehrwalze D, see Philip Marks, 'Umkehrwalze D: Enigma's Rewirable Reflector',
Parts I, II and III, *Cryptologia* (2001) vol 25, pp. 101–41, 177–212, 296–310.

Page 211   'The wheels sometimes moved backwards': see further, David P. Mowry, *German Cipher
Machines of World War II*, National Security Agency, Fort George G. Meade, MD, 2003,
pp. 25–7.

Page 212   'The first two groups and last two groups in its traffic were identical': GISK 6 in
'Descriptions of German Cipher Types GISOS, GIMP, GISK and GISKXY'.

Page 212   'A variable "kick" to the inner disc's movement': see Cipher A. Deavours and Louis Kruh,
Machine Cryptography and Modern Cryptanalysis, Artech House, Dedham, MA, 1986, pp.
151–170, and, for photographs, the Crypto Machines website <http://jproc.ca/crypto>
and Louis Kruh, 'The Kryha Liliput Ciphering Machine', *Cryptologia* (1985), vol. 9, pp.
252–261, which includes a copy of the drawing for the US patent.

Page 212   'An overstatement, but one erring on the side of caution': IL 3675, Fried Report F-74, p.
6, quoting a signal from Berlin: 'Capt. Walter J. Fried Reports/SSA Liaison with GCCS',
HCC, Box CBMH15, Nr. 2612.

Page 212   on Hagelin machines, see David Kahn, *The Codebreakers: The Story of Secret Writing*,
Macmillan, New York, 1967, pp. 427–432; Deavours and Kruh, *Machine Cryptography*,
ch. V.

Index

Note: The abbreviation DK is used for Dilly Knox. The suffix *g* after a page number denotes a glossary entry. Pseudonyms are indicated by the use of single quotes – e.g. 'Asché'.

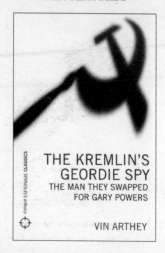

Also available from Biteback

CODENAME RYGOR
MIECZYSŁAW ZYGFRYD SŁOWIKOWSKI

The spy behind the Allied victory in North Africa

Major General Mieczysław Zygfryd Słowikowski, codenamed Rygor, was a Polish intelligence officer who helped establish Allied spy networks in occupied France and, later, in German-occupied North Africa.

In July 1941, Słowikowski was transferred to Algiers, where he set up and ran one of the war's most successful intelligence operations, providing the vast bulk of the intelligence for Operation Torch, the 1942 Allied invasion of North Africa.

Although not as well known as the later operations in France and Italy, Operation Torch provided a turning point in the war against the Axis powers. Słowikowski lit the fuse.

His immense bravery and effort were later rewarded with the American Legion of Merit and the Order of the British Empire. This is his extraordinary story.

352pp Paperback, £9.99

Available from all good bookshops or order from
www.bitebackpublishing.com

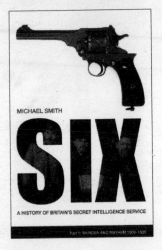